The Handbook of Work Based Learning

The Handbook of Work Based Learning

IAN CUNNINGHAM, GRAHAM DAWES
and BEN BENNETT

GOWER

Published by
Gower Publishing Limited
Gower House
Croft Road
Aldershot
Hants GU11 3HR
England

Gower Publishing Company
Suite 420
101 Cherry Street
Burlington, VT 05401-4405
USA

Ian Cunningham, Graham Dawes and Ben Bennett have asserted their right under the Copyright, Designs and Patents Act, 1988 to be identified as the authors of this work.

British Library Cataloguing in Publication Data
Cunningham, Ian
    The handbook of work based learning
    1. Education, Cooperative 2. Employees – Training of
    3. Experiential learning
    I. Title II. Dawes, Graham III. Bennett, Ben
    658.3'124

ISBN: 0 566 08541 0

Library of Congress Cataloging-in-Publication Data
Cunningham, Ian, 1943–
    The handbook of work based learning / Ian Cunningham, Graham Dawes, and Ben Bennett.
        p. cm.
    Includes bibliographical references.
    ISBN 0-566-08541-0
    1. Employees--Training of--Handbooks, manuals, etc. 2. Career
development--Handbooks, manuals, etc. 3. Experiential learning--Handbooks, manuals,
etc. 4. Active learning--Handbooks, manuals, etc. 5. Mentoring in business--Handbooks,
manuals, etc. 6. Employer-supported education--Handbooks, manuals, etc. 7.
Organizational learning--Handbooks, manuals, etc. I. Title: Work based learning. II.
Dawes, Graham. III. Bennett, Ben. IV. Title.

    HF5549.5.T7C853 2004
    658.3'124--dc22   2003057019

Typeset by Owain Hammonds, Ceredigion.
Printed by MPG Books Ltd., Bodmin.

Contents

Foreword

Over the last decade politicians and educators have given a great deal of attention to the importance of learning as a lifelong activity. Within the context of lifelong learning the learning that is required by work and which takes place at and through work has a predominant role. Such is the significance widely ascribed to this 'work based learning' that it is seen as central to a paradigm shift from an 'industrial society' to a 'knowledge society'.

Recognition of the importance of knowledge and learning from work is not new. The nature of knowledge and the relationship between knowledge and work was much contested by the philosophers of Classical Greece. As long ago as 1890 the economist Alfred Marshall wrote 'Capital consists in a great part of knowledge and organization...knowledge is our most powerful engine of production'. Yet it is in the latter years of the 1990s and the start of the twenty-first century that it has frequently been demonstrated that wealth is generated through knowledge and there has been a growing realization that people are the source of organizational knowledge. Today, in a time of increasingly rapid change driven by technological innovation and knowledge based competitiveness, it has never been more important to understand and proactively engage in work based learning.

Work based learning is by design and necessity concerned with knowledge which is often unsystematic, socially constructed and is action focused by the worker in order to achieve specific outcomes of significance to others. The importance and complexity of the work based context for learning makes work based learning different from formal classroom-based training or education. It is a truism that we learn from experience but unplanned, unstructured and often accidental learning alone is at best unlikely to enable the individual to reach their potential and at worst may be drawing upon negative experiences resulting in future negative behaviour. Work based learning is just too important for the individual worker or their employer to leave to chance.

The Handbook of Work Based Learning clearly and concisely identifies why we should take work based learning seriously. This is important as, despite the commonplace rhetoric of 'lifelong learning' and the 'knowledge driven society', a recent national survey of UK employers and employees by the Professional Development Foundation found that the majority of workers do not see themselves as learners and feel that their professional development is the responsibility of their employer. At the same time a majority of employers see learning as something which has value for the individual and is essentially the responsibility of the worker in order to retain and enhance their personal competitiveness in the job market. Both perspectives are catastrophically narrow and shortsighted!

This handbook provides the employer with a clearly argued case for the strategic as well as tactical management of work based learning and provides clear and well reasoned guidance about how this might be achieved. Particularly valuable is the linkage between work based learning and organizational decision making. The practical approach adopted in the handbook is to present and discuss work based learning as a range of choices: strategic (for example, action learning, mentoring, self managed learning), tactical (for example, buddying, coaching, projects) and methods (for example, discussion, learning log, peer review, shadowing).

The handbook clearly makes the case for the personal benefits of employees managing their own work based learning and then goes on to explore how this might be achieved. The significance of individual learning styles is explored and a range of different ways of learning are identified. In each case the strengths and limitations of the approach are identified and discussed in order to empower the reader to make informed choices. This is a practical approach that marks this handbook out from much of what has been written about knowledge, learning and work.

The authors draw upon their extensive practical as well as research knowledge of work based learning to move beyond traditional stereotypes of work based courses as they fully recognize that work based learning is not purely about the individual; it is about learning in the social, cultural, political and economic context of work. This makes the workplace a complex learning environment where, left unguided, individual or collective work based learning will take place but it is unlikely to be focused on the strategic aims of the employer and may actually be counter to the goals of the collective work enterprise. It is in the context of this complexity that the section of the handbook aimed at the work based learning developer is of particular value as it provides a solutions-orientated approach to the complex people, process and problem issues which are at the core of work based learning.

The Handbook of Work Based Learning is a valuable and above all a practical resource for the manager, the training and development specialist and the individual work based learner.

Professor Jonathan Garnett
Director, National Centre for Work Based Learning Partnerships
Middlesex University

Preface

Who is this handbook for?

We have written this for people who are in work and who see learning to be more effective at work as an important activity. We believe that this should ideally include all people who work. Note that we are talking about work, not necessarily employment. Some readers may work but not be employed in an organization. While we have used examples that usually refer to organizationally based work, we are clear that much of what we cover in this handbook is of general relevance.

Most of the books in this field are written explicitly for professionals employed to help others to learn – trainers, developers, tutors, lecturers, and so on. We have oriented the main body of the text to those not in professional roles. However, we assume that development professionals also want to carry on their own learning so we hope that most of what we have produced will be relevant to all readers.

Introduction

Work based learning is becoming more recognized and accepted. Increasingly organizations are realizing that learning in the work context is crucial for organizational success. For many people this can be a liberating notion. In our research we have often found that people have had less than ideal experiences in school and then linked learning with such settings. That is, they associate learning with something unpleasant. Yet in their everyday lives they could be learning to play a sport, learning to drive, learning to be a parent, and so on. Recognizing that learning is just a natural human process that goes on all the time inside and outside work can free people from the constraints of imagining that learning only takes place on courses or in other controlled, formal settings.

People can also see that much of the learning that they undertake in their private lives is both enjoyable and rewarding. However, at work this may not always be so. Learning to use a new piece of computer software or to apply some new health and safety rules might be tedious. Yet we usually recognize that it has to be done. And that we can't perform our work effectively without it. On the other hand, learning new skills that increase job satisfaction is stimulating and enriching. People are learning creatures and the lack of interesting new learning can be associated with boredom and low morale.

Yet there are still undertones in official circles that, while work based learning is a good thing, proper official learning takes place on courses and is the domain of education and training. We will show in Part 1 that all the research evidence says that work based learning is more important than education and training. Indeed we will quote evidence that suggests that for most people at work, education and training contributes only about 10–20 per cent of what makes the person effective. And this applies to secretaries and senior managers, cleaners and chartered accountants.

One problem is the language that is used. Again we will go into this more in Part 1 where we explore the rationale for using work based learning. However, we can indicate just a few problems here. First there is the distinction that is made between formal and informal learning. The hidden assumption is that, while informal learning does occur, formal learning is what really counts, especially where it is linked to a qualification. The problem with this distinction is that it doesn't make sense in practice. To take one example. Suppose you are signed up for a qualification course and you happen to meet friends in the pub. You might mention a problem that you are having learning some new piece of knowledge. A friend might chip in and give you some suggestions.

In this example, the conversation is in an informal setting and it could be argued that you have learned something informally. But when you repeat this in an examination that is clearly a formal setting, or you were motivated to learn this by being on a formal course, was the learning informal or formal? We'd suggest that it is an irrelevant question. People learn in hugely varied ways and one advantage of taking a work-based focus is that it allows us to do justice to how learning really occurs.

Another strange use of language is the idea of a non-learner. Official UK government documents suggest that a non-learner is someone who has not been on a course in the last three years. That makes pretty well the whole of the UK government non-learners – and probably almost all heads of state around the world. Isn't it scary that we are governed by non-learners? Except that, of course, the whole concept is basically faulty. People learn all the time every day of their lives. Much of this learning is quite simple. We might go into work and find that the design of a form has changed and we have to learn how to use the new one. A more challenging situation is one where we might have a new manager to report to and we have to learn what their expectations are about working practices. Or we change jobs and have a whole heap of new things to learn. And so it goes on. Learning is central to being human and is a universal human activity. So non-learning is a nonsensical concept.

Another linguistic error is where people talk about structured and unstructured learning. The assumption is that proper learning is structured, as exemplified by the training course, and that while unstructured learning occurs it is of lesser status. However, as the examples in the previous paragraph show, most useful learning happens in what can be called unstructured situations. But let's take this supposed distinction a bit further. A PhD is a qualification that is highly valued. Yet doing research for a PhD can be quite unstructured. There may be no lectures to go to or any formal (structured) events that the PhD student will use. Compare this with someone who is allocated a work-based mentor. They may meet regularly with the mentor, be working to a personal development plan or learning contract and in general have quite a structured programme of learning. Yet mentoring usually gets put into the unstructured category and the PhD would go in the structured category. It doesn't make a lot of sense.

What does make sense is the notion of work based learning. There are elements at the edges where some activity might or might not be categorized as work based. But overall we can be reasonably clear about what learning is work based and what isn't. Hence this handbook.

In the material that follows we have attempted to give a structure to what we have covered. Some of the distinctions are a bit arbitrary, but overall we have started from the big picture and moved gradually through more specific approaches into very precise methods and techniques. Our intention is that the handbook be of use to anyone at work. It can be dipped into where you want to find out about a specific technique. However, you may find it useful to at least read Section 1.1 in Part 1 first as that gives the rationale for the rest of the handbook.

In saying that this handbook can be useful to anyone at work we are aware that some people have a specific role to help others with their learning. Such people may be called Human Resource Development professionals or consultants or mentors or careers advisers. We offer some ideas for them to consider and have identified separately material directed at them. This is covered in Section 1.3.

The other key role in developing work based learning is that of the top management of an organization (and others in strategic roles). Section 1.2 is addressed to those in this position. The focus of this section is on those who are in leadership positions who can influence learning decisions such as resource allocation. The section offers advice on choices for supporting learning at a strategic level.

Changing attitudes to work based learning

Despite our critical comments about the British government we can see signs of change here. For instance, in a Department of Health report on Continuing Professional Development (CPD) they suggest the following:

> An important principle of CPD is that it includes much more than going on courses. All health organisations need to develop a learning culture with work based learning at the heart of this. Work based learning involves a wide range of activities. For example, it includes learning from the results of clinical audit and putting in place service improvements based on audit. It includes learning on the job how to make better use of information systems and how to apply the results of research. Work based learning should also include the process of reflection within a team about untoward incidents which may have occurred and how to learn the lessons from these. Creating a learning environment in every health organisation should mean that an increasingly large proportion of CPD is work based. (Department of Health, 1999)

We couldn't agree more. This quote leads us to add ideas about learning organizations and the creation of learning cultures in organizations to the consideration of work based learning. It is clearly important in fostering work based learning to have such learning valued and for people to feel that they are in a culture which supports learning. Many of the approaches that we offer do depend on such support. If people want mentors or opportunities to go onto the Internet while at work, they are likely to need a sympathetic management. Getting buy-in to work based learning is one of the subjects of Section 1.1 in Part 1. If you work in an organization where there is wholehearted support for learning and development at all levels in the organization, then you may not need all this material. However, we have found that, even in organizations that are committed to learning at work, there are pockets of resistance and often there is not wholehearted practical support for all staff.

Structure of the handbook

We have already indicated that Part 1 provides the rationale for work based learning and for its centrality in organizational performance. There we cover the issues for individuals and how learning at work is vital for career development. We also introduce the model for how the rest of the handbook is organized. Basically we suggest that once you are clear about the purposes of using work based learning, you next need to consider some strategies that are open to you. This is the focus of Part 2.

We take a learning strategy to be about the big picture and about planning for learning over the longest time horizon across which you can think. For some people, their career plans indicate the need for long-term planning and for support with this. For other people they may have quite short-term needs and have no wish to think long term. We don't intend to take a stance on what is ideal. However, we suggest that preparing for different eventualities in life could be important and therefore learning a range of useful skills and capabilities can ensure a greater range of choices for the future. We take the notion of preparing to be an important one and we suggest ways in which individuals can adopt this approach.

Having gained a clear strategy you may need to use particular tactics to meet your needs. We take tactics to be the short-term implementation of strategy. The root of this language is in warfare. Strategy is about winning the war; tactics about winning battles. You can win battles but lose the war, so strategy has to be the bedrock for tactical decisions. (We appreciate that work may not best be compared with war, but it may at least be useful to recognize where this language comes from. We use it only because it has become common parlance in most large organizations.)

An example of a link from strategy to tactics might be the following. You are fortunate enough to be allocated a mentor who works with you over a period of time to support your development. You and your mentor may come to realize that you need to broaden your experience in order to progress your career. An idea that may come up is to undertake a project at work which will take you out of your normal duties. The mentor is here behaving strategically with you and the project may prove to be a useful tactic as part of your overall learning strategy.

However, you might find that, in pursing the project, new learning needs are thrown up. Hence you may need to consider the methods by which you will learn them. For instance, you might need to learn project management skills – and there could be a range of learning methods open to you. There may be a computer-based package that you can use, or a video tape to watch, or a book to read, and so on. Hence while Part 3 of the handbook covers tactics that you could use, Part 4 goes into methods and techniques. Figure 1 shows the progression diagrammatically.

Therefore you can see that we have tried to create a logic to the different parts of the handbook. Part 1 lays the foundations; Part 2 provides the strategic options; Part 3 shows the tactical choices available and Part 4 indicates a range of methods to put the tactics into practice. The flow is from high level, more abstract ideas through to quite specific and concrete advice. However, if you just want to know how to use a particular method, because you already have a clear strategy and tactics, then there is nothing wrong with skipping directly to the section you need.

You will also notice that the parts and the sections are not of equal length. The parts grow larger as you go through because there is more to say on each. Also each section varies

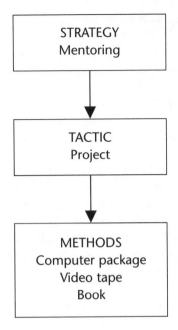

Figure 1   The flow through from strategy to methods

in length because some need more explanation than others. You will notice that each section after Part 1 has a similar structure. We have generally structured each section as follows:

- A description of the strategy, tactic or method
- Examples
- Possible benefits
- Possible limitations
- Operating hints.

All the items that we cover have been tried and tested and offer a wide range of approaches to suit different learning needs. Also we recognize that people have different preferences for how they learn so you will no doubt want to see what fits your own style of learning.

Our approach to writing the handbook has been to cover learning approaches that can work in real organizational settings. Everything we discuss has been shown to work. However, any approach to learning can be badly implemented. A good coach can be of real value; a poor one can be a hindrance. A poorly delivered lecture may be a waste of time while an inspiring one can stimulate learning. No method in and of itself is foolproof. However, one problem that we have observed is that sometimes someone has experienced a learning method that has been badly implemented and so they generalize and assume that such a method has no value.

An example of this which we encountered recently was where an organization had implemented a sloppy, ill-considered mentoring scheme. It didn't work, so some people started to say that mentoring was a useless approach to development. It isn't, of course. Well-run mentoring schemes have been evaluated and shown to be of considerable value. Hence we hope that in reading about particular approaches you will consider the evidence and not be put off any method because of previous bad experiences.

In trying to keep to tried and trusted approaches we have not attempted to be encyclopaedic. There is already an 'Encyclopaedia of Development Methods' (Huczynski, 2001). Our aim has been to give advice and support for using work based learning that can be readily applied rather than mention every variant of a particular approach for the sake of completeness. We have also had to keep explanations within bounds. For example, approaches such as coaching and mentoring have had numerous texts written about them. We haven't tried to match that level of detail. However, we have indicated, at the end of the handbook, some sources of further reading for those wanting more information.

The last part of this handbook contains three appendices. The first one reproduces the Declaration on Learning that one of us (Ian Cunningham) was involved in creating. This appendix provides an overview of learning issues in organizations and can be consulted to get a wider picture on the background to much of what we have produced in the body of the handbook.

The second appendix outlines one university's approach to providing qualifications for work based learning. It is provided here as the growing acceptance of work based learning has been helped by universities recognizing that such learning is not academically inferior to classroom-based learning. Indeed the more universities that accept this the more we will get a sensible balance of state resourcing for learning, as at the moment in almost all wealthy countries there is an imbalance which favours institutionally-based learning.

The third appendix elaborates on the reasons why people do not seem to grasp the importance of work based learning and why they do not act on the findings of research on learning (or the ideas expressed in the Declaration on Learning). We believe that eventually the case for a more coherent and sensible approach to learning in organizations will succeed. However, for the time being we are aware that, for the reasons explored in this appendix, progress is slow. We hope that this handbook will be a contribution to the changes we would like to see in the future.

We make no apology for taking this more campaigning stance in our work. The evidence of the centrality of work based learning is there and those of us who know this have an obligation to continue to demonstrate its importance.

Ian Cunningham, Graham Dawes and Ben Bennett, 2004

1 *The Rationale for Work Based Learning*

Introduction

This part of the handbook contains three sections. The first one is designed to provide a rationale for work based learning. It introduces the topic in a general way and it covers aspects such as definitions as well as research evidence on the use of work based learning.

The second section is written for those in strategic leadership roles, for example, Board members, Directors, senior HR professionals, and so on. It provides a basis for considering strategic choices about learning and makes the case for various approaches to work based learning that all strategic leaders need to consider. The section can be skipped if you don't see yourself in this role.

The third section is primarily for those who need to assist learners either from a professional position such as an HR Development specialist or a learning consultant, or as an individual manager who takes seriously their role in supporting the learning of the people around them. The sections specifically for developers may be of less interest to managers and could be safely skipped over, if necessary.

After Part 1 the next three parts of the handbook are written for learners. We assume that everyone is a learner and so Parts 2, 3 and 4 should be relevant to all readers. Part 5 is a short concluding piece of a more general nature.

A CASE OF WORK BASED LEARNING

Delia Smith is the best-selling cookery author ever in the UK, with some books of hers selling over one million copies each. She has undoubtedly influenced more people on their cooking than anyone else. She has also been a much watched TV star. So how did she learn to do this?

As she comments: 'I want to learn and I want others to learn'. Note that she is not thinking just of herself. Learning is a shared activity in her mind (and in the mind of other excellent learners who we have studied). She clearly has helped others to learn, through her TV shows and her books. But how did she learn?

Her career started with working in a restaurant kitchen washing dishes. She took the job in order to learn how this restaurant produced such high quality food. She spent time looking at how the chefs worked, asking them questions and making notes on how dishes were cooked. She went away and read avidly about cooking, including tracking down obscure recipes in the British Library.

As she developed her ideas she used all sorts of contacts to further her learning. For instance, she talked to people who ran speciality food shops in Soho in order to learn more about the use of particular ingredients. On top of this she experimented widely, trying out methods and techniques.

In all this she never had any training. She learned through work based learning and the kinds of learning methods she used are ones that we will emphasize in this handbook. It is also worth noting that other great cooks/chefs have followed a similar path to Delia Smith. Keith Floyd uses all the approaches that Delia Smith used and in addition he quotes travel as a key learning mode, especially travelling in France in his early career.

According to the UK government, these people are non-learners. They have learned through work based approaches only and they therefore don't count as learners. Yet we can see that Delia Smith, Keith Floyd and other great chefs are brilliant learners. They are passionate about their work and learn avidly all the time through their work. Note that it is this passion and motivation that is a key. Lyn Davies, a former Olympic gold medal-winning long jumper, commented that if someone devotes four hours a day every day to practising something, they will become good at it. But of course in order to do that the person needs a high level of commitment.

1.1 *The Basis of Work Based Learning*

This section is a general opening to the subject of work based learning. In it we will show how work based learning is the central and most important aspect of learning to impact on performance at work. We want to make a case for work based learning before showing the practical approaches that can be used. So often when people at work think about improving their knowledge or skills, they think of going on a training course. Yet the research evidence suggests that this knee-jerk reaction is usually unhelpful and that more cost-effective learning approaches may be available to meet a particular need. That is to say, it might be a case for work based learning.

We are not intending to knock training per se. Off-the-job training has a place – it's just that it occupies a minor place in supporting learning and organizational improvement. For example, at a conference of trainers, we asked about 350 people who were attending a particular session, who used Microsoft Office. Over 90 per cent of the people put their hands up. We then asked how many people had been on a course to learn how to use Office. About 30 per cent of the audience put their hands up. We then asked how many people had learned all they needed to know on such a course. No hands went up. And that is not surprising. Most people learn how to use computer software through reading the manuals, experimenting directly, getting coaching, talking with colleagues, and so on. (Even if you have been on a course, these methods are likely to come into play at some time.)

These latter methods are amongst the work based learning methods that we will explore later. Suffice it to say that in many areas of work people learn all they need through work based learning alone. However, before getting into the issue of work based learning itself we need to say a little about this commonly used verb 'to learn'.

Learning

The UK's Campaign for Learning defines learning as follows:

> Learning is a process of active engagement with experience. It is what people do when they want to make sense of the world. It may involve an increase in skills, knowledge or understanding, a deepening of values or the capacity to reflect. Effective learning will lead to change, development and a desire to learn more (p. 2, 2002).

It's possible to quibble about aspects of this definition – and it's also possible to wheel out numerous other definitions. But, for the sake of a quiet life, we'll accept the general tenor of this definition. Our own simple formula is as follows:

$$U = G + P + L$$

That means that you (U) are equal to what you are born with (we'll call this G for genes and we'll leave aside the possibility of aspects such as 'soul' or 'spirit' as this will lead us into contentious waters), how you develop physically (P) and what you learn (L). That's it. There is nothing else that we know for sure makes up a human being. We are either born with particular attributes or physical maturation changes us or we learn things. Since, for the time being at least, we can't do much about G and P, the only way in which we can reasonably change for the better is through learning. There is no other process available to us.

This makes learning a ubiquitous process. Indeed the verb 'to learn' crops up all the time in our language. 'I learned today that the train timetable has changed for the summer'; 'I just learned something new about our neighbours'; 'I learned how to grow tomatoes', and so on. What is strange, then, is that the UK government and other official bodies talk about many people being 'non-learners'. Indeed on the same page of the Campaign for Learning's definition appears this quote from a research study:

> ...the vast majority of people who have not engaged in any learning since school, 33% of the total, have no intention of taking up learning.

Strange. Indeed it's totally nonsensical and, juxtaposed with the Campaign's own definition of learning, makes no sense whatsoever. People learn every day of their lives and in all sorts of ways.

So what's going on here? The answer seems simple. The authors of the Campaign for Learning document, along with many in the education and training establishment, do not accept that proper learning can occur unless they sanction it through official channels, usually via a 'recognised course'. Hence real work based learning can disappear from official recognition.

However, we also find many official UK government reports referring to learning at an organizational level. The Department of Health's website for 'Area Protection Committees' mentions 'The lessons to be learned from Serious Case Reviews' (DOH, 2002). The use of the verb to learn in this and other cases seems to refer more to learning at a higher, more macro, level. Yet it is arguable that we are dealing with a similar process to that which goes on at an individual level. People change as a result of learning and in the process hopefully the organization benefits.

Given the continual reference to 'learning from experience' in organizations, we might expect a more rigorous analysis of what is involved. However, more often than not, official documents seem to imply that the learning needed is a simple process that needs little further comment. Is it possible that the obsession with formal, recognized courses as a vehicle for learning stops the authors of official reports from being able to make a more useful analysis of what is required, namely, work based learning?

TYPES OF LEARNING

Another problem with the verb 'to learn' is that it can imply that learning is all one process. We have already mentioned how the term can be used differently at the individual and the organizational level – and we will return to this issue later. Another factor is to recognize that learning to be more self-confident is quite a different process from learning a specific date – say, the date of the Battle of Hastings. The process of memorizing a date is quite different from what is usually seen as longer term and deeper learning, namely, to be more self-confident.

In the context of work based learning one particular distinction can be important, namely, between learning that is dependent on context and learning that is less so. To take a specific example, learning to use a laptop computer is largely independent of social context. If you use the laptop in a hotel in Hong Kong, Hamburg or Harrogate, the skills and knowledge required are pretty much the same, and are not affected by other people who may be present at the time.

However, if you learn to lead a tribe in Africa and then hope to transfer that learning to leading IBM (or vice versa) then you would find that context is dominant. In work based learning this distinction is important, namely, between learning independent of social context and learning dependent on social context.

Later we will return to the issue of transfer of learning as this has a bearing on what we have raised here. For the time being we merely want to log that the verb 'to learn' can actually cover a range of processes (further discussion of some of these distinctions can be found in Cunningham, 1999).

THE CASE FOR LEARNING AT WORK

'*Reductio ad absurdum*' is the process of proving a proposition by showing that its opposite is absurd. The use of *reductio ad absurdum* as a method in maths has always appealed to us, so it occurred to us that we could use it in our field. We therefore intend to prove that investment in learning at work is essential by using this tried and tested logical methodology. We will do this by showing that not investing in work based learning is genuinely absurd.

Let us first take an organization that is opposed to learning. In this organization people would be forbidden to learn anything. When a person is recruited they would be forbidden to learn how to do the job. This would only be a slightly more extreme version of the organization that claims only to recruit those who are already competent in the job. Also this organization presumes that all the processes and rules in place in the organization are 100 per cent the same as those in the organization the person left – that is, no learning at all is needed.

Let's assume that the recruited person really can do everything required in the new job. What happens when some new technology arrives? They would be told not to learn how to use it. What happens when they face a new customer? The answer presumably is 'don't learn about them – just treat them the same as all previous customers'.

We could go on but we hope it's not necessary. An organization that forbade learning at work is logically impossible – it could not exist. However, we now need to address the next issue. The leadership of a business could say that they don't forbid learning but that they will not invest in it. So let's see how this organization would fare.

If we go back to the new recruit the organization would not provide any induction into the new job. They would also not allow more experienced members of staff to waste time coaching the person or even explaining any of the organization's rules and procedures. Because, if a more experienced person were to take time out from their work to brief or coach someone, that would constitute an investment in learning. The experienced person would, for that time period, be unproductive, so there would be a real cost to the business.

If a new piece of machinery were to be introduced into the company no coaching would be provided. The leaders of the business might expect people to read a manual to learn how to use it. However, the time that the person takes to read the manual is unproductive time and constitutes a cost to the business, that is, there is a real investment in learning even if the company does not recognize it. If no manual was provided and the person was told to learn by trial and error the chances are that there would be at the very least poor productivity and most likely actual damage or safety problems.

Again we could go on with ever more absurdities. We hope the point is made. Organizations invest in work based learning whether they recognize it or not. And the organization that did not would be impossible to imagine. We may, though, need to take the issue beyond *reductio ad absurdum* into the real world of organizations. If all organizations have to invest in learning then are their current investments wise? The muddling-through mode seems to be very wasteful. Relying on learning to take place by happenstance looks pretty inefficient.

To go back to the organization that claims not to invest in learning but is actually doing so, we could make the case for a more effective investment. When new machinery arrives people could learn to use it more efficiently if they were, say, coached in its use. The investment in a coaching session is likely to be less than the investment in happenstance learning. Unproductive time wading through a manual or learning by trial and error could be reduced greatly. All of this is basic stuff and hopefully does not need labouring.

To put some hard evidence on this, a Scientific American study reckoned that the cost of a computer terminal could be doubled if one took into consideration learning costs (IT people's time in advising people, colleagues providing informal coaching, and so on).

So why do organizational leaders make critical remarks about investing in learning? The main reason seems to be that they (and many HR professionals) equate learning with training and education. The government does not help when it talks about people not in education or training as 'non-learners'. So when the notion of investing in learning is mooted the image for many business leaders is one of increased spend on training or sending more people on educational courses. And the education and training establishment has a vested interest in promoting this view – this is how they make their money after all.

But all of this is totally wrong headed. Most learning that goes on in organizations has nothing to do with education or training. It is work based – as it should be. However, one major point we want to make is that the cost effectiveness of work based learning could be improved in most organizations.

DEFINING WORK BASED LEARNING

Having made the case for learning at work, we now need to say how we intend to use the term 'work based learning'.

The first issue is to distance this handbook from the use of 'Work-Based Learning' as an approach purely designed for school children to learn outside the classroom for part of their time. Naylor (1997) says that work based learning 'is part of a three-pronged approach to school-to-work transition that also includes school-based learning and connecting activities'. This is not how we use the idea. We are interested here more in adults in work rather than school children learning *about* work prior to leaving school. (This doesn't mean that many of the approaches we describe later could not be used with children. Rather we want to establish a specific focus for this handbook.)

When we refer to 'work' we do not just mean paid employment in organizations. Many people, for instance, work in the home or are self employed or do unpaid voluntary work. We are therefore interested in work in its broadest sense, though our examples will be drawn primarily from organizational life.

We also focus on learning linked to real work. We therefore distinguish our approach to work based learning from the way some writers use the term 'workplace learning' (for example, Matthews, 1999). Workplace learning may include a university or training organization running a standard course in the workplace but primarily using standard teaching methods such as case studies, lectures, simulation exercises and role plays. Such activity could just as easily take place in the university or a hotel. And even where material is supposedly tailored to the needs of the organization it is still delivered in a teaching/training mode.

To take the example of Matthews (1999) as a typical writer on workplace learning, she implies that workplace training is central to workplace learning. As she says, 'Managerial commitment to workplace learning needs to be secured at the beginning of the training process. Managers should be involved in needs analysis, identifying skill deficiencies in employees, and deciding what type of training would be best' (p. 25). From our perspective training is only one option for meeting identified needs. To be fair to Matthews she does acknowledge the role of 'informal learning' but our concern is that such informal learning gets downgraded compared with 'formal learning'.

Another cause of the problems of definition comes in official documents from the UK government. An example is in the report of the Adult Learning Inspectorate (July, 2002). In this report the terms 'work based learning' and 'work based training' get used almost interchangeably. Hence the report's criticisms of much work based learning provision seem, on careful reading, to be more about training courses and less about learning through real work. Similarly the Department for Education and Skills in its 20 June 2002 Statistics Release comments on 'Work Based Learning for Young People' (WBLYP) as covering Advanced Modern Apprenticeships, Foundation Modern Apprenticeships, Other Training (sic) and Life Skills. That's it. If you are a young person and not signed up for one of these formal programmes you are not counted as doing work based learning.

In our approach we are closest to the definition of work based learning which Woodall (1999) used in her research on work based management development, namely 'development that occurs in the course of or as a consequence of the real work activities that constitute a manager's job role' (p. 24). This definition is different from that used by Levy (1987) who adds in the use of off-the-job training, that is, his definition is closer to what we have called workplace learning.

Some research evidence

We conducted a research study that involved in-depth interviews with 140 people in ten organizations in the UK. Our aim was to explore the reality of how people learned to be more effective and to progress their careers. The research was conducted by a team that included two other colleagues, Jane Cooper and Caroline Cunningham. The advantage of the use of the team included the opportunity to share material and to develop ideas – we were learning together as a team throughout the research programme.

The first result to quote is that we confirmed the findings of other research studies (for example, Burgoyne and Reynolds, 1997; Eraut, 1998) that most learning that is of relevance to work is not achieved through education or training. The figure that comes out as a general average from all the research studies is that at most 10–20 per cent of what makes a person effective comes from education and training.

The following is a typical quote from our research. It comes from a former secretary in the National Health Service.

I was very lucky to work at (x) Hospital in the (y) unit where there was very much an atmosphere of, you are not just here to do typing but can get involved in what is going on, 'If you want to help us with the research or if you want to stay late and sort out the computer, that's great' and I learned an awful lot there and it was that experience which motivated me to get on and make a career. I put a lot of my time into it, using weekends and evenings working on the computer database we were using for the research. I also learned an awful lot from (z) who was in the unit and let me do a lot of the administrative work that was part of her job.

The atmosphere of the unit was very motivating. Everybody in that unit was in it because they wanted to develop their career and they were very motivated to get on, and this just motivated everyone else. My particular boss, I think, had the confidence in me to let me do things that she was responsible for and the fact that she let me do them increased my confidence.

So in the unit I was seen as the person to go to first of all, especially by the nurses. My boss would tell them to see me if there were things they wanted to know. So they came straight to me, they didn't even bother to go to her first, so my role in the unit was much more than that of a secretary, and I think I was seen as more than a secretary as well. Sometimes my boss would pass on things to me, she'd say, 'I'll hand all this over to you to sort out' and I would often have to go to other people to find out information I needed to know, and then I'd get it all sorted out.

It was a close unit. Although I was a junior I sat with the senior staff in the coffee room and joined in their conversations. They would talk about things in front of me and they obviously trusted it wouldn't go any further. The job I'd had before had been as secretary in a laboratory in another place and there it was just a matter of putting in the allotted hours. I got very bored, very quickly. There was no motivation at all and I left after six months. I need a challenge. If I stop learning, then I'm not going to be motivated, and that means I couldn't be doing my job very well.

On reading this extract from the research interview it is easy to see some themes, such as the interviewee's use of the word 'motivation'. She also describes neatly a contrast between a poor learning climate and a good one, and how she learns from others around her. Similarly, she indicates how she had developed her ideas about a career. Overall, in an unstructured way, she started to be more strategic about her learning; she developed a big picture/long-term perspective.

None of the learning this person described as significant for her had come from courses. And, of course, she would be categorized in official documents as a non-learner.

We could repeat the story told above many times. Our research provided rich evidence of work based learning. However, we also had examples where the support for work based learning was lacking. The secretary in the example mentioned her previous experience as being one where she was not stimulated to learn. This was unfortunately all too common a finding in our research. Yet even in difficult circumstances people could still find ways to learn through work.

Woodall (1999) carried out extensive research on HR professionals to explore their attitudes to and perceptions of work based learning for managers. She quotes that they saw the following challenges as definitely developmental:

high profile responsibility
developing new directions
unfamiliar responsibilities
influencing without authority (p. 26).

We would agree with this, from our research. However she went on to quote challenges that were seen as 'definitely not developmental' (p. 26). These were:

handling adverse business conditions
dealing with a lack of top management support
dealing with a lack of peer support
handling a difficult boss (p. 26).

What is interesting is that these are the *perceptions* of HR professionals. Our research explored how people did learn in reality. And we had examples where the supposed 'not developmental' challenges did prove developmental for some people. For instance, one interviewee mentioned that she had had a very difficult, authoritarian boss. He would, for instance, demand material for a Monday morning on a Friday afternoon. She said that, while this was unpleasant at the time (and not the way she would ideally have liked to learn new things), the pressure from her boss did actually make her learn. Because she would have been in trouble if she had not delivered, it pushed her to develop more than she might have done.

We are not here suggesting that everyone would learn through this kind of treatment. And we certainly do not want to champion authoritarian bullying. Rather, what we want to show is that people appear to learn at work through many different means – and that learning is not always via a pleasant or enjoyable route. Indeed Woodall herself quotes the research of McCall *et al.* (1988) where they found that successful managers did learn from difficult bosses. That being said there is no doubt that some work contexts do provide more congenial support for learning – and the extensive quote from the NHS secretary cited earlier indicates this.

Planned versus opportunistic learning

The research we conducted confirms that of others in the field (for example, Woodall, 1999; Burgoyne and Reynolds, 1997; Eraut, 1998), in that most work based learning is opportunistic and unplanned. People learn from things as they happen. However, many organizations have used more planned and structured approaches. We found, for instance, that there was a growth in planned mentoring schemes in some of the organizations that we studied. Other organizations had planned assignments to provide developmental experience for particular individuals.

One reason for this handbook is to promote the more explicit use of organized and thought through learning processes in work. It's clear that the learning from day-to-day activity will just get on and happen. However, it's also clear that many organizations are missing the opportunity to maximize learning from work contexts. For instance, we have found that people were sent on time management courses which did little good, when the organization had people who were excellent at time management and who could coach others to be more effective.

Coaching is just one of the many methods that we will mention later. We could have also suggested other approaches to meet this need. What we want to promote is the notion that the first option that needs considering, when looking at a development issue, usually ought to be inside the organization. In Appendix I (the Declaration on Learning) we make this point quite explicitly.

Modifying training

Reynolds (2002) makes a neat distinction between what he labels the 'traditional approach' and a 'business-focused approach' to training. An example shows the distinction he makes. He postulates how the two approaches would deal with a specific topic:

> **Customer care**: *Traditional* – Lecture people on why customer care is important. Do a few role plays.
> *Business-focused* – Give people a phone and a list of customers. Have them ring up real customers to find out what they want and how that compares to what they get. Have people ring up real customers with real complaints and resolve them. Bring in a real customer into the training room and have people find out what he or she wants (p. 9).

Reynolds is commenting here on improving traditional training but it does not take much imagination to see that the activities he suggests could be detached from a formal training course and integrated into working practices. Indeed, one has to wonder why he invokes the use of the training room in the second example. Just bringing in real customers to an organization to talk to them (or, even better sometimes, visiting them at their workplaces) is highly effective.

The problem we face is this continuing commitment to the training course and the training room. Gallwey (2000) quotes an excellent example of what works and what doesn't in improving customer care. He worked with telephone operators in AT&T and he developed approaches that did not require traditional training. He first of all went to see the operators and found that they were bored with their work. As one commented: 'After the first six weeks, there's nothing more to learn on this job. We've heard all the problems and know how to handle them. I could do this job in my sleep and sometimes that's just how it feels' (p. 37). Note the reference to the lack of learning.

One of the things that Gallwey did was to get learning back into the work. However, he did not try to impose the wishes of senior management to get the operators to improve 'courtesy, accuracy and productivity' (p. 37). Rather he started to work with them to address the problems that they had identified to him, including boredom and stress. He sat with a group and asked them simple questions like 'What can be learned besides mere data by listening to the customer's voice?' (p. 38). Initially the operators were not sure what his questions had to do with their jobs. However he asked them to try an experiment.

> We asked them to rate on a scale of one to ten the degrees of 'warmth'; 'friendliness' or 'irritation' (in the voices of customers). The next step was for the operators to learn to express different qualities in their own voices... The operators began to see that by choosing to express different qualities in their voices, they could have an impact on how they felt as well as how customers felt (p. 38).

To cut this part of a long story short, his approach produced a marked improvement in courtesy ratings and the operators demonstrated less boredom and less stress in their work. However, this was not the end of the story. The supervisors of the operators were less happy as they were less in control. So, increasingly, supervisors were put in charge of what became a more standardized training programme – and the results of this were poor, hence killing the process of learning that Gallwey had introduced.

There are a couple of lessons in this. One is the use of job based learning driven by the workers themselves. The other is the need to involve more senior people in order to get support for something that does not fit the traditional mould. Both issues raise the problem of power and control. The operators learned to improve when empowered to take charge of their own learning; the process was undermined when supervisors and managers wanted to re-assert their control.

This leads us into providing another rationale for more self directed or self managed processes of learning. Daniel Goleman has become well known through popularizing the idea of Emotional Intelligence (EI). In a recent text (Goleman *et al.*, 2002) the idea of resonant leadership is a feature and the following four aspects of Emotional Intelligence are suggested as important, namely: self awareness, self management, social awareness and relationship management. Gary (2002) provides a good summary of this work and he quotes Goleman and his colleagues as arguing that:

> Most training programmes that seek to develop EI and leadership skills fail because they target the neocortex, the part of the brain that governs analytical and technical ability, rather than the limbic system, which controls feelings, impulses and desires (p. 5).

Goleman argues that a more self directed process is needed to help the limbic system learn, as the latter requires, among other things, a slower learning process that taps feelings and values. His approach is very much the same as what we call 'Self Managed Learning', namely, that the learning process needs to give the learner a chance to explore their own strengths and weaknesses, to discover where these came from and to set their own learning goals. This then can lead the learner to experiment for themselves with new behaviours, though they will need a supportive context within which to do this.

Note that Goleman's ideas are close to Gallwey's, even though both come at the issue from different directions (Goleman as an interpreter of brain research and Gallwey as a successful sports coach). Where both lead is to a particular interpretation of work based learning. That is, they show that certain characteristics will make work based learning effective and other features may inhibit good learning. (Appendix I, reproducing the Declaration on Learning, provides another example of principles that have been proven to be important.)

Transfer of learning

The simplest definition of transfer is 'the degree to which behaviour will be repeated in a new situation' (Detterman, 1993, p. 4). Transfer of learning is therefore a key issue. One reason for supporting work based learning is that, properly carried out, it can often make the problem almost redundant. If you have a work problem and you learn to solve it there is no transfer of learning involved: you have learned precisely what you need in the situation in which you work.

The major transfer problem lies in the education and training world. In this context people go away from their work, learn things on a course and then have the issue of transferring this learning to real situations back at work.

The Detterman and Sternberg (1993) collection of papers is one of the best and most rigorous expositions of the issues of transfer. Research quoted there suggests that, from US evidence, useful transfer of training to work may be as low as 10 per cent. In other words, billions of dollars a year could be wasted on the model of taking people out of their work contexts and exposing them to information, ideas and new skills that are not used at all, ever.

The issue of transfer in work based learning is a bit different. We may want to know not just that a person has learned a particular skill, but whether they can use it in a new situation. So we might well be interested in transfer of learning. However, it may be that what happens is that people undergo new learning as they go from one situation to the next, that is, little transfer may need to occur. We will look at this and other related issues in the next section.

KINDS OF TRANSFER

Much of the literature (and common parlance in organizations) assumes that transfer is all one process. However, it can be useful to separate out a number of aspects. First, we can distinguish between *near transfer* and *far transfer*. Near transfer is where the learning is close to the job requirements. So learning to use particular software on a PC at someone else's desk may transfer to you using the same software and hardware at your desk. This is near transfer. Far transfer would be where you learned to speak German and this helped you to learn Japanese. Both are languages but they are quite dissimilar and if learning one helped you to learn the other it would be a case of far transfer.

An example of the claim for far transfer was the notion in schools in the past that learning Latin was a training of the mind that would transfer into learning other things more effectively. The problem with the notion of far transfer is that the balance of research evidence suggests that it is very difficult to justify many of the claims made for its existence. Certainly there is no evidence whatsoever to support the assertion about learning Latin (see Detterman and Sternberg, 1993). Learning Latin may help you to learn other languages that have Latin roots to their vocabulary but the idea that Latin is a special training of the mind has long been discredited. Like so many of these claims for far transfer, it can be traced back to special pleading by those with a vested interest in maintaining a fiction (in this case educationalists and especially Latin teachers).

The strength of most of what we will cover in this handbook is that it is about learning which often requires little or no transfer. A good coach helps a person to learn precisely what they need and often no transfer issues come into play. If, for instance, you are struggling to learn how to use a new piece of software, someone may coach you at your computer on using it. It is direct learning linked to a specific need. They may also show you how to use the help facility so that you don't need to ask them in future. None of this requires transfer to new situations or assumes that by learning to use a piece of software you will transfer what you have learned to some unrelated task.

Let us, though, look at some of the research evidence on transfer. For instance, the Detterman and Sternberg (1993) collection of papers quotes how students may learn statistics in the classroom but then not use what they have learned to solve a statistical problem outside the classroom. They also show how learning mathematical methods in a maths class does not transfer to the use of maths in physics. These would be examples of transfer that did not look 'far' but may turn out to be so because the context changes.

Some of the research evidence also challenges assumptions about the role of intelligence. For example, in some tasks, the ability to respond to a new situation is not related to intelligence at all.

One surprising piece of research is quoted by Detterman and Sternberg (1993). Here, an experiment was conducted where people were faced with making a choice from circles and squares on a page with each in a different colour and in a different position. The problem was presented to two groups: students and people with learning disabilities. The correct choice that people had to learn was to choose a circle (irrespective of colour or position). After a number of rounds (in which, not surprisingly, the students learned quicker) the experimenter changed to another problem without telling people. This time the correct dimension was position – colour and shape were not relevant. The students found this difficult (and sometimes impossible) whereas the people with learning disabilities solved it almost immediately. There are good reasons why this is so (for people with learning disabilities, position is a more important stimulus). The reason for quoting this research (which has been replicated) is that we can make erroneous assumptions about learning capabilities.

Theorists such as Argyris (1990) and Bateson (1973) have argued that there are different kinds of learning. If we learn in ways which are specific to situations then transfer becomes very difficult. However, if we learn about learning in more fundamental ways, then we may be able to operate effectively across different contexts with greater ease. For instance, Herb Simon (1991) won the Nobel Prize for economics yet he was not a trained economist. He claimed that as a young man he 'learned' that he could learn anything that he put his mind and energies to. And he proved this throughout his life, publishing outstanding material in psychology, artificial intelligence, political science and economics.

Our interpretation is that what Simon learned as a young man was not the same as learning the academic subjects that he used in his work. Bateson (1973) made a clear distinction between these two kinds of learning: learning a subject and learning how to learn. Argyris has developed these ideas further. One of his pieces of work supports the case that intelligence is not the sole determinant of learning ability since he has been able to show that supposedly intelligent management consultants can also use their intelligence and articulacy to resist learning.

It is not our intention to discuss the wider implications of the work of Bateson and Argyris here. However, we can take the case of Herb Simon and say that just learning one academic subject did not make him better at learning others. The fact that he had learned to be a good learner was not in any way related to his undertaking lots of learning of theories and skills. Our case here is, then, closer to that made earlier by Goleman. Learning which involves feelings, desires, values and beliefs is quite different from skill and knowledge learning. And it is likely that if far transfer is to occur it will be via the route that Goleman (and we) suggest, namely, through self managed or self directed learning.

Another distinction in the cognitive psychology literature is between surface structure and deep structure. An example of how this distinction applies in relation to transfer is cited by Detterman and Sternberg (1993). Car dashboards all give similar information, for example, speed, but their dial configurations are different. The deep structure is the same but surface structure is different. On the other hand, an aeroplane dashboard contains dials similar to those in a car but the information presented on them is different, for example, altitude. For the car and the aeroplane there is a similar surface structure but a different deep structure.

We can see that in this example it is easier to transfer learning from one car to another than from a car to an aeroplane. This can be important in thinking about transfer of learning. Indeed, anyone thinking that it would be easy to transfer their learning about car driving to flying an aircraft could be dangerous. The difficulty that we see in much of the discussion about transferable skills is that there is an attempt to create far transfer of deep structure whereas we know that we may be on much safer ground when using near transfer of surface structure.

One example where easy transfer might have been assumed was our experience of helping social workers to learn selection interviewing. They had all been well trained in carrying out counselling-type interviews. They were beautifully non-directive and non-judgemental, helping the client to air their problems and being generally nice and supportive.

When it came to selection interviews, they had to learn to be focused and judgemental – a selection interview is centrally about getting information in order to make a judgement (do you hire the person or not). They almost had to start all over again in learning to interview in this new context. Some of their skills could be seen as transferable, for example, gaining rapport, but the context was so different that it was not about skills so much as developing a mind set for information gathering and judgement. Thus a skill called 'interviewing' could be seen as transferable, but when, in a selection situation, the social workers spent their time being nice to the applicant without getting enough evidence to make a good judgement, it became clear that there was a transfer problem.

The situation we have described could look like near transfer – especially when the label 'interview' is used to describe two different situations. However, it was clearly not so. Indeed, some researchers have suggested that often we want to stop transfer. The social workers needed to avoid transferring aspects of their counselling approach to the selection situation.

THE ORGANIZATIONAL CONTEXT FOR TRANSFER

We have so far only looked at transfer as an individual activity. And we have only mentioned barriers to transfer at this level. However, there is much evidence that there are wider social factors to pay attention to. For instance, a classic paper by Fleishman (1953) showed that supervisors could attend a one week course on how to be better at dealing with their staff. The course trained supervisors to be more people-oriented.

And from day one back at work it seemed that the key lessons had effectively transferred to the work context. Supervisors were more people-oriented. However, when the researchers went back some months later the supervisors had mostly reverted to their previous behaviour. The reasons for this were simple. The managers of the supervisors wanted them to behave as they had before the course.

We also know that other factors in the work context can affect the transfer of learning. Some factors that we identified in our research as barriers to transfer in work contexts include:

- the person's manager;
- the general culture of the organization – for example, one where people are discouraged from trying something new;
- technology, for example, less than user-friendly computer software;
- resources, for example, there is no money to try out a new way of working;
- markets – they are not ready for a new approach;
- the work team – peers can be a bigger influence than the manager in blocking new learning;
- professional barriers, for example, a nurse learning a new approach that the consultant will not let her use because of assumed professional roles;
- fear of feeling foolish, for example, where a person learns a new technique but fears the response of others.

TRANSFER OF LEARNING AND THE INDIVIDUAL

Our own research supports the review of research studies in Yamnill and McLean (2001), namely, that the individual has a large impact on transfer. The key issues are:

- the extent of self management by the individual;
- the setting of goals by the individual.

To take the first issue, the research suggests that where people feel in control of their own learning and are motivated to learn because it fits their needs, then transfer occurs more readily. This does, then, link to the second factor. Random learning, even if controlled by the learner, may be significantly less effective than if the person is working to clear learning goals that they themselves have committed to.

These research findings are in keeping with evidence already presented in this section. For example, we quoted an extract from an interview with a former secretary in the health service on her learning experiences and we indicated that this self managing of learning was a common finding in our research. We also quoted writers such as Goleman who have made the case for a self directed approach.

In the research on the problems of transfer we mentioned studies where attempts were made at transfer of learning and where failures were evident. For instance, in the case of people learning statistics in a classroom and not transferring their knowledge and skills to other situations. Interestingly, we have evidence from our research of people realizing that they needed statistical skills, going off and learning precisely what they needed and then using the skills in their work.

Note the key differences between the two cases. In the first case individuals were learning statistics in the abstract in a classroom and were not in control of their own learning. The teacher was in charge. In the second case, the individual was in charge – they drove the learning process and had a clear reason for learning statistics. The lessons seem obvious to us but are ignored daily by trainers and educators around the world.

Summary

This section has made a general case for the value of work based learning. There are more cases and more research studies that we could have quoted but we imagine that an overload of information could get boring. Suffice it to say that we know of no credible research that would contradict our general position.

We can summarize aspects of our case as follows:

- Work based learning is essential – an organization cannot survive unless people continuously learn at work.
- There is no such thing as a 'non-learner' – learning is part of being human and people learn all the time at work.
- Learning is not all one process – there are different kinds of learning.
- Just learning at work does not guarantee that it will be effective – there are ways of maximizing the value of work based learning.
- Education and training have a minor role to play in supporting learning for work – the role is enhanced if learners can drive what is provided on courses.
- Learner self management enhances effective learning.
- The transfer of learning across contexts is important but not always easy.
- The organizational context may support or hinder work based learning (but it can't totally prevent it).

In later sections we will return to some of the themes that we have introduced here. In the next section we will focus more on the role of organizational leaders and decision makers.

1.2 *Work Based Learning and the Role of Decision Makers*

This section is specifically addressed to those who make top level decisions that affect learning and development issues. We assume that people in the following leadership roles might be involved:

- chief executives, managing directors and other senior directors/Board members
- human resources/personnel directors
- human resource development managers/directors (who may also be called Training and Development Directors, Learning and Development Directors, and so on)
- other senior managers in strategic positions.

The above list is obviously mostly relevant to larger organizations. However, we would also like to address those in smaller organizations, where it may be an owner/manager who is the person who makes decisions on these matters. Whoever it is, we are specifically concerned here with providing advice to managers and directors so that they can make the most cost-effective decisions about learning and development.

One reason that we see this as a serious issue is that our research has shown that senior managers and directors often make poor decisions about development and learning issues. This has been confirmed in other studies. For example, Woodall (1999) found that organizations used only a narrow range of work-based approaches to management development. She commented: 'Surprisingly, HR professionals responsible for management development were often unclear about what other work-based management development tools might be used, and when and how to use them' (p. 25). Woodall's study covered a wide range of organizations, many of whom had supposedly good records for management development, so her findings, coupled with our own and other studies, indicate that there is a real problem here.

We hope that the opening section has provided an unanswerable case for work based learning. Just to reiterate four points, though:

1 Usually the only means that you have to improve performance is through learning.
2 People learn at work all the time. However, the efficacy of this work based learning could be significantly improved in every organization that we have studied.
3 Organizations invest in learning and development, whether they realize it or not. So why not get the best from this investment?
4 Much training and education is wasted effort and the knee-jerk reaction to learning needs of 'put on a training course' is often misguided.

Investing in learning and development at the organizational level

We assume that you, as a senior decision maker, recognize that you have a responsibility to continue your own learning, and therefore Parts 2, 3 and 4 are relevant to you. However, here we want to look at your responsibility to your organization for promoting effective learning. We will use one specific report from the UK government to exemplify many of the concerns that we have at this level. The report is entitled 'An Organization with a Memory' and was produced by the Chief Medical Officer for the Department of Health (2000).

While a report on the health service might not initially seem relevant to, say, private sector organizations, we hope to convince you that it is. One reason that we believe this report has very wide validity is that it looks at issues of organizational learning across many sectors and analyses disasters in the airline, rail and sports industries, for instance. The report shows how across all sectors the lack of organizational-level learning impacts negatively on performance.

The report is clear that the National Health Service (NHS) is not an effective learning organization and that it is poor at learning from experience. The NHS, we should remember, is one of the world's largest organizations and it employs a highly educated workforce which has usually undergone extensive training. What we are dealing with here are inadequacies of their approach to work based learning. The report says 'the failure to learn reliably from adverse events is illustrated by seven simple facts', of which we will quote just four. (Note that when the report refers to 'adverse events' this is a polite way of saying that there was a major, sometimes life-threatening, error/mishap. Often people died who shouldn't have.) Here are the selected four 'facts':

- 'Research suggests that an estimated 850 000 adverse events might occur each year in the NHS hospital sector, resulting in a £2 billion direct cost in additional hospital days alone; some adverse events will be inevitable complications of treatment but around half might be avoidable'.
- 'The NHS paid out around £400 million in clinical litigation settlements in the financial year 1998/9 and has a potential liability of around £2.4 billion from existing and expected claims; when analysed many cases of litigation show potentially avoidable causes'.
- 'Over 6600 adverse incidents involving medical devices were reported in 1999, including 87 deaths and 345 serious injuries'.
- 'At least 13 patients have died or been paralysed since 1985 because a drug has been wrongly administered by spinal injection' (p. 5).

The report goes on to chronicle the human misery caused by failures to learn, as well as the billions of pounds it costs the NHS. Learning is a very serious business. If we take the last of the examples mentioned above, the report points out that the circumstances of the errors were similar and that there is a clear failure to learn from experience. We should re-iterate that we are talking about highly trained people making these mistakes. The Chief Medical Officer was emphasizing that without improved work based learning, such mistakes would continue.

The report does, though, show how such learning problems need to be addressed systemically. The report suggests that the NHS has a blame culture which does not help learning. Clearly errors are made by individuals and, in some cases, it is right to identify such individuals. However, the report comments: 'When an adverse event occurs, the important issue is not who made the error but how and why did the defences fail and what factors helped to create the conditions in which errors occurred' (p. 21).

In later parts of the report there is a clear recognition of the need for a more effective learning culture in the NHS. The report outlines many of the barriers to learning and most of them can be laid at the door of the NHS leadership. A simple example comes from research on maternal deaths. As the report comments: 'A recurring theme [of the research] has been the dangers of inadequate senior supervision and problems with delegation. A report in 1995 concluded that both were still factors in a number of maternal deaths' (p. 69). Put bluntly, women die because managers do not manage the learning process effectively. Inquiries into child deaths due to social services errors come up with similar conclusions.

Further on in the same report is the following damning indictment of the current education system as well as aspects of the work context.

> There is little culture of individual self-appraisal. The education of NHS professionals depends to a variable, but generally significant, extent on clinical apprenticeship – that is, on learning by example. This process rarely counteracts a burden of public expectation of infallibility, and may often reinforce it. Yet for the NHS to learn effectively from experience, these individuals must be able to admit that perfection is not always attained: firstly to themselves, and then to their fellows. Where the ability to self-appraise openly and frankly is absent, the negative effects of the 'blame culture' will be reinforced (p. 77).

The report shows graphically just such a situation. Our own research on learning and development in organizations confirms that the NHS in not alone in having these problems. For instance, we found an engineering-based company with similar issues that hindered learning and, as a result, their safety record was poor. We would argue that senior managers have to look differently at learning issues. And such learning has to be work based. The reduction of errors and mistakes comes through people learning not to make them. Such learning is best driven from the problems encountered in real work. Classroom-based exhortation to improve has a poor record.

Also what the NHS report shows is that the educational system acts as a disincentive to 'self appraisal'. When people sit exams or submit dissertations, academics impose their criteria and their judgements on the individual and there is usually no encouragement for the individual to make their own assessment of their own work. Hence, when the individual enters the workplace they are not used to assessing their own capabilities in work tasks. This can lead to all sorts of self delusions and defensive behaviours (see, for example, Argyris, 1990).

This factor is identified by the NHS report in relation to the apprenticeship that professionals receive. Clearly the technical aspects of such an apprenticeship are valuable. It is useful to learn tips and techniques from more experienced practitioners. And this applies just as much to car mechanics as to clinicians in the NHS. Apprenticeship is also a way of absorbing the culture of one's trade or profession. However, as the NHS report indicates (and our research confirms), there can be aspects of the culture that support poor performance and the wrong kind of learning. This is an area that managers need to address.

How to change organizational culture is a major issue and it is beyond the scope of this handbook to deal with all the dimensions of this topic. What we want to draw attention to is the learning dimension. Leadership, if it's about nothing else, ought to be about tackling cultural issues. And we want to make the case that to get cultural change requires organizational learning – and that such cultural change needs to be in the direction of creating a better climate for learning.

Later in this section we will make reference to some of the specific processes that organizational leaders/decision makers could use. Some of these will have a contribution to make to cultural change, so we will leave aside further discussion of such issues until later.

Measuring, assessing and accrediting learning

We have worked with company boards where there is a desire to get a fix on learning. This prompted one organization to do a competency audit of its managers. All managers were assessed against a series of competency categories and this information was aggregated and presented to the Board. It showed that X per cent of managers possessed competency Y – and so on. When the Board received this information they clearly did not know what to do with it. The original idea was to identify learning needs and, through this competency measurement, to create a strategy for management development. However, the figures were so general that it gave no indication of precise action to take.

Other organizations rely on the appraisal or performance management system to handle the measurement of individual needs. We will comment later on such schemes. Suffice it to say here that many such schemes are less than cost effective. Where they do work is where there has not been an attempt to institutionalize centralized control.

Some organizations have looked to external benchmarking to get a fix on their own development processes. Many of these organizations have looked to the UK government's 'Investors in People' (IiP) scheme. This approach assumes that such external accreditation might not just assess the quality of learning in organizations but might also be a spur to action for an organization not judged to be an investor in people.

By July 2001 more than nine million people (about 40 per cent of the UK workforce) were in organizations that had IiP recognition, or were aiming for it. On this basis it can be seen as a success. Also the IiP organization claims that companies with IiP recognition are more successful than those without it. However, we have to be careful about interpreting this. Bell *et al.* (2002) are not the only researchers to suggest that government agencies such as the former Training and Enterprise Councils cherry picked the better performing organizations to get them into the IiP scheme. The implication is that the process was not

* a company improves learning processes, gets the IiP badge and then its performance improves;

but rather

* a company is seen as a high performer and therefore it is encouraged to carry out formal processes in order to get the IiP badge, hence enhancing the status of IiP, that is, the IiP award may have had little or no impact on performance.

Bell, Taylor and Thorpe (2002) carried out research to look at the impact of IiP. Their findings show that organizations can strait-jacket themselves into the IiP framework and hence neglect, for instance, learning that is seen as about 'soft' skills. They raise serious concerns about the bureaucratization of the processes encouraged in the IiP framework and the lack of responsiveness to organizational differences. One organization that we studied had been turned down for IiP precisely because it did not fit the pattern. The Chief Executive was criticized for his role, yet this was an organization where the CEO was a passionate (and genuine) advocate of learning; it's just that he did not want to bureaucratize his own processes in order to play a game to get a badge.

This latter case is an example of the evidence gained by Bell *et al.* (2002), namely, that going for IiP badging could actually inhibit the wider aspects of organizational learning. If we reflect on the evidence we presented from the Chief Medical Officer, it is not apparent that IiP badging would necessarily assist with the problems he and his team identified. Indeed, as Bell *et al.* (2002) assert, the rigidity of the IiP framework could encourage organizations to neglect important aspects of learning that fall outside the IiP model. Not withstanding the concerns that we have raised, it is possible for an organization to use an IiP assessment in a positive way. The better IiP assessors can give useful feedback to senior management and they sometimes do identify important areas for change. On the other hand, poor assessors can encourage the kind of rigidity that we have criticized.

Our summary advice on the basis of the evidence we have seen is that there may be nothing wrong with picking up an IiP badge so long as your organization does not:

a) delude itself into thinking that this is all there is to solving learning problems;
b) distort your learning strategies to fit the IiP requirements;
c) devote too much time and energy going for the badge.

Cost of learning

We have presented a case for the need to invest in learning. However, senior managers sometimes merely translate 'investment' into expenditure on training courses. And there may also be a case made inside the organization that some work-based approaches, such as one-to-one coaching, are too expensive compared with training courses that can accommodate large numbers. The response of the Chartered Institute of Personnel and Development to this is in their 2002 Training and Development Report. They state, from their research, that very few organizations have any real idea of the cost of training as they are poor at making good calculations on such matters. As they say: 'most training budgets concentrate on the explicit costs of running activities, such as costs for external courses... Opportunity costs such as salaries of those involved in training activities tend not to be covered. Thus training budgets as a measure would mean seriously underestimating the true costs of training' (p.16, CIPD 2002).

Our case for work based learning is made on cost-effectiveness grounds, not just cost. Many organizations are now looking for the cheapest apparent solutions to learning needs. We say 'apparent' in part because of the CIPD evidence; an apparently cheap training course can be more expensive than people imagine. And there is then the issue of effectiveness. Even if a course can be proved to be inexpensive there is still the problem of transfer of learning to the workplace.

In making our case we do, of course, recognize that work-based methods can be used badly and therefore not be cost effective. This is one reason for this handbook; our research threw up many examples of work-based methods being badly applied.

HR policy and learning

Learning issues are seen in many organizations as part of an HR approach. If people are seen as resources then by helping them to learn better they become more valuable resources. In other organizations, learning and development is a separate function from HR. Often this learning and development function sees itself as not treating people as resources but as people. And this can lead to a different orientation to learning.

For the purposes of this handbook, we will look at learning as an issue that should be taken on board in designing strategies for improving people's performance in the organization. We will leave aside issues of whether 'Human Resources' is an appropriate label. Also we will put to one side the issue of internal structures in relation to 'People Development' and concentrate instead on policies and strategies.

To put it crudely there are two strategic arenas to address. We can either align people with roles or align roles with people.

ALIGN PEOPLE WITH ROLES

This assumes that the roles in the organization are relatively fixed and that the interventions we can make are around making certain that people play out these roles for the benefit of the organization.

There are three parts to this strategy, namely:

- recruitment, selection and placement
- learning and development
- career support and guidance.

The strategies here will be readily recognizable. If we have performance problems we can recruit/select better people; we can place people in more appropriate roles; we can develop them; or we can give people career support in order for them to choose better work contexts. If we are looking at aligning people with roles these areas are the key.

If we are to improve these processes from a learning point of view then we can consider the following:

1   With **recruitment and selection**, the organization can put the ability to learn as a fixed criterion in all selection decisions. Many organizations now recognize that it's best to recruit for attitude and develop skills after recruitment. If you have a good committed learner they may be able to learn what is needed for effective job performance. Hence at a selection interview the applicant would be asked questions about how they have learned in the past. This usually means asking about issues in their current job and then seeing how they learned to improve or to cope with change. Note that we are recommending focusing on work based learning. If most learning of value occurs in work then it makes sense to explore such factors in an interview. Too

often interviewers focus their attention solely on courses and educational qualifications. We are not suggesting that such evidence is irrelevant; merely that to ask about learning from courses and not from work experience would be misguided.

2   In **promoting** people, they can be assessed as to how well they have learned in their current or previous roles. Indeed we'd argue that unless a person shows a commitment to learning, why should they be promoted? In their more senior role, for example, as a supervisor or manager, they are likely to have a significant responsibility for the learning of others. If they can't demonstrate a commitment to learning in order to improve their own performance, should they manage/supervise others?

3   Clearly **learning and development** is central to 'aligning people with roles' and other parts of this chapter address this.

4   **Career** issues can be addressed from a learning point of view. For instance, it can be important for people to consider the developmental opportunities in going into a new role. Evidence from research on graduates shows that they are increasingly looking at the development opportunities in an organization when they choose their first job and first employer.

ALIGNING ROLES WITH PEOPLE

The idea of aligning people with roles is only half the story. The other side of the coin is to align roles with people. Here the assumption is that people are fixed and that we can manipulate other variables in order to improve performance. These variables include the following:

- organization design
- role/job design
- methods design
- the design of rewards
- equipment design
- environmental design.

Note that we are suggesting that the key activity is one of designing.

The headings above are not exhaustive of the options that are open to an organization, but they are probably the most used. We will take them in turn – and indicate the implications for learning of any design decisions that the organization might make.

1   **Organization design.** Many organizational design activities ignore the implications for learning. One feature to consider is the extent to which the organization's structure and procedures create:

a)   **Opportunity structures** – allow, permit, encourage, facilitate, require interaction/collaboration, for example, structures which provide opportunities for productive interaction between people and opportunities for learning. These structures might include the opportunity for cross-departmental projects, the use of matrix structures, and so on.

b)   **Constraint structures** – inhibit, discourage, prohibit, block interaction/ collaboration. Here we find the classic organizational silos that can create barriers to collaboration and mutual learning. However, even inside the silos we can see barriers to learning, especially where a manager tries to keep people isolated on a divide and rule basis through the rigid use of a pyramidal organization chart.

2   **Role design.** We deliberately use the term 'role' here rather than 'job'. Role is a broader notion which moves the focus more towards social relationships and away from a narrow task-based perspective. It's clear that role freedom is conducive to learning, for example, where the person can negotiate work relationships and not be confined by a job description. Also the research evidence shows that unless people have the opportunity to use new learning, they can be frustrated and performance suffers. If, for instance, a person is coached in order to learn a new technique it seems wasteful not to let them use it in the work context. Yet this happens.

3   **Methods design.** The methods of work can help or hinder a learning based climate. Business process re-engineering (BPR) was promoted as a magic solution to performance issues through an approach to method redesign. Yet most BPR projects failed. In many cases the learning issues involved in new methods of working were not addressed effectively. Changing methods of working impacts on the need for learning. And the evidence is that if the people affected are given the chance to drive their own learning process, the changes work better.

4   **Rewards.** In one organization, when a person is promoted they are given a budget of £1000 to distribute to the people who helped them to learn, for example, through providing coaching or mentoring. This is an indirect reward to the person (in that they can't keep the money for themselves) but it is a direct monetary reward for those who have assisted learning. In other organizations there are direct rewards for learning, for example, at Johnsonville Sausage in the USA, hourly paid workers receive an increase in pay for every new skill that they learn. At the top level in an organization, we were involved in bringing in a rewards scheme whereby salary increments were tied to learning. Bonuses were related to performance but performance was not linked to salary. The argument being that performance can go up or down but learning is an irreversible change and an ever increasing value to the business. And that learning contributes to long-term strategic value.

5   **Equipment.** Here the most obvious example can be the computer. For instance, if the organization is promoting e-learning, does everyone have access to a PC or terminal in order to access learning materials? And is the computer software user friendly so that it makes learning easy?

6   **Environment.** In a recent example we were working with a major retailer that wanted to get purchasing, logistics, merchandizing, and so on, to work together. The company created a matrix structure, but the real cross-functional learning only occurred when people were co-located. So, instead of having purchasing on one floor, logistics on another and merchandizing on another, teams were put together on the same floor and in an open plan office. This meant that the purchaser, logistician and merchandizer were next to each other and could rapidly learn about each other's work, to the benefit of the team and the business.

Bringing it together

If a company wants to link HR strategies and policies to improved learning, it may be important to consider all the factors that we have mentioned and look for a coherent synthesis of these. However, we recognize that a manager may not be able to make all the decisions on their own. Hence there is an issue of how, from their domain, they influence others to take these matters seriously. For instance, a line manager who loses a key member of staff may focus narrowly on getting in an immediate replacement without thinking of the longer-term implications, for example, are they a good learner such that they will cope with changes, does the job meet their career aspirations, and so on.

A major problem in organizations is that many HR matters are 'today problems' and learning seems like something that can be put off until tomorrow. The manager who has to attend an industrial tribunal to defend a company decision may be more interested in that than the development of people in the business. This means that creating clear strategies for work based learning becomes even more important. Without a strategic focus on learning it is easy for organizations to neglect such matters in the heat of daily action.

Eraut et al. (1998) suggest that the most important strategic decision is the appointment of managers who take work based learning seriously and who see it as their duty to foster a learning climate. They point out that one problem is that management development activity usually neglects to pay attention to this issue. Managers get instruction in a range of tasks that are seen as important, but the Eraut et al. research confirms our own findings in identifying that skills in areas such as coaching have been sadly neglected.

Another dimension of the problem of HR policies and activities was identified in the Woodall (1999) research. Her findings are in keeping with our own in identifying that HR systems and procedures can be a major issue. For instance, it is the policy of many organizations for people to have Personal Development Plans (PDPs). In reality, very little usually happens with these. As Woodall comments, there is very little follow up even if PDPs are written and usually support for the learning indicated in them is sadly lacking.

In our own research we can recall one organization that claimed to have a widespread use of PDPs. Since this was out of keeping with many other organizations we had studied, we asked to see those produced by the training and development staff. This, in reality, proved a problem and a number of the trainers admitted that the PDP was only in their heads – they had not written anything down at all.

Another area that we identified was 'learning inhibitors' in HR policies and practices. This was confirmed in the Woodall study. For instance, performance management systems, to use her words, 'obstruct work-based management development' because they focus on short-term deliverables and 'squeeze out long term development' (p. 27). Even if organizations focus on selecting and developing managers for their ability to develop others (as Eraut et al., 1998, suggest), organizational systems can inhibit effective learning. As Woodall comments, 'Many organisations were so task-focused that the use of time to reflect on learning was perceived as an indication of individual underperformance' (p. 28).

Having shown that current arrangements in most organizations are sadly lacking in providing support for learning, we want now to move to some positive things that you could do. We recognize that even at the CEO level it is not easy to make all the changes that we suggest, so you will need to evaluate what is feasible in your own context. Our first recommendation is for senior decision makers to take seriously the need for a coherent strategy for learning and development.

Learning strategy

In the preface, we introduced the notion that there needs to be a logical flow from strategy to tactics to learning methods. We are focusing in this section on strategic-level issues but we are aware that they may have little meaning unless they are implemented. There has to be a link from strategic decisions to tactics as the first stage. This is often done by being clear about long-term strategy so that tactical decisions such as budget allocations can follow from the strategy.

Too often we see tactics dictating action. For example, an organization may have invested in specific training courses and each year tactical decisions are taken to shuffle them around (a bit more of one and bit less of another, and so on). We found in our research that these budgetary decisions about expenditure on training are usually taken in isolation from other investment decisions that could affect learning and development. For instance, in one organization there was a supposed strategy to develop all managers as coaches. Yet the investment in coach development was so small that it would have taken over 40 years just to develop all existing managers. No one looked at the link between the espoused strategy (all managers as effective coaches) and the tactical decisions about budgets. In effect therefore the real strategy was not to develop coaching capability at all.

A new development in the last few years has drawn attention to the problem of maintaining a strategic focus. This is the growth of so-called bite-size learning. The UK's Learning and Skills Council has been promoting this approach in a national campaign, and consultancies have been quick to jump on the bandwagon. The idea is to provide short sessions of training that may be delivered in a lunch time. Such sessions may last around 90 minutes and seem generally to be packaged modules.

As part of an overall learning strategy, short sessions that brief people on issues can be useful. But what is being promoted by some consultancies is that this is the way to do learning of all sorts. Michael Stark of the Learning and Skills Council is quoted as saying that 'people do everything in small chunks these days' (Roberts, 2003) as a justification for the approach. Mike Cannett of the Chartered Institute of Personnel and Development suggests that 'What people have realised is that we all learn much better in short bursts' (Smith, 2003). Now both these generalizations are quite false.

The fact that there has been a societal trend in wealthier countries to more rapid communication and shorter attention spans does not mean that, in general, learning has to be all in short bursts. Mathematicians struggle for years solving complex problems and their learning may at times vary in pace but it doesn't all occur in short bursts. Learning to be more emotionally intelligent was shown in the last section to be a slow process and other qualities can be seen to take time to learn.

The need for a strategic approach that encompasses different learning tactics and methods is clearly an important issue as there is a danger that gimmicks such as bite-size learning can appear cost effective and easy. In reality, just relying on quick fixes can be low on cost effectiveness as they neglect the complexity of learning processes in organizations.

We will elaborate later on eleven criteria, or factors, that characterize a strategic approach. First, though, we will give a brief outline of other approaches.

From research we conducted on a range of small, medium and large organizations, in the public and private sectors, we identified four main organizational approaches to management learning, development and training, only the last of which is strategic.

APATHETIC/ANTAGONISTIC ORGANIZATIONS

These organizations were especially characterized by top management apathy or outright antagonism to supporting and resourcing learning and development. Many small firms fell into this category. The boss was adamant that funding and giving time to such activity was either a waste or downright harmful. The latter position was taken by those who felt that supporting training and development would lead people to learn things which would make them more marketable (especially if they obtained qualifications) or raise their sights to look elsewhere for a job. The apathetic (the larger group) tended not to see learning as a priority. They felt that in difficult economic times their business survival was linked to other activities (for example, more aggressive selling) than to their employees learning new skills and abilities through organized development activity.

Not only did organizations in this category not sponsor people for courses, they also didn't foster a learning environment. There was minimal coaching and mentoring; induction of new employees was haphazard and there were no rewards for learning.

REACTIVE ORGANIZATIONS

These organizations did provide support for learning, but purely (or mainly) on a reactive basis. If employees pushed their managers they might get funding for an external course. If individuals took initiatives they might find someone to coach them, or at the very least share knowledge and expertise. At one extreme, reactive organizations are close to apathetic; at the other extreme, they could be quite supportive of individual learning.

However, there was no strategic imperative guiding learning, and little or no evidence of attempts to evaluate courses or other developmental activity. Learning was hit-and-miss with no systematic planning (though there might be a designated training budget in the better examples of this type).

BUREAUCRATIC ORGANIZATIONS

These organizations (typically relatively large) did have a training budget and either ran internal training courses or sent people on external courses (or both). Internal courses were highly standardized and often linked to particular grades or levels in the organization. In many organizations, people had to go through a particular course when they reached (or were about to reach) a particular level in the hierarchy.

The main overt commitment to learning in these organizations was through training. People were sent on courses if learning needs were identified (for example, in an appraisal interview). There was usually little emphasis on work based learning (projects, secondments, mentoring, and so on) – though this would, of course, go on informally. In large organizations with regional offices, we found considerable resentment towards head office driven training. The training department would carry out a mechanistic questionnaire-based training needs analysis and then design courses for the whole company based on an averaging of the identified needs. Managers outside head offices usually felt that the standardized offerings that resulted were unresponsive to their needs, and provided little added value to the business (and were certainly not cost effective). However, the bureaucracy required that they conform to head office systems.

STRATEGIC ORGANIZATIONS

These were the minority. They encompassed small, medium and large sized companies and they were characterized by Board-level commitment to learning and development. In the medium and large companies there was an active personnel/HR/management development function which had access to the CEO. The people in HR/development were typically energetic, able, committed people who cared deeply about the business and its success. Senior managers respected them and their expertise was regularly called upon. They sometimes directly supported line managers in coaching and counselling their staff. They were good networkers, well connected inside the organization and outside. They could readily access external sources of expertise as needed and they were knowledgeable about current thinking on management, organizations and learning.

In taking a strategic approach to learning, these organizations would look for direct linkage between business needs and learning activity. They would pragmatically support learning methods that met specific needs, especially those that were work based. They were flexible and responsive to the differing needs of different parts of the organization.

Criteria for strategic learning

In order to exemplify further this strategic approach we suggest eleven criteria by which to judge if an organization is taking a strategic view.

1 *Organization-wide commitment*
   Learning needs to be high profile, centrally resourced, and across the board. There should be no sense of it being a marginal or peripheral 'extra'.
2 *Top management giving demonstrable support*
   CEOs and Directors especially need to show that they are continually learning.
3 *Linked to strategic direction and cultural change*
   A learning approach should be directly integrated into the change process at all levels. If there are any changes planned then what people will need to learn forms an integral part of the strategic planning.
4 *Large-scale development*
   It is not a case of picking a few people to go off on a course, but rather there is an integrated, strategic approach which considers the needs of all staff at all levels.
5 *Development of organizational capability*
   Developing coaches and mentors is often a starting point for widespread development of organizational capability to support and foster learning. With the growth of flatter organizations (and the concomitant reduction in time that leaders can spend with people who report to them), peer group support for learning is starting to loom larger as a priority in strategic learning.

6 **Multi-functional development**
There is enormous value in bringing together people from different functions in the organization to address learning issues. In a learning group (discussed later in more detail) people get to know each other in depth and learn how to support learning across different departments and disciplines. This encourages an integrated approach to learning across the organization through networking. This isn't just a spin-off from a programme (as is often the case on training courses). Such shared learning encourages the open exploration of live issues. This is infinitely superior to telling 'war stories' in the bar between sessions on a training course as a way of getting to know people in other departments.

A strategic approach to learning has to encompass the development of a learning culture across the whole organization. It may seem paradoxical to focus on the personal learning needs of individuals, but when people in a learning group start to see the similarities of some of their problems this enhances the in-depth development of a learning culture. People feel less isolated and more able to be open with colleagues.

7 **Long term not quick fix**
Learning in depth can take time. If people need to learn new ways of working it won't necessarily happen overnight. The creation of a learning culture in an organization takes time and effort.

8 **Cascading down the organization**
Strategic learning means involving everyone in appropriate learning. New development approaches need to cascade down the organization involving other staff. Strategic learning does not stop with managers (though it usually needs to start there).

9 **Part of the organization's competitive advantage**
Strategic learning is becoming a key part of an organization's competitive advantage. Top managers are realizing that unless their organization is learning better and faster than ever before, they will be at a disadvantage. Organizations are starting to make this more explicit.

10 **Visibility**
Strategic learning is being made visible externally as well as internally. It is recognized as part of the strategic direction of an organization, and is something organizations feel proud of.

11 **Integrating strategy and tactics**
Strategic visions and missions are unhelpful without a link to tactical action. The long term and the short term need to be synchronized. Motivation to stick with long-term goals can come from short-term pay-off (which is seen as part of a bigger picture).

In the following material we will indicate some areas that could benefit from strategic consideration. As with other sections in this handbook we are not attempting to be encyclopaedic. Rather, we want to give a flavour of strategic dimensions that we have found to be of value. In later sections we focus on strategic decisions for the learner and the tactics and methods that they might use. We have left aside any analysis of tactics and methods in this section as we want to emphasize your role as a decision maker at the strategic level. However, we hope that you would want, at the very least, to dip into other sections to assess the options for actions that are in line with the issues discussed here.

Developing a learning climate/culture

THE LEARNING ORGANIZATION

We can't progress this section without making reference to the idea of a learning organization. It's a concept that grabbed senior managers in the 1990s but seems now to be less at the forefront of organizational strategy. However, we often find that senior managers will still cling to the idea that they are a learning organization – or at least want to be. And that last point leads us to our first dilemma. Is there such a beast as a learning organization? Many senior managers will say: 'Well, of course we are not yet a learning organization but we are striving to be one'. In this they reflect the comments in the NHS report that we discussed earlier, where the view was that the NHS isn't a learning organization – but the implication is that it ought to be. And maybe it is aiming in this direction (other NHS reports do say this more explicitly).

In this handbook we take an agnostic line on the value or not of the concept of the learning organization. We will not take a stance on whether an organization should be using the idea of a learning organization or not. For one thing, a fuller discussion of all the issues surrounding this idea is beyond the scope of this handbook; we want to keep focused on work based learning. However, there is no doubt that the need to develop a climate or culture for learning is a crucial aspect of the role of senior decision makers in organizations. Hence we will use the notion of climate or culture (and use these two terms interchangeably) as well as making reference to learning organization ideas, where this is appropriate.

There is no doubt that top-level decision makers can have a significant impact in this area. If the organization is to take learning and development seriously there are a wide range of activities that can be undertaken. Some specific ones are discussed below. One simple issue that we would raise at this point is your role in modelling good learning – and the way that you raise learning issues with others.

One famous CEO is reputed to have encouraged people to talk to him about what they had learned. However, when someone mentioned some key learning that was of some value to the business, he would ask 'And who else have you shared this with?' Woe betide anyone who didn't have a good answer to this question. We quote this example to show how, even in seemingly minor ways, a CEO can keep learning high on people's minds – and maintain awareness of the need to share learning. This is as much part of the creation of a learning culture as the grand plans and strategies.

In the appendix containing the Declaration on Learning, there is reference to the role of those in leadership positions in organizations. We reproduce here that section (though we hope that you will refer to the whole text in the appendix).

Leaders in organizations should:

1   Commit to, proclaim and celebrate continual learning as one of the organization's most valuable capabilities.
2   Include the right to learn and develop continually in all contracts of employment.
3   Build into the agreed roles of all managers the primary need to focus on encouraging others to learn and reinforce this through personal support and coaching.

4   Be a role model for learning, by doing such things as asking questions you do not know the answers to, demonstrating how you have learned from your mistakes, articulating and sharing your own learning.

5   Have effective strategies to link individual and collective learning, both within and between groups and organizations.

6   Routinely encourage curiosity, inquiry and diversity of thought as the norm to ensure dialogue about strategy and decision making at all levels.

7   Encourage people to challenge, innovate and experiment.

Much of this can look a bit 'motherhood-and-apple-pie', though we would suggest that there is considerable bite in some of these statements. For instance, in reference to number three we are not aware that many organizations do actually explicitly write into job descriptions this need to encourage learning. Also we know that most managers are not good role models for effective coaching. In item number two, the idea of committing the organization to support work based learning in employment contracts is not met by any of the organizations that we have studied and we doubt that there are any large companies that do this. So it is not quite as bland as it might at first look.

LIFELONG LEARNING

This does not refer to a specific learning programme or to a particular approach to learning. The term is closer to a slogan and advocates the recognition that learning does not stop with the end of formal education. As a term it has been taken up by governments and by the European Union.

We are living in a time of transition and the old view, that after schooling or vocational training the development of ability was due to 'experience', remains a significant influence on how we think of learning. Basically, that view does not recognize learning. The assumption is that ability is gained, through experience, by a sort of osmosis. Today, what is gained from experience is seen as being gained through a process of learning. That focus on learning enables us to consider the variety of ways in which learning may be approached, and to make our choices among them. The big difference is that while our gaining experience 'just happens', we can take control of our own learning.

The idea that learning is a continuous, lifelong process has moved into the foreground at the same time as the world has moved further into the Information Age, and as we discover what this means for us all. From our current perspective, we can see that the more change occurs in the world the greater the importance of learning. Today there is little that we can look at in the social world where learning is not central.

As an example, Ericsson has committed itself, as a company, to lifelong learning. They state that 'We have an environment of continuous learning and development that fosters lifelong learning for our employees.' One programme that we were involved in was to use Self Managed Learning processes to help the company make this ideal a reality. More detail on the use of Self Managed Learning is covered in the next section.

Because lifelong learning is a powerful idea, and is given currency by national and international initiatives, it can be usefully adopted by those who advocate learning. It can support almost any focus on learning, and can therefore be invoked by anyone wishing to position a learning initiative within their organization. The basic concept that learning needs to continue throughout life is hard to deny in today's world. The value of the concept of lifelong learning is that it carries within it the exhortation to us all that we each need to be learning all our lives.

The limitations of the phrase and concept lie, as does its value, in the fact that lifelong learning advocates learning, alone, without pointing toward any particular way of going about learning. In consequence, the phrase can be used as justification for instituting 'learning days' in the workplace. Typically, this means quite conventional educational or training events which, in addition to the inherent limitations of such approaches, carry the unfortunate implication that learning is something which is done on one special day of the week. In other words, such activities fly against the whole idea that learning is linked with life; it is not just a matter of learning continuing throughout the lifespan, perhaps in the guise of serial evening classes in hobbies, but that learning should be seen as being a natural part of the process of life. The whole orientation of this handbook is based on the idea that learning is something which is woven into working life. It is not a separate activity in which you go out of working and into learning. What are being offered here are ways in which learning *is* a way of working. We might step aside from our work in order to engage in a learning activity, but it is our work that provides the focus for our learning and our learning is a way of working on our work.

The same issue, where out-of-date orientations toward learning are brought to bear on present learning needs, can also be seen in many of the national and international initiatives which have sailed under the flag of lifelong learning. There, too, the weight of the past and, perhaps, a distrust of learners' ability to manage their own learning has led to some stiflingly bureaucratic initiatives. These will do nothing to encourage people to become active learners, nor to embrace learning as the pathway to a fulfilling future.

In the Declaration on Learning, which we have already mentioned, the following assertion occurs:

> Lifelong learning should be about a learning approach to all life and work experience, using formal education and training as a last resort. It should not be about ongoing compulsory formal learning events and monitoring against competency requirements.

We agree with this view and we are aware of the dangers of lifelong learning being equated with continual course attendance. One problem is that many in the education and training establishment have a vested interest in getting people on to courses. That's how they stay in business. But such an orientation can be incredibly wasteful as well as demotivating for staff who get turned off learning and development by irrelevant course provision.

Developing individuals is not enough

THE IMPORTANCE OF DEVELOPING SOCIAL CAPITAL

Just investing in developing individuals isn't enough. Organizations need more than good 'human capital' – the development of 'social capital' is even more important. Just having lots of bright people working in an organization does not guarantee success. Witness some of the dot.com disasters. Or note that, as one commentator put it, 'you can have a team with individual IQs of 150 – and a collective IQ of 50'.

If human capital is about having individual talent, social capital is about organizations having the capability to leverage it. As the World Bank says, social capital is about 'the norms and social relationships embedded in the social structures that enable people to coordinate action to achieve desired results' (Dasgupta and Serageldin, 2002). Social capital has been shown to be a genuine asset in organizations – it does contribute to profitability and growth by mobilizing the capabilities of the organization more effectively. But it needs strong relationships based on trust and mutual concern. And these can only be learned through work based learning.

The cost of low levels of social capital include:

- poor sharing of ideas – hence reducing innovation;
- defensive emails as everyone covers their backs (and the ensuing information overload reduces productivity);
- poor sharing of resources – and hence increased costs of duplication;
- lengthy unproductive meetings;
- increased stress due to poor working relationships;
- increased control costs due to lack of trust;
- missed market opportunities due to the lack of high quality shared information;
- higher HR costs due to increased turnover, more disputes, and so on;
- people don't help each other to learn new skills or how to operate the latest computer software – hence increased errors and/or increased training costs;
- poor internal co-operation produces lower quality customer care;
- lack of united commitment to the organization's strategy/vision/mission – hence creating confusion and low morale.

The list could go on. And anyone who has been involved in a failed merger or acquisition will recognize that some of these factors will have contributed to such a failure. As most mergers and acquisitions do not live up to the promised increase in shareholder value we can see that this issue of reduced social capital in such organizational changes is not an esoteric irrelevance. And even if we ignore mergers, there is plenty more evidence of the impact of reduced social capital through mismanagement.

In Table 1.1 you might like to see which side your organization favours. If most answers are to the left, you may have low social capital and the organization may be at risk in the long term. If your organization is closest to most of the right-hand side, you may have higher social capital and therefore have a lasting and valuable asset. However, high social capital is not a magic solution to organizational performance problems. It's one important part of an organization's capability, but you still have to utilize it for the benefit of the business.

Some people read such material and assume that the level of social capital is a given and that it can't be increased. Not true. It is possible to increase social capital by investing in collective development and reducing investment in activities such as individualized quick-fix training, shallow recruitment practices and short-termist rewards methods. Developing social capital requires coherent strategies that are owned from the top and integrated with business needs. These strategies will need to use the kinds of tactics and methods covered in this handbook.

Work based learning is at the core of social capital development. Indeed, taking people away from work and into a classroom where the focus may be only on individual development can harm the social capital of the business. In Table 1 we have alluded to quite

Table 1   The characteristics of social capital

Low Social Capital Characteristics	High Social Capital Characteristics
People are expected to stick to their job descriptions and their defined tasks.	People are expected to support others in the organization and not stick to a rigid job description. (Indeed there may not be any job descriptions.)
The overall strategy of the organization is seen as a top management issue only.	People also have a good understanding of the organization's strategic direction and see themselves as working and contributing to that.
Performance management is only about increasing individual performance.	Performance management is about increasing individual, team and organizational performance.
People are expected to meet individual performance targets any way they want. How they behave to colleagues or customers is irrelevant.	People are expected to behave in appropriate ways with others. People are not just judged on WHAT they achieve but HOW they achieve it. Ego-driven self-centredness is discouraged.
People are expected to stick to their own work areas and keep their heads in their work.	Moving around the building is encouraged. Managers take time to wander around and chat to staff.
Empowerment means people doing their own thing.	Empowerment means the freedom for people to collaborate for the common good.
Managers are judged (and rewarded) purely on delivering short-term results.	Managers are expected to pay attention to the long term and the short term. This includes developing their staff to take on wider roles.
Managers cling on to good people and do not encourage career development.	Managers are happy to develop people so that they can move on to other parts of the business.
Managers can be promoted even if they are poor at managing people.	Managers cannot be promoted if they have not proved that they are good at managing people.
If the organization invests in team building this is purely for the benefit of specific teams.	The focus is on team development where people learn to work in any team (not just one team).
People are recruited against a narrow range of required skills or competences that mainly reflect short-term performance needs.	The top two factors in recruiting are: 1 Is the person trustworthy and able to collaborate with colleagues? 2 Is the person a good learner, so that they can change to suit changing needs?
Mistakes are met with disciplinary action or total inaction (such as avoidance behaviour).	Managers rapidly pick up on mistakes and help people to learn to be more effective. Coaching others is a normal part of managerial behaviour.

Table 1.1 *continued*

Resources belong to the person or their team.	Resources belong to the organization. Sharing across teams occurs naturally.
People do not admit if they do not know something. They don't ask others for help.	Asking for ideas, for information and for help is part of the culture. Admitting ignorance is seen as a mark of maturity.
Rigid mechanistic succession planning is imposed.	Flexible approaches to succession that allow, for example, for late developers, are encouraged.
Short term and/or sheep dip approaches to training are the only formal development activities that are supported.	Strategic approaches to assisting people to learn and develop are viewed as key. Training is only one part of this strategy.
Structure and organization design limits opportunities for lateral and diagonal ways of communicating and working.	Structure and organization design encourages cross-functional and multi-level communication and working.
Morale issues are not taken seriously.	Morale is seen as important and is explicitly addressed by managers.

a range of strategic choices, such as the role of team development. These are discussed more in the next section.

Conclusion

This section has deliberately focused on those in strategic leadership positions. We have wanted especially to address those in senior management positions outside the learning/development/HRD functions. The next section is geared more for those who see themselves in a professional role vis-à-vis learning and development, for example, trainers, consultants and HRD professionals. However, as we have not gone into detail here as to how to tackle the issues we have focused on, it may be that those with a general interest in the subject will find the next section of value.

We have, in this section, developed the case that we made in the first section. We have shown that a focus on learning is an essential dimension of ensuring high quality organizational performance. Much of what we have discussed has raised more general issues than the mechanics of work based learning. Our reason for this is that, given that most learning is in any case in the workplace, any general discussion about learning in organizations is bound to be about work based learning. We used an example from the UK's largest organization, the National Health Service (NHS), to show the impact of poor work based learning and this case raised a range of important issues.

Later in the section we invoked some concepts and ideas that are important in work based learning. These included:

- the importance of learning climate/culture
- the learning organization
- lifelong learning
- the development of social capital.

If you reflect on the NHS case, it is clear that all the above are exemplified in the problems identified in the NHS. The NHS has had a poor learning climate, it is not a good learning organization, it has not invested sufficiently in lifelong learning and it has neglected the development of social capital. Note that this interpretation is based on the facts as elaborated by the report we mentioned – it is not merely our view.

But we should not especially castigate the NHS. The report of the Chief Medical Officer also showed how private sector organizations have faced similar problems. Our case is that all leaders in organizations cannot be complacent about work based learning.

1.3 *Work Based Learning and the Role of Developers*

Our customers on the sales floor are an endlessly valuable source of learning. They teach us so much with the questions they ask and the comments they give us. They teach you a whole lot more than you'll get in any internal memo. (Ingvar Kamprad, IKEA)

To learn about a new job, it would be better to follow people in their daily work than to have presentations. (Catarina Bengtsson, IKEA)

This section is focused more on the role of developers, trainers, consultants and others who get paid for assisting learning in organizations. However, as with other sections, it may be of interest to anyone who cares about learning in organizations. (We will use the term 'developer' as a generic term to cover anyone who assists the learning of others as a professional role, unless we want to make a specific point about, say, training or consulting.)

The first thing to clarify is our use of the verb 'to assist' in the last sentence. We picked this verb deliberately. People in organizations will choose what they want to learn and any trainers who believe that they control the learning of others are deluding themselves. A lecturer may deliver a brilliant lecture but people attending it will take from it what they choose. And, as everyone is different, what they take away will vary. Thus, in many respects, what might be considered traditional learning in a classroom could be seen as 'work based'. By this we mean that good learners will attend lectures and go on courses with their own agendas and these will, from an organizational point of view, be driven by work-based needs. Hence, we see the developer role as assisting others in their learning: it is not about imposing on others.

We find that effective learners may be told to go on a course that has little relevance for their work but they will use it to think about work issues and ignore what the trainer wants to put over, if it does not fit their needs. This is as it should be. Good learners are expert about their own work and usually know best what needs to be learned. In the case where people are not good learners then maybe the role of those of us who assist learning is to help them to become good learners. This may be more important than inculcating particular knowledge or skills.

There is not the space to do justice to the notion of what makes a good learner or what constitutes good learning. Our views are elaborated in Cunningham (1999) though we will say something about the notion of 'good learning' later, but only as it affects this handbook. In a way it does not matter what view you take as to what makes a good learner as we would argue that the approaches to learning that we suggest are not, in themselves, dependent on a theory or model of what makes a good learner. All we want to establish here is that our research has shown that people vary greatly in their ability to learn. Therefore, when we are asserting that good learners generally know what they need to learn, we also accept that poor learners may not. And the latter may need different kinds of support from the former.

Our research in organizations has also shown that these good learners are not likely to have been on more courses than others. Rather, they are better at learning from everyday experience – they are work based learners. This section will, then, explore some issues that might be relevant to this agenda. The rest of the handbook has a wide range of approaches that anyone (including developers) can use directly. And many of these approaches are second nature to good learners. Indeed, some of the sections may seem irrelevant to those who take it as read that they will be focused and strategic about their learning.

This latter point leads us to revisit the model that we proposed in the Preface.

Strategic learning

We have suggested that having an overarching strategy in relation to learning can be important. Just randomly using learning approaches without a clear sense of why you are using them can be wasteful and inefficient. We would argue that developers may be of most help in assisting learners to clarify their learning goals and then helping them to make their own choices about learning methods. Too often we see in official documents and reports that people 'need to be trained in X, Y and Z'. The assumption seems to be that training people means that they will automatically learn what is required, and that training is the only learning mode allowed.

The following is an example of more sensible practice. The driving test is, by and large, seen as an effective means to make as sure as possible that we have safe drivers on the road. We don't care if someone has been intensively trained in car driving or if they have just had a few trips round the block with their parents. So long as the person can show, in a live situation (that is, in a real car in real traffic), that they can drive safely, we have no interest, as a society, in how they learned to do that. One person could have had a hundred hours training from a reputable driving school and still fail. Another person could have done a few hours driving with parents and friends and pass. In the context of the driving test we accept this. So why, in an organization, should anyone care how a person learns to be effective (so long as it doesn't cost too much and is in line with company policy and company ethics)?

We can therefore make a simple comparison between:

1   A training controlled, input-based, non-assessed model

and

2   A self managed, outcome-based, assessed model.

Relating the first model to driving a car, one would insist on X hours of training for everyone but not assess the outcome, that is, all people who have done the X hours training would be assumed to be competent and allowed to drive.

The second model says that individuals self manage their learning and we only care about outcomes. You have to be assessed, that is, pass the driving test. We know which one works so it always seems odd that so many organizations favour the first model.

This point is important as it justifies the basis of this handbook, that is, that by showing a range of ways of learning, individuals can be best placed to make sensible choices for themselves. So what's the role of the developer? So far we may be seen to be doing the developer out of a job. Indeed we have been told that our advocacy of the position that we have taken so far in this handbook is a reason why many developers are wary of work based learning. After all, if people can choose for themselves how to learn – and if courses have a minimal impact on organizational performance – this can seem like a recipe for redundancy.

Our stance would be that developers are more at risk in the long term if they do not recognize the need for work based learning. We know of a number of blue chip companies that have made many instructors/trainers redundant because their activities were not seen to contribute to organizational performance. Our case is that developers should be well placed to take a strategic overview of learning issues and help learners to make good choices for learning. It may be that they are no longer deliverers of training but are able to fulfil other roles that we will explore shortly.

Before doing that we want to return to our strategy model. In the Preface we have suggested that a learning and development strategy provides the basis for making tactical choices. For example, such a learning strategy might include embedding support for learning in the role/job descriptions and activities of all managers. That strategy needs interpreting into tactics. These latter are typically driven by annual budgets. Hence, such a strategy might require the allocation of budgetary sums to the development of coaching capability. The allocation of funds could extend over a period of years. These budget decisions would then need further interpretation into method decisions. What methods will be used to develop coaching capability? The choices here might include workshops; novice coaches shadowing effective coaches; the use of learning packages; the use of the Internet; and so on.

Figure 2 shows the process diagrammatically. Note that what is shown here is just to demonstrate the logical flow from strategy to tactics to methods. It is not meant to cover all possibilities for meeting the particular strategy. Throughout the handbook we elaborate on many of the options available.

Hopefully the example we have just mentioned shows the importance of making the link from strategy to tactics to methods. Given that we know that managers are increasingly busy and often highly focused on delivering short-term results, the role of development professionals in facilitating the creation of learning strategies is even more important than ever. And then there is the role of making certain that the strategies are implemented through tactical decisions and the choice of appropriate development methods.

The views of learners

The 2002 survey by the UK's Chartered Institute of Personnel and Development (CIPD) on 'Who learns at work?' shows that the most used forms of training/structured learning in organizations are classroom-based modes. Yet the survey found that these are one of the least popular with learners, who favour on-the-job learning. This is a problem to which

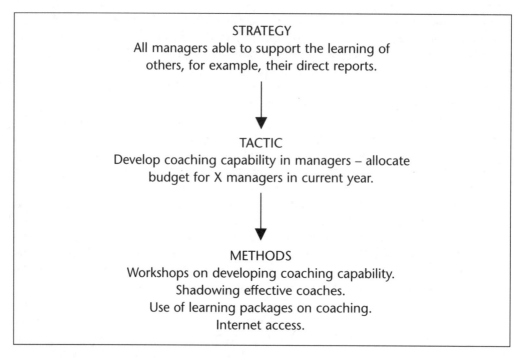

Figure 2   Strategic action

other researchers have referred. There is a mismatch between what people prefer and what is being provided.

When people were asked, in the CIPD survey, what learning method was best, 'being shown how to do things then practising them' was quoted by over 50 per cent of respondents and 16 per cent cited learning from colleagues and others at work. When asked about the least appealing learning methods the following were at the top of the list:

- watching videos
- reading books or articles
- correspondence courses
- Internet
- classroom-based learning.

The evidence quoted from this survey is matched by all other serious research studies. What is particularly interesting about the CIPD report is that here is a major professional body representing trainers, saying to them quite explicitly that they are investing their time and resources unwisely. The CIPD is clear that the balance of investment in learning activities in the average UK organization is wrong.

The issue for trainers ought to be, then, to explore how to shift their work to make it more cost effective and learning effective (to coin a phrase). Later in this chapter we will indicate ideas for the roles of developers in organizations, with specific reference to work based learning. Before moving on, though, we need to mention the issue of diversity.

Dealing with diversity

Another factor that the CIPD survey articulated was the extent to which organizational investment in learning is biased towards those in the higher social groups and those who have already been favoured with greater state investment in their education. As the report states: 'Better educated people and those in higher social classes are more likely to receive training' (p. 3). These inequalities raise serious issues for development professionals. If we know that there is a link between learning and performance, then to get increased investment for those from classes C2DE (where investment is lowest) needs new policies and strategies in organizations. The CIPD report makes the explicit point that 'because on-the-job training is by far the most popular method among trainees, especially the lower skilled and less well educated, those responsible for training may wish to consider whether more resources should be put into on-the-job training *at the expense of classroom training* [our emphasis]'. Note the last point – there is an explicit plea to divert resources away from classroom training. This is obviously significant to those who have a vested interest in maintaining the status quo.

This point is linked to the problems of other disadvantaged groups. For instance, investment in development for ethnic minorities may become a more recognized issue. The danger is that classroom learning is organized in a way which favours white middle-class able-bodied males. Our research has shown that, for instance, ethnic minority groups may have different learning approaches and this is confirmed by Hofstede (1985) and others.

When we consider those with severe physical disabilities it's again clear that much organizational (classroom-based) training does not make it easy for anyone in a wheelchair, with hearing or sight problems, and so on. This is another reason for more individual, work-based modes. Similarly, those with caring responsibilities (for example, for elderly relatives or sick children) may be disadvantaged in not being able to attend extensive off-the-job training, especially if it is residential.

It is also interesting that the CIPD survey showed that there are gender differences. Women were even more in favour of work-based approaches than men. Is it possible that the men who decide on budgets for development may not recognize this gender difference? There are, of course, many other suggested differences between men and women as regards learning, though a full discussion of such issues takes us beyond the domain of work based learning so we will not pursue it here.

The final difference we want to mention here is age. It's clear that older people can learn but that they may learn in different ways. The silly reference to 'you can't teach an old dog new tricks' only buys into the misguided notion that teaching is the prime mode for encouraging learning and that older workers cannot learn. The evidence of our research is that older employees may prefer work based learning modes that allow them to learn in ways that respond to the wisdom they bring to the workplace.

All of the issues we have mentioned above need to be at the forefront of the thinking of any development professional. We hope that the climate will continue to move in the direction of addressing diversity and equal opportunity issues. If this is so it will be dangerous for development professionals to continue to focus on white able-bodied heterosexual middle-class males aged 25 to 45 as this group constitutes less than 4 per cent of the UK population (and an even smaller percentage of the US population). Work-based approaches demand that developers focus on the interplay of the person and their work context as opposed to the creation of ever more superficial ways to entertain people in the classroom. The latter strategy appears to be pursued in a desperate attempt to avoid the research evidence of the need for a move away from the classroom.

Learning styles

The case we have made above links to what is commonly called 'learning style'. Here the notion is that people learn in different ways and have different preferences. Indeed, one could re-label this area as about 'learning preferences' in that we are dealing precisely with how an individual *prefers* to learn.

The commonest model used in this area emanates from the work of David Kolb, though the modification of his ideas by Peter Honey and Alan Mumford has gained wide appeal (Honey, 1997). In this latter approach people are assumed to prefer particular modes and, in this modification, are labelled as Activists, Pragmatists, Theorists or Reflectors. Many trainers operate as if these were the only variations in people's preferences. This is clearly misguided. Below we will indicate just a few of the many factors that influence learning preferences. The importance of this issue is that, as we have mentioned above, there will be an interplay between a person's work context and their preferred learning mode.

An example of this would be where a person is faced with having to learn about a new piece of computer software. Their preference may be to consult others and to get coaching (a more interactive learning mode). However, if they were in an isolated location they may have to learn via the manual and through trial and error on the computer. Hence, learning preferences may not totally dictate the learning approach chosen. This points towards an ideal of a person being able to adjust their learning style to suit circumstances. This objective might indeed be one that developers could address (instead of focusing more narrowly on people learning a specific skill, say). The common term used for this approach is 'learning how to learn'.

Allowing for the fact that the situation might not allow a person to learn in their preferred way, it is still useful to consider learning styles/preferences. If a variety of learning modes are available, one role for the developer is to assist the person to think through what may be most appropriate for them. Honold (2000) makes a stab at suggesting learning methods to fit learning styles and her analysis is worth consulting for those who like the Honey/Mumford model.

In the later parts of this handbook we offer some advice about the use of particular methods. However, our view is that there are so many variables in an individual's learning preferences that it is better to leave aside any notion of being prescriptive. Below we indicate just a few of the choices that are available so that you can consider how to assist an individual learner in their choice of methods.

1 **Sensory preference.** Neuro-Linguistic Programming (NLP) practitioners are likely to be interested in the extent to which a person has an orientation to one particular sensory mode. For instance, one person may prefer a visual mode – they like to see things and want pictures, diagrams, models and flow charts. Another person may be more auditory and prefer to hear new ideas or to read about them. People in reality normally have a mixture of preferences, but there is no doubt that some do have a very dominant preference – and this affects their learning style.

2   **Immersion versus spaced.** Some learners prefer to get a new chunk of knowledge in one piece; they like to be immersed in the topic over as short a period as possible. Others want to absorb new knowledge over time, perhaps bit by bit; they hate trying to learn new material in one go and prefer to take it in over time.

3   **Alone or with others.** Some people welcome learning with others and enjoy the social interaction; they would commonly be labelled extroverts. Introverts may, however, prefer more solitary learning processes. Also sometimes people have had bad experiences as children in a classroom with others, for example, because they have been ridiculed by teachers or other children. This may predispose them to dislike social contexts where they might fear such ridicule.

4   **Courses or not.** Some people like courses and we are not in favour of stopping all course provision (rather, we favour redirecting resources to balance investment in other forms of learning). However, the research says that most people prefer not to learn on courses and our case is that this should be recognized and provided for.

5   **Coached or not.** There has been a growth in coaching provision in organizations and this clearly meets a need. However, not everyone needs a formally allocated coach. In athletics, most successful performers have had coaches. However, there are examples of brilliant athletes who have been self coached – Ed Moses, possibly the greatest 400 metre hurdler of all time, did not have a coach.

6   **Holistic versus analytic.** Some skills lend themselves to be learned best in a holistic way. Bicycle riding is one such skill – you have to get on the bike and experience it as one event; there is a mathematical equation that shows what you need to do on a bike to keep it upright but if you were actually cycling you would have fallen off by the time you had done the calculation. The analytical mode does not work. In organizations, many managers learn by osmosis from the managers around them – for instance, they may adopt the time management skills of their colleagues. If such processes are highly effective then that may be a good thing. However, if they are not, the ability to step back and analyse such processes and improve on them may be required. It's clear that some people are less inclined to do this and prefer the holistic mode. In this case it would be useful to help them to be more analytical learners. On the other hand, the highly analytical mode may get in the way of the holistic. Many successful managers reported to us in our research that they just learned certain things 'from experience'; they couldn't analyse where particular qualities had come from.

7   **'One piece' versus piece-by-piece.** Some skills lend themselves to a piece-by-piece mode; one example is car driving where we learn one element of driving at a time and then have to put it all together. Some sports people clearly develop their abilities in different ways. For example, one world-class football player claimed that he could see another player do something once and that he could replicate the move perfectly the next day on the training ground. However, other players will learn the same skill but have to take time to break it down into its component parts in order to learn it.

8   **Pressure versus relaxation.** In our research we found that some people only learned certain things if they had to and they were up against deadlines, for instance. Others found deadlines inhibiting and needed a more measured approach that fitted their moods or their energy levels. They were more likely to be intolerant of managers who exerted pressure on them to perform than the former group. However, it was also apparent from our research that these preferences (as with others) could change over time or in relation to a particular work context.

9 **Friends versus strangers.** Some people have mentioned to us that they like to use friends to assist them with learning certain skills, such as using a new piece of computer software. Others said that they preferred someone they didn't know; they seemed to feel more relaxed working in a neutral climate.

We could go on adding to the above categories. Certainly our research showed that people varied greatly in the way that they preferred to learn. All we want to do here is to signal that the developer role may, in part, require sensitivity to such factors in order to assist people learning at work.

Roles for developers

We have suggested that the role of a trainer/developer may need to change to operate in a context where work based learning is central and courses are peripheral. We will suggest a model which describes four roles that are needed in this kind of environment. Given our focus on work based learning we will not explore all the nuances of this model (if you are interested, the reference for more information is Cunningham, 1999).

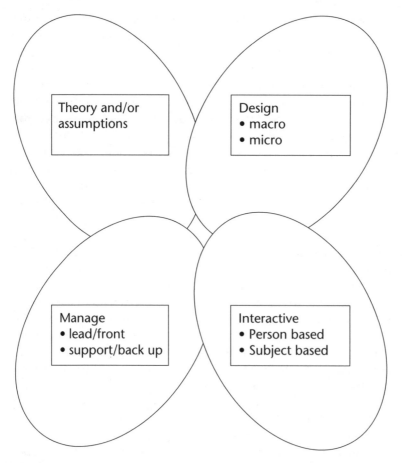

Figure 3   Roles for developers

Our model suggests that there are four basic roles for a developer and we will indicate each in turn. Figure 3 shows these roles in summary.

DESIGN

Developers need to design learning strategies and tactics as well as specific programmes and activities. We therefore divide the designing role into two.

First there is the need to do *macro design*. This is about the big picture, strategic arena. Here you might be working out a total system for supporting work based learning that could include, say, developing coaches and mentors, creating an intranet-based learning support system, developing a learning resource centre, and so on. This activity we see as designing – it requires design capabilities that include innovating where necessary as well as taking ideas from others.

At the macro level the design activity crucially requires systemic thinking. There is a need to picture the total learning environment and to plan how to keep the whole system synchronized. In the e-learning world an aspect of this has been called 'blended learning'. It suggests that you can't provide e-learning on its own but that it needs blending with other methods. We would take a wider view; it's not sensible to start with the idea of blending two or more learning methods. Rather, the whole environment for learning needs to be considered. This is what the best learning organization practitioners do.

Following from the macro design there is a need for *micro design*. Here we are looking at the design of specific events or processes. For instance, with one client where we were assisting them to develop a better learning culture, we started with team events with the senior management and then we ran some large group events to get the whole organization involved. The macro design was about sequencing some activities to move the culture on. The micro design was about creating each specific event such as the one with the senior management and then the large group events.

In working with this client we were challenged to create an effective macro design and then do the micro design that followed it. We should emphasize that built into the macro design was a notion that the actual work based learning was in no way controlled by us. We created structures such as learning groups (see later) so that people could come together to support each other's learning, but what people did in those groups was driven by them. Our notion of design was not to try to direct people's learning but rather to create spaces where they could collaborate and support each other's learning.

The key point about this work is that it isn't about creating syllabuses and curricula for courses (or other controlled learning methods). The micro designs that we have mentioned above, such as large group events and learning groups, did not have a syllabus or required learning outcomes or competences to develop (or any of the other modes used by trainers to attempt to control the learning of others). They were structures that gave participants the freedom to address live issues from their work.

MANAGING

Work based learning can be inefficient without effective management. Developers can provide some of this. (Some of the management will ideally come from line managers or the Board.)

First, there is what we have identified as a leadership role. It requires fronting up the implementation of learning designs. This can include such activities as presenting a case to the Board or marketing new ideas about learning within the organization. Many people, including Board directors, are confused about learning issues and as a result work based learning can be undervalued compared with training courses. Developers may need to have the courage to step out and champion approaches that will support the business and people in it but which may not initially make sense to those who see training as the only solution to learning problems.

The other aspect of managing that is required of developers is more of a supporting or back-up role. For instance, developers may need to manage the link between what an individual needs and the resources that are available. Much of this can be seen as a brokerage role. For instance, a person might be struggling to learn something and the developer can put them in touch with a coach who can assist them. Note that the developer here is not doing something that looks like development. What is required in this context is the ability to understand the learner and their needs and to have the knowledge of appropriate resources.

INTERACTING

Developers may need to interact directly with learners. They may take on coaching and mentoring roles or they may assist learning groups. We call this part of the role the 'P Mode'. In this mode you are assisting learning by focusing on a number of factors such as:

1   *Persons*. The idea is to understand the person so that you can assist them with their learning.
2   *Problems*. Part of the need is to understand the problems that the learner faces in their work and therefore to be able to assist them in identifying what they need to learn.
3   *Processes*. You are working in the context of real organizational processes. People do things in particular ways because that's the accepted process. And their initial learning may be around understanding such processes in order to change them. A good example is time management. Many managers and professionals complain that there are not enough hours in the day to do all that they need to do. They may discover that they have dysfunctional work processes that they could learn to change. The error that is often made in training is to offer hints and tips as to how to manage time better without getting to the root of why the person has a problem. Hence the person may get little from a course as it does not connect to their personal problem.

The 'P Mode' may need balancing with the 'S Mode'. Here we are attempting to assist the person with a problem to get the required help. The need is to start with 'P' – people, problems and processes – and look for the 'S'. Some aspects of 'S' include:

1   *Solutions*. People want solutions to their problems. Developers can therefore help the person to identify new learning that will, for instance, solve performance problems.
2   *Skills*. New skills may need to be acquired.
3   *Subjects*. The person may need to gain subject knowledge to support their learning.
4   *Specializations*. There may be specialist assistance that the person needs, for example, the IT specialist who can help them learn how to use a new piece of software.

We are clear that one of the key facets of work based learning is that it almost always starts with 'P' and then may move to 'S'. (This is an important defining characteristic of work based learning and could be added to the definition that we discussed in the first section.) For instance, in the last example about learning how to use computer software, it may be that a developer can assist the person to have a clear understanding about the exact problem and also to identify the best process by which to learn. It may transpire that the IT specialist is not the solution and that some other way needs to be found to solve the problem.

We recognize that this notion of how to conduct their interactions with learners is quite threatening to many developers. Hence one reason for the continued reliance on directive training methods. If we start in the 'P Mode' we are starting from what can seem the unknown. If we sit down with someone and ask them about what they need to learn we are not in control. In the classroom the trainer plans the lesson and imposes on participants the case study or the simulation exercise or the role play and can run these to predefined plans. If we start with a blank sheet it can seem pretty scary to trainers who are used to dictating content and process in training sessions.

Within the training context, the trainer is considered, and considers themselves, responsible for the learning. The work based learning approach is bound to be scary if a trainer imports that feeling of responsibility but doesn't any longer have control. What trainers may not grasp is that in the work based learning mode the responsibility for learning remains with the learner. In fact it can't really go anywhere else; we could even enunciate an aphoristic principle: You can't be responsible for what you can't control.

There are no easy answers to this problem. The one that we find ourselves engaged in is to say to trainers who want to run courses that they have a role in delivering the 'S Mode' provided learners need it. If they do then there is a role for trainers who can work to the requirements passed on to them by learners or that come via a developer operating in the 'P Mode'. However, it is not always apparent that a trainer is needed to deliver the 'S'. For instance, in one organization time management was a major problem. However, one of the Directors was known to be very well organized and efficient in his use of time. So he agreed to coach people and he also ran some workshops on specific issues. He made a much bigger impression on people than a trainer would have done because he was an acknowledged role model.

THEORY

You need to operate on the basis of a theory when doing development work. Sometimes this is labelled 'assumptions', that is, what you believe to be true (in this case, about work based learning). It is important to have some explicit insight into the assumptions you have about learning. If your learning theory is based on the notion that the only real learning takes place in the classroom, this will affect your practice. Our theory about learning takes a different perspective and was outlined in earlier comments in this handbook.

What is necessary is to be able to articulate a theory to users (especially senior management). Also each of the other three roles previously discussed are dependent on your theoretical assumptions. If you carry out design work, this is always underpinned by theory. For instance, our reference to the use of large group processes is based on theories about organizational learning and about the nature of change. Our use of learning groups is based on the theory of Self Managed Learning (see Cunningham *et al.*, 2000).

INTEGRATING THE ROLES

The reality of working as a developer requires the coherent synthesis of these four roles. Often it needs a group of developers to be able to carry out all these roles. One person may be excellent at macro design but poor at undertaking a managerial/leadership role. Someone may be great at interacting with learners but poor at articulating theory to senior managers. This should not be a problem if developers recognize the need to work with colleagues and to draw on other assistance as needed.

Roles in practice

Linda Honold (2000) suggests that the kinds of titles that are used for developers with a work-based focus include:

- Personal Development Co-ordinator
- Employee Development Zealot
- Jumpstarter
- Learning Manager
- Architect of Learning.

She makes these suggestions because, as she says, 'simply using something like "training director" will probably send the wrong message' (p. 63). However, there are various roles emerging that also might report into a learning and development director and that exemplify an organizational remit for aspects of work based learning. One that we have seen emerge, and which has proved highly successful, is the 'strategic development adviser' role.

In outlining the role of the strategic development adviser below, we have deliberately incorporated the structure that we will use for most of our comments about work based learning in the later parts of this handbook. This hopefully provides an introduction to our treatment of the approaches we explore later.

STRATEGIC DEVELOPMENT ADVISER

The essence of this role is to see that the capability of people matches the demands of the business. It is therefore a strategic role. The activities it involves, however, may include those of a mentor or coach or, in general terms, a facilitator. The difference is that those activities are undertaken from a strategic perspective. The strategic development adviser operates with both the organizational imperatives in mind and the learning and development needs of the individual. These are brought together in a synergistic way, to the advantage of all parties.

While actual coaches and mentors might widen the remit of their roles, those roles are defined in relation to the needs of an individual. Yet, those needs do not exist in isolation; they are situated in an organizational context. Account needs to be taken of the twin requirements, and the artistry of a strategic development adviser is to ensure that neither is narrowly interpreted. It might be easy to mistake the remit of the strategic development adviser as being the rigid alignment of individual to organizational objectives. The result of this could well be that only learning and development goals of immediate and certain relevance to the organization were to be pursued. What the role requires, in contrast, is a sensitivity to the way in which an individual's development can contribute to the development of the organization, not simply to the organization as it currently operates but also to how it may need to operate in the future, or how its culture may need to change in order for it to have a future.

Some of the time the strategic development adviser is acting as a broker. They may identify needs in the 'P Mode' (see above) and then help to broker ways in which the person can solve particular needs. In this sense they are likely to know about most of the options in this handbook and be able to assist individuals and their managers to access resources to support learning.

Example

In a major accounting firm, one of the trainers was seconded to a part of the firm in order to play the strategic development adviser role. This required him to learn about the business areas that this part of the firm was dealing with. It also meant that he needed to get close to and understand the partner in charge, who acted in a way as the CEO of this part of the firm. The strategic development adviser himself had coaching and other support both from inside the firm (from an experienced HR partner) and from an external consultant. The aim of this support was to help the person move from a training focus to one where he would not be doing much training, if at all.

In this new role, he had to draw on the whole panoply of learning and development provision to support any given individual. Consequently, at times he has operated as an internal consultant, a facilitator, a broker and resource finder, a diagnostician, a confidant to the firm's managers and partners – and more.

In terms of the four roles that we identified earlier, the following capabilities have been demanded of him:

- **Design**. He is not usually required to undertake micro design work. Rather, he has a macro (strategic) role in developing a learning strategy for this part of the firm and putting together methods of learning that often already exist. He used the strategy model that we introduced earlier in order to develop a coherent learning strategy for this part of the firm.
- **Managing**. This is a key part of his work. He has to get buy-in to ideas and to manage relationships with learning providers, such as the coaches he hires in.
- **Interacting**. He takes on some of the mentoring and coaching work directly, as well as facilitating meetings. He provides the occasional workshop as part of the overall training activity of the firm.
- **Theory**. He had thought through the issues about learning in organizations and was already moving away from the didactic trainer role when this opportunity came up. He is clear about the 'P to S' distinction and has been able to articulate that and other aspects of learning theory to managers and partners.

Possible benefits

In effect, a strategic development adviser becomes a 'one-stop shop' in terms of responding to learning and development issues. They may draw upon other professionals, within or without the organization, but they will be the one person overseeing development and learning issues.

Because the nature of the role requires that the strategic development adviser keep informed of the ever-changing landscape within the organization and in the sector in which it operates, they become a source for dependable information. In that role, they act as 'makers of meaning' able to integrate, interpret and draw implications from the swirl of information, rumour and gossip that floats around an organization. Given the prevalence, in large organizations in particular, of people feeling they do not know what is going on, this can be a valuable function.

Possible limitations

The most obvious limitation revolves around the question of whether a given organization has sufficient people able to take on this role. It is a demanding role and it cannot be assumed that just because someone works in an HR or training and development role they will already have the requisite abilities nor, come to that, that they will readily be able to develop them. Over and above matters of skill sets and qualities, what is involved is a different mind set.

An obvious point is that in order to fulfil the demands of their role, a strategic development adviser needs to be aware of the strategic direction of the organization. All too often in large organizations even senior managers are unclear about strategic imperatives. Sometimes the lack of clarity within organizations is due to the lack of a strategic focus in the first place. In either case, the strategic development adviser will need sufficient knowledge of the organization, and its context, to be able to supply enough sense of the strategic direction even when it is not being made explicit or even when it is simply not there. In times of extreme turbulence, the fall-back position would need to be an organizational variation on the Boy Scout motto, 'Be prepared', that is to say, being prepared for the unknown and the unexpected. (Lest this should seem an impossible task it should be remembered that enhancing your ability to learn is, itself, a useful preparation for the unknown and unexpected.)

A final, axiomatic, limitation on the role is when it is not recognized as being distinct from other roles which it encompasses. A strategic development adviser who is viewed, within the organization, as just a coach, for instance, will be limited from bringing full value to their role.

It is worth mentioning one limitation which exists outside the parameters of the role. This is that the strategic development adviser's work can become too focused on the individual. Thus it will not address, at least directly, the relationships between individuals and functional and other workplace groups nor, therefore, the social capital aspects of the organization.

Operating hints

It is clear that in order to take on this role effectively, a strategic development adviser will need to have integrated very many of the abilities expected of coaches, of mentors, of consultants, of those with sensitivity to what makes people tick and a facility for getting to the bottom of things. Because the role encompasses so many other roles it presents a development challenge, in itself, to those who would take it on.

However, viewed as a strategic possibility, in the context of this section of the handbook, having strategic development advisers offers many benefits:

- Coaching and mentoring activities gain by going beyond merely an individual focus to include the organizational context and strategic direction.

- Individual managers are able to draw on a wide range of abilities and perspectives through a single strategic development adviser.
- Awareness of, and contribution to, the overall strategy of the organization will be disseminated in a form which has personal and practical relevance, rather than being somewhat abstract and theoretical.
- People can know that the development they undertake will be in line with the needs of the organization and, therefore, with what is valued within that organization.

Links to HR/personnel practice

The strategic development adviser role suggests an important overlap with wider HR/personnel practice in an organization. There is an important need for a two-way flow of information at the very least. Ideally there needs to be a better integration with HR policy in order to maximize the benefit of the role (and of work based learning in general).

Woodall (1999) makes some important points from her research on work-based management development. She identifies, for instance, HR practices that inhibit work based learning, such as mechanistic performance management systems. These may masquerade as providing sufficient impetus to work based learning via the use of personal development plans. However, such plans are rarely properly implemented and are often poorly created as the people involved are usually not aware of the range of learning modes available. Hence such plans too often fall back on training as a solution to performance problems.

Woodall suggests that, emanating from such problems: 'First [HR professionals] need to be made more aware of the full range of work based management development interventions... Secondly, if greater reliance is to be placed on work-based management development as part of management strategy, then professionals need to assemble the resources required for support and facilitation... Finally HR professionals need to scrutinise other aspects of HR policy and practice...to ensure that they complement and do not impede the effectiveness of work-based management development' (p. 29).

Woodall suggests that performance management systems need to change to allow for more thorough development review processes so that line managers can develop their people better. This is a noble aim but we have found few organizations that do this even moderately well. This is where the strategic development adviser can come in. What they can do is to carry out much more professional reviews of learning needs than most managers are capable of. And they are better equipped to assist the person to get the assistance they need.

One strategy we have favoured is to take the development review process out of the line manager's performance review. Admitting to a 'development need' in a performance review is the equivalent of saying that you have weaknesses – and that might not be a wise tactic. A development review needs a context where a person can discuss development needs in a non-defensive way. In separating the two processes, the results of a performance review can then be taken by an individual to someone like a strategic development adviser who can do a proper job on carrying out a development review. Hopefully this shows how development professionals do have a key role in work based learning.

Resources for learning

A key role for developers is making certain that appropriate resources are available for learners. The other parts of this handbook focus on approaches that in many cases do require resources to be arranged. In recent years e-learning has become a fashionable area. Our research evidence matches that of many others in suggesting that there can be problems with a rush to buy into such material.

This is not the place to make an exhaustive analysis of e-learning. Rather, we'll just mention a few examples of the problems occurring with it.

1   Most web-based training has increased the dropout rates on 'courses' (see for example Frankola, 2001).
2   People complain of boredom. Many of the references cited below contain comments by learners that much of the material provided under the e-learning banner is boring and badly presented.
3   Staley and MacKenzie (2000) found 'many examples' that 'simply automate existing curricula and reinforce learning processes that have existed for centuries' (p. 1). In other words, the use of the technology may change little in such areas as the empowerment of learners.
4   The 'technolust' syndrome causes many people to fall for the technology without evaluating it. This has been going on for decades – witness the failures of teaching machines, programmed instruction, interactive video, and so on.
5   Print material is often easier to deal with. Throp (2000) quotes research from Russ Brown of the University of Toronto that people will only wait eight seconds for information to arrive via the web; 79 per cent of users do not read every word; on-screen reading is 25 per cent slower than print; and only 10 per cent of users will scroll.
6   Material is often not easy to find – and most users just want to get what they want and don't want to be bothered with what they see as extraneous material (see Rajani and Rosenberg, 1999).
7   Motorola (and other companies) have found that it's the young people (18 to 30) who are most anti web-based training (see Westerbeck, 2000). This is counter to the common assumption that those who have grown up with computers would be expected to love having their training coming to them via a computer. It seems that young people are more sophisticated than that, and less tolerant of the mechanistic irrelevances that characterize much web-based training.
8   Liedholm and Brown (2002) found that economics students using e-learning fared worse in examinations than those learning through traditional means. They claim that e-learning is fine for basic concepts but that people did not learn complex analytical skills.
9   Most e-learning has a solely individualistic, human capital focus and ignores the value of social interaction (and the development of social capital).

Some commentators have suggested that the blended approach is the answer, that is, integrating e-learning with existing training activity rather than replacing one with the other. This does not necessarily solve some of the fundamental problems mentioned above. We would reiterate our 'P to S' model. Any resources that are provided need to respond to the problems and processes that real people have. Resources should be demand led not supply led. Too many trainers have supplied material that they think is useful without having properly assessed the demand.

This problem has also bedevilled the provision of learning resource centres. Our research suggests that many of these are underused white elephants. Organizations have invested in fancy facilities only to find that very few people use them. Our experience is that learning resource centres again need to be demand led. If individuals are assisted to undertake a serious review of their learning with someone like a strategic development adviser, the latter can suggest the purchase of appropriate learning resources to whoever manages the learning resource centre.

One approach that we have found to work well is to give individuals the right to a budget for their own learning. This right is restricted to those who have conducted a serious review of their own learning and have signed off a learning contract. (We will indicate later the nature of such a learning contract where we discuss the use of Self Managed Learning. Suffice it to say here that such a document is unlike a personal development plan in not being just 'personal' or just a 'plan' but a rigorous strategic document with built-in commitments from the learner.)

If the person has a functioning learning contract they have the right to access finance for it. In one organization, for instance, the sum was £500 per person. This money could be used for visits, workshops or whatever – but it could be used to drive purchases in a learning resource centre, for example, books, tapes, CD-ROMs, and so on. Later in this handbook we comment, from a learner's perspective, on the use of various resources like this, so we will not repeat that information here. Rather, we want to signal to developers that there are some important decisions to be made about resourcing to support work based learning. If work based learning is to be taken seriously, learners need to be empowered to influence decisions that previously trainers often took without involving learners.

Using learning resources – the developer role

In the following paragraphs we want to mention the link from this section to later material. We have emphasized that we have left exploration of the detail of particular learning approaches until later. We have also mentioned that our description and analysis of such approaches is addressed to learners. Here we want to indicate to you, the developer, how you might need to consider your role in relation to such approaches.

It seems to us that there are a range of responses that you could make to the later material. These include:

- I have used this approach in my own learning and feel fully confident to assist a learner to use it.
- I have limited personal experience of using it but I have observed enough or read enough to feel reasonably confident in advising a learner.
- The material in the handbook is sufficient for me to feel confident to recommend this approach, even though I personally have not used it.
- I would need to consult others before feeling fully confident to recommend this approach.
- I am not skilled in this area but I know someone who is and therefore I can recommend this person to the learner.

Note that we are not suggesting that developers have to be skilled in all aspects of the approaches we suggest. An important ability is to know that you don't know and that you can refer someone on to an expert. On the other hand, it is dangerous if you don't know about an area and try to pretend that you do. The mark of a good professional is not necessarily to know everything but to be able to assist learners to get to the help they need. A good GP recognizes that they don't know everything and they are quick to refer a patient to a consultant when it's needed.

Conclusion

In this section we have focused on the role of developers, whether they are trainers, HR professionals, consultants – or whatever. We have emphasized that we see a changing role for trainers who are still wedded to the (wrong) assumption that the classroom/training room is the only place for proper learning. We are, however, confident that there is a continuing (indeed growing) role for developers in organizations. Just because most learning is work based does not mean that developers have no role. On the contrary managers are usually unaware of the wide range of learning approaches available to them and the people who report into them. They desperately need the help of development professionals who can assist them to promote learning that benefits both the individual and the organization.

However, developers may need to be more strategic in their approach and to make certain that they can integrate with the strategic direction of the organization. Also, work based approaches are able to respond to diversity and equal opportunity issues, if developers grasp the opportunity. In this context, work based approaches can more easily respond to different learning styles and preferences. This handbook is indeed dedicated to that proposition.

We explored in this section the actual roles that developers can play and showed how important the design of work based approaches is, along with the managing of the process and the interaction with learners. We also emphasized the importance of being able to articulate a coherent theory of learning related to work based practices.

We have shown one role (that of the strategic development adviser) in order to exemplify our position, though we in no way want to suggest that such a role is the only one that is relevant. We also showed that the link to HR practice is vital, as well as practical matters such as resources for learning.

We concluded with some notes on your role vis-à-vis later material. We would urge the value of a careful reading of such material though we do not intend that what we have produced should be an encyclopedia of approaches. There is space for much creative design work in this field and we hope that you would wish to rise to such a challenge.

2 Strategies for Work Based Learning and Development

Introduction

In this part we have outlined various strategies for work based learning and development. We recognize that the distinction between a strategy and a tactic can be fuzzy. We wanted to divide this handbook into parts rather than just throw down lots of ideas. In doing so we wanted to move from big picture approaches (strategies) to tactics and methods that can be used to implement these strategies.

One common characteristic of the approaches covered in this part is that the time horizon for applying them is typically many months if not, in some cases, years. In choosing a particular strategy to follow you will be committing yourself over a significant period of time.

One example of a fuzzy area is that of mentoring and coaching. We have taken mentoring to be a strategic approach as usually the mentor takes an interest in the whole person and supports the individual in their longer term development, often linked to career development. Coaching is, for us, more a way of assisting a person to learn specific skills or abilities. It may be quite short term, such as one person showing another how to do a budget. However, we are aware that some coaching activity is long term and may be closer to mentoring.

We have largely written the material as though it is for a person wishing to use that strategy for their own development. However, we assume that if you are reading this as someone looking to utilize that strategy from the position of a trainer, developer or senior manager, then you will be able to interpret the advice offered.

For instance, in the section on **Apprenticeships** we have suggested that potential apprentices check to see if they will get sufficient support for their learning and that the learning opportunities will not be too narrow. Clearly, if you are organizing an apprenticeship scheme we would hope that you would take these points on board. Hence it is fairly easy to extrapolate from our comments what might be needed.

In developing a strategy for learning you will probably use some of the tactics and methods mentioned in Parts 3 and 4 respectively. We have indicated in **bold** references to other material so that you can plan to implement any strategic approach through relevant tactics and methods. For instance, in the section on Apprenticeships we have suggested that an apprentice might create a **Personal Development Plan**; they might carry out **Projects** and they might be given **Coaching.** All of these are covered in Parts 3 and 4.

2.1 *Action Learning*

Action learning is an approach to learning in which individuals, with the support of colleagues in a small group, address problems of importance to them, take actions to resolve those problems and learn from the process of doing so. Action learning is a work based approach to learning which requires a strategic commitment – at its best it is not about quick fix solutions.

Reg Revans (who died in January 2003 aged 95) developed the ideas behind action learning during the middle of the last century. For those who are less familiar with his work, here are a few quick highlights.

After the Second World War, Reg Revans worked for the National Coal Board in Britain along with a team of highly creative and able people. He had already been thinking about learning issues and how to get better performance from, in this case, coal mines. His research was thorough and ground-breaking. He found that by getting managers of coal mines together they could learn with and from each other without the need of a teacher. Indeed, he went on to believe that the teacher/lecturer/professor could get in the way of effective learning by denying managers the chance to engage in dialogue with each other. This realization has led to the proliferation of the use of action learning sets – small groups of learners using their real work experience to learn as 'comrades in adversity' (as he put it).

Revans' antipathy to the academic establishment (which was reciprocated) ended with him leaving Britain to work in Belgium, where his action learning methods received more support. On Revans' return to the UK, Arnold Weinstock happened to see him interviewed on TV and, having sought him out, decided to use action learning in GEC (which Weinstock was running at the time). The 'Developing Senior Managers' programme started in the early 1970s with the aim of developing future managing directors and other top managers for GEC companies. This programme was probably more instrumental in getting the notion of action learning accepted than any other.

Some of Revans' assertions about the learning process included:

- There can be no learning without action and no, sober and deliberate, action without learning.
- For an organization to survive, the rate of learning should be equal to or greater than the rate of change.
- There is a distinction between puzzles (where there is a known solution) and problems (where there is no immediately obvious solution). Action learning is about managers tackling problems.

Key features of action learning

- **The Learning Set**

  Five or six people meet for up to a day every month or so for a period defined by the provider of the action learning programme or by the learning set during its first meeting. Some programmes are based around the whole set working on a project. In other programmes individuals carry out their own specific projects. A third variant is where learners come together to discuss work problems.

  Sets develop different procedures but typically each meeting will include time for each member to report on progress in achieving action and other goals decided at the previous meeting. Through their questioning, listening, supporting and challenging, other members may help the person to articulate what they have learned and to set new goals or actions for the forthcoming period.

- **Set Adviser**

  The set adviser is the person who helps the learning set to function effectively and to make the learning and the learning process explicit.

- **Sponsor**

  The sponsor is someone who supports one or more set members in tackling their problems and provides assistance in evaluating outcomes. They can sometimes fulfil a general mentoring role or be concerned with the detail of the person's problem where this is framed and tackled as a project, for example, they may take the role of 'client'.

- **Conferences**

  These are when several sets in an organization come together for, say, a day to share and report on learning in the presence of more senior managers. They can be used to begin and end a programme. Quite often conferences that end programmes include presentations from individuals and/or sets about what they have done and learned.

Note that these may not be the only elements of an action learning programme. For instance, some of them include classroom-based training as one part.

Examples

The GEC programme mentioned earlier was structured roughly as indicated below. We say 'roughly' as the precise design changed over time. About 15 senior managers were nominated for each programme by their Managing Directors or other Directors. Often these sponsors indicated the projects to be undertaken by participants and hence became clients for the work of the relevant manager. The senior managers were typically in learning sets of around five participants with one set adviser from outside the company and one internal to GEC. The programme started with a residential event of around one week where participants not only met in their sets but also looked at a variety of company issues and undertook business games.

After the residential period, sets met for about one day per month, usually on the premises of one of the GEC companies. Sponsors/clients were keen to see real problems solved. Unless it was really necessary participants did not write lengthy reports, but rather were judged on the extent to which problems were solved. In earlier programmes participants might be full time on the programme (which typically lasted six months). Later programmes were less likely to have full-time participants.

Possible benefits

☑ Problems can be solved with measurable outcomes (including those that hitherto had seemed intractable).

☑ Learning can occur at different levels and be integrated by the person; not being just abstract or a matter of technique.

☑ People can learn about the process of learning (learning to learn).

☑ It can encourage the development of networks and networking skills.

☑ People can develop their abilities to assist others, for example, to question and listen, support and challenge.

☑ People can learn about others, their problems and situations.

☑ Using sponsors can mean that senior managers get more involved in supporting and assisting learning than they otherwise would.

Possible limitations

☒ There can be too much attention paid to action, that is, more action than learning.

☒ Where problems are framed as projects this can limit both action and learning, for example, when the project is or becomes no more than an investigation into a problem without actually solving it.

☒ There is the possibility for participants to focus on issues and learning at tactical and operational levels only.

Operating hints

➲ Gaining top management commitment is important, for example, to attend conferences at the beginning and end of programmes, to take the role of sponsor (or to ensure that those appropriate for the role take it), to ensure that attendance at set meetings has sufficient priority, or that there is access to resources for individuals' problem solving if needed.

➲ Set advising is a demanding job, so due consideration should be given to having good people in that role.

⮑ If you are offered the chance to take part in an action learning programme, try to make certain that you can work on issues that really matter to the organization (as opposed to invented projects that are not central to the organization).

⮑ You get the most out of set meetings if you take a real interest in others in the set; the opportunity to practise listening and supporting others is really valuable – for example, in learning to be a better coach or developer.

2.2 *Apprenticeship*

The time-served apprenticeship is one of the oldest forms of structured work based learning. When formalized in England by the Statute of Artificers of 1563 it was already an old practice. Apprenticeship (in the old time-served model) peaked in the mid-1960s and has been in decline ever since. This has been partly because of the shift from manufacturing to service industries and the growth of new technologies. Also from the 1960s onwards there were concerns about the length of time taken to qualify (as much as six years in printing).

It was said to support boundaries between trades that were no longer relevant and there was a view that standards varied considerably between firms. Further, it was felt that the quantity and quality of recruits were not planned adequately. The most significant criticism of traditional schemes was that there was no guarantee of competence. What this led to was the assumption that the only guarantee of competence came from systematic (classroom) instruction and the passing of vocational examinations – the opposite of work based learning.

The time-served model could be viewed as the 'proper way' to think about apprenticeship. However, there is a looser way in which people use the term. This is where a person might refer to doing their apprenticeship in a trade or profession but just mean that they are learning the trade over a period of time. In that sense it is still a strategic approach to learning as we are here considering the totality of learning for a field of work as opposed to just learning a few specific skills. Also there is something about apprenticeship which is to do with absorbing the values and ideals of a particular trade or profession. For instance, newly qualified doctors in a hospital setting are absorbing the culture of hospital work and their role in it, as well as specific skills related to their future career.

In recent years the UK government has attempted to revive interest in an updated version of apprenticeship, through schemes such as 'Modern Apprenticeships'. However, the numbers of people involved in such schemes is not large in comparison to the need for more in-depth learning by young people.

Examples

A typical example of apprenticeship has been the placing of a young person, often straight out of school, with an older experienced craftsperson. In this model the idea is for the expert to transfer knowledge and skills to the apprentice. However, other variants have included the placing of a new learner in a team where the support for learning comes from a range of people.

There are a number of features of the traditional apprenticeship that have relevance for work based learning and its organization today at strategic and tactical levels and with regard to methods. With regard to methods, there can be many opportunities for apprentices to use a wide range of work based learning methods. The implication here is that as well as learning a craft or profession, the apprentice has the opportunity to become a more capable work based learner.

The following is an example of how apprenticeship can draw on work based learning methods:

- There is a clear agreement between the apprentice and their employer that they will be inducted into the craft, occupation or organization and that their learning will be resourced and supported over a period of time (see the section on **Induction**). This agreement is a form of **Personal Development Plan** (see later).
- The apprentice learns on-the-job in part from '**Mistakes**' and can do so through '**Projects**' (see later).
- The learning period can incorporate monitoring arrangements like '**Appraisal and Performance Reviews**', 'Learning Reviews' and '**Learning Logs**'.
- As the apprentice grows in their skills and knowledge they might be involved in '**Job Rotation**' and '**Deputizing**'.
- They learn with assistance from qualified practitioners. On the part of the apprentice this requires '**Observation and Listening**', '**Questioning**' and, very probably, '**Shadowing**'. On the part of the practitioner this can require '**Briefings, Presentations and Demonstrations**', '**Coaching**' and, given the comparatively long apprenticeship time period and a potentially pastoral relationship with the apprentice, '**Mentoring**'.
- In addition to craft apprenticeships, what happened in higher or premium apprenticeships is informative. These had their origins in the sixteenth century. In return for a premium paid to the firm the apprentice received all-round learning encompassing a wide range of different skills, trades or functions. Perhaps most importantly, this sort of apprenticeship could provide an overall view of the whole organization and business to put the apprentice potentially on an accelerated route to senior management or independence as an entrepreneur.
- Of particular significance in apprenticeship, and an aspect of it that doesn't appear to have occurred to critics of apprenticeship in the 1960s and subsequently, is the fact that apprentices become members of '**Communities of Practice**' with opportunities for '**Buddying**'. Importantly then, as well as contributing to the organization's stock of human capital, apprenticeship can contribute to the development of social capital.

Possible benefits

☑ Apprenticeship is about making a serious commitment to a body of learning – it encourages a strategic approach.

☑ People gain considerable job satisfaction from mastering a coherent body of capabilities and skills.

☑ Society benefits from having people who are real experts in their field – the concern about the poor working practices of 'cowboy' plumbers and builders is evidence of the societal need for people who have gone through a rigorous apprenticeship.

Possible limitations

☒ Apprenticeship takes time – and the length of time can be off-putting to many.

☒ Just by virtue of spending a great deal of time learning does not guarantee quality – a person may still be less than capable even after extensive apprenticeship.

☒ Apprentices need support from others, for example, mentors and coaches – this is a drain on the resources of an organization. It make apprenticeships especially unappealing to small organizations.

☒ In addition to the above there are usually financial costs associated with an apprenticeship scheme.

☒ People can learn bad habits in poorly organized apprenticeship schemes – old timers can inculcate out-of-date approaches in young people if a scheme is not well managed.

Operating hints

➲ Recent approaches have linked apprenticeships to the gaining of qualifications. This can ensure that there is some measure of learning and gives you a qualification to assist in your career. However, many of these schemes, such as National Vocational Qualifications in England, have gained a poor reputation due to excessive bureaucracy and the mechanistic approach to assessment.

➲ If you are looking to take up an apprenticeship, whether through an official scheme or more informally, it is important to check on the support that you will get from the organization.

➲ Try to make certain that the learning opportunities that you get provide sufficient breadth as well as depth – a narrowly based scheme can prove restrictive for the future, for example, if the skills become obsolete.

➲ Assuming that you get on a good scheme, it's important to use the opportunity to the full. For instance, it may be a unique opportunity to learn from really able practitioners and too often apprentices do not ask enough questions of the experts so that they can really learn the heart of the work.

2.3 *Career Advice*

Career advice that is given to an individual can be of various kinds. It can include information about future opportunities, in terms of descriptions of potential roles and what these will require, feedback about relevant aspects of their current behaviour, performance or capabilities, and recommendations about the actions they could or should take. The sources of this advice can vary from informal conversations with others drawn from a potentially diverse range of people inside or outside the organization, to participation in some of the tactics and methods covered in this handbook that are designed to lead to learning that is related to, or can have an impact on, the individual's longer term aspirations. Examples of the latter include **Development Centres** to provide individuals with data and analysis about their current abilities, **Personal Development Plans** to provide a means of grounding longer term career aims in relevant work based learning over the medium term or **deputizing** to give live experience of a role that could constitute a career step. Whatever formal means are used to impart career advice they may together make up a career development programme or system provided by the organization for its staff. If this is the case then the 'programme' might be a constituent part of the organization's workforce or management development strategy, which itself might be linked purposively with its business strategy.

The substance of the career advice that is actually received, the manner of its provision and the extent to which it is integrated strategically at the organizational level will depend on a number of factors. Notable among these are the different meanings associated with the term 'career'. Such meanings have changed over recent years in association with a number of other developments. These include changes in the nature of the psychological contract between individuals and their employers, a broadening of the perspectives adopted by many individuals in considering their futures, changes in what counts as success in career terms, and shifts in the responsibility for career management from the organization to the individual.

The changes and their practical implications can be captured in two contrasting career models, the Traditional Model and the Contemporary Model, and in a third, the Cross-Boundary Career, that flows from and complements the second. This is not to say that the first and second models represent a straight either/or choice. It is more that their use can help clarify our thinking about the appropriateness of different ways of providing career advice.

Examples

TRADITIONAL MODEL

The traditional model can be represented by the image of an individual progressing through predetermined steps within a hierarchical structure in one, or at most a small number, of medium-sized to large organizations. Success in career terms is seen as advancement through promotions up the hierarchy. The employment relationship is typified by a psychological contract in which loyalty on the part of the individual is exchanged for security of employment. The organization is likely to want to meet its staffing requirements largely internally rather than externally and thus the emphasis on career advice is likely to be on early career entry and, subsequently, at the appropriate points along defined career paths or ladders and linked to succession plans. Historically this model has been associated with medium-sized to large commercial organizations operating in stable market conditions, or to government agencies or other public sector bodies.

CONTEMPORARY MODEL

More recently the tall, pyramidal, multi-level structures that typified large organizations in the past have altered considerably in response to the increasing pace of worldwide social, economic and technological changes. Organizations have reduced staff and flattened structures alongside moves towards greater decentralization and devolvement of decision making and more flexible, cross-functional and team methods of working. Those within organizations have had to adapt to these changes in terms of increased job responsibilities, work demands and needs for flexibility, together with reduced promotion opportunities. To some extent the large organizations typified above can be seen to be catching up with smaller ones that are well used to operating in more turbulent competitive environments.

Whether the organization is a large but down-sized and out-sourced one or a small adaptable entrepreneurial one, career advice in such circumstances is much more likely to be associated with preparing for a future that is essentially unpredictable, rather than with planning careers by making predictions based on past experience. The employment relationship is different too. Rather than being based on an exchange of loyalty on the employee's part in return for advancement and security, the psychological contract is now much more likely to focus on performance in return for opportunities for continuous learning. Here the learning to be gained can be seen by the individual as being of equal if not greater value than the increased monetary and other rewards associated with promotion. Certainly it can be seen as contributing to enhancing the security they gain from knowing that they are and will continue to be employable. In this way their security of employability is intended to be a substitute for the security of employment in their current role or organization that they might have enjoyed in the past.

Just how secure staff actually feel about their present or future employability will vary from person to person, depending on the marketability of each individual's blend of experience and abilities coupled with their capacity to seek out appropriate new opportunities. Security through employability is not something that can be provided for the individual by their employer but, so the model proposes, something that with their employer's help the individual can create for themselves. Logically the notion of employability is likely to go hand in hand with a desire on the organization's part to see staff taking greater personal responsibility for their own development. However, this should mean more than just exhortation to do so on the organization's part and should be backed up by sound career advice delivered in such a way that staff are supported and encouraged to take more responsibility in this area.

An extension of the notion of employability is the concept of self management. If employability merely means the ability to get another job, then there are those who may not wish to have a job in the traditional sense. They may be self employed for large parts of their career, or work part time (including in a job share) or have what Charles Handy has called a 'portfolio career' – a collection of activities that are not dependent on working for just one employer at a time.

The ability to be self managing appears to be growing as the traditional career route reduces in importance. Self managing is linked to the model in the following section.

CROSS-BOUNDARY CAREER

As a result of the changes in organizations and to the psychological contract, there are now many more people working outside the traditional model of orderly progression within the boundaries of a single or a limited number of organizations. The contemporary model suggests the idea of the cross-boundary career. The boundaries can include different organizations or occupations. They can also include boundaries between and within roles inside the organization as in the traditional model. However, these boundaries are likely to be crossed with much greater frequency. In addition, the boundaries themselves are likely to be more fluid and changeable, and certainly far less clear or so tightly prescribed. There are a number of important implications of the cross-boundary career for the provision of advice. These cover the frequency with which boundaries are crossed, the numbers and kinds of people who can be sources of career advice, and the ways in which the organization can enable networking.

Frequency of boundary crossing

The greater the frequency of transitions across boundaries the more there is likely to be a need for relevant and up-to-date career advice that is tailored specifically to meet the individual's particular needs and interests.

SOURCES OF CAREER ADVICE

The traditional sources of career advice open to the individual, such as their immediate manager or supervisor, or the human resources function, are unlikely to be sufficient on their own. Those needed to provide relevant and tailored advice are people who know the individual well and with whom the person feels they have reasonably open and trusting relationships. These people are likely to be found in a much wider network of relationships that includes colleagues, friends, and other peers outside the organization, all of whom can at different times be providers of career advice, information, opportunities and contacts. The use of **mentors** has, in part, grown because of the need for career advice from someone to whom the individual does not report.

ENABLING NETWORKING

The successful development and use of such **networks** is a good example of what can be achieved by the individual on their own behalf and is illustrative of how taking greater responsibility for one's own career management can be demonstrated in practice. Clearly one way in which the organization can ensure the provision of relevant career advice while encouraging and supporting staff to do this is to promote the use of work based learning tactics and methods that enable the development of networking within and outside the organization. Examples here include **projects, attachments, benchmarking** and **secondments.** This approach can be of particular value in the cases of individuals working in traditional organizations who might be facing the prospect of voluntary or involuntary changes of employer, especially if it heralds a transition to more of a cross-boundary career. In addition, this way of facilitating the provision of career advice can have the added business benefit of developing social capital more generally within the organization.

Possible benefits

☑ It can contribute directly to better informed career decisions and actions – without such support you may end up making poor decisions about career choices.

☑ It can lead to stronger feelings of confidence and security when facing role and organizational change.

☑ It can lead to higher levels of job satisfaction – if you are developing your career through your work you are more likely to get satisfaction from your work.

☑ It can lead to enhanced job performance where it contributes to the establishment and fulfilment of more realistic expectations in the psychological contract.

Possible limitations

☒ You may not be able to rely on the accuracy of career advice, particularly in those organizations that match the contemporary career model and where actual changes in organizational practices are likely, continuously, to outpace current knowledge about them.

☒ Advice can be offered from the perspective of the advice giver and not be based on your needs.

☒ Even with good advice there may not be the support in your organization for you to pursue the career development that you need – this may be especially true where you want to learn new skills that don't fit the short-term needs of the organization.

Operating hints

⮑ Think through which career model is most representative of real employment relationships in your organization and try to get career advice which fits your needs – look beyond immediate colleagues and managers to see if there are wider perspectives to draw on.

⮑ There are numerous books available on career development and these can be a source of new ideas. If you are looking for a book, one that also provides exercises and practical material may be the best bet. Some organizations also provide career development workshops and these can be really helpful.

➲ Use existing work practices to assist you. For example, through **deputizing** for your manager or **observing** others you might get useful insights into career options.

➲ Note that where career advice is being provided alongside the operation of succession plans, these are increasingly being shared between the organization and the individual. It can be useful to tap into any succession planning information that is available.

➲ Develop your **network** – not necessarily for direct career advancement but more for seeing what others are doing, and for accessing informal information about career options.

2.4 *Continuing Professional Development*

Continuing Professional Development (CPD) is a growing area of interest. If we interpret the term 'professional' quite loosely, then we can include not just the traditional regulated professions such as medicine and law under this heading but also include management and similar fields of work.

The requirement to continue to keep up to date has been the starting point for CPD. In medicine, for instance, there are new drugs and procedures appearing all the time. Doctors need to keep on top of this and therefore they need to continue to learn. Indeed, the UK government is proposing that General Practitioners will have to be revalidated every five years in order to maintain their licence to practice. However, the emphasis on just knowledge learning has broadened over recent years. Now we find the pressure is for professionals to increase their skills and capabilities to cope with a changing world.

We see this clearly as a strategic area as the best CPD is a process of continuing to learn in one's professional arena for as long as one is employed in that profession. It cannot be just a short term, quick fix activity. However, many professional bodies still see it in the latter terms. This is especially so when CPD means no more than attending some seminars or conferences in the year and ticking off boxes on the form you send to the professional body and then getting the approval for doing CPD.

This input-led mode clearly does not work. We have attended professional conferences and observed some individuals either sitting at the back reading newspapers or just not turning up for sessions (they were too busy on the golf course). The reason for this behaviour is that the professional body requires a certain number of learning events in the year to be attended – and there are people attending in order to get their tick in the relevant box. They have no interest in learning.

When working with a professional body in order to change their CPD scheme, one person we interviewed mentioned that he had set up his own business and entered some totally new areas of work. He commented that he had learned more in the last year in his profession than at any other time. But he was failing his CPD requirements because he had not been on enough courses.

The answer to this silly situation is that CPD needs to be based on outcomes and outputs; schemes need to measure what is learned, not what has been taught.

Examples

We will focus on examples of individuals carrying out CPD. In the best schemes, professional bodies provide a range of support mechanisms for CPD. These include:

- online support systems to help people find learning activities and to record their learning;
- a CPD person at local level who can encourage CPD (the UK's Chartered Institute of Personnel and Development is encouraging this);
- mentors who can support newcomers to a profession in their CPD (see later in **Mentoring**);
- learning groups that can provide peer group support for CPD (see **Self Managed Learning**).

If you are fortunate enough to belong to such a professional body then this kind of support obviously makes it easier to do CPD. However, even without it this handbook provides many ideas for doing CPD. If most learning occurs through work then utilizing work-based approaches makes sense. However, this is not to say that courses and conferences should be neglected. The key issue is being clear about what you need to learn and then looking for methods that can help.

Possible benefits

It could be argued that CPD is an ethical requirement of any professional; if you are not keeping up to date and continuing to develop, should you expect to be calling yourself a professional?

There are some clear benefits that ought to come with CPD. These include:

☑ increased job satisfaction due to being on top of the work;

☑ increased security in one's professional field – if you get out of date you are more vulnerable to redundancy (if employed) or lack of clients (if you are self employed);

☑ possible increased income due to higher level skills being used.

Possible limitations

☒ Time – this is the biggest issue – people are so busy these days that they say that lack of time is the real problem in continuing to learn.

☒ Lack of support from one's professional body.

☒ The professional body is still in the input oriented, box-ticking mode and hence CPD becomes a bureaucratic chore.

☒ Resources – some development approaches cost.

☒ Geography – in our research a number of people said that they lived too far away from where professional meetings were held and hence could not attend them.

Operating hints

➲ Some of the other approaches in this section can be used for CPD so it does not have to be a separate activity. Ideally it should just be an integral part of working practice to monitor one's own learning.

➲ If your professional body is one of the many that continue to use input measures, try to keep the focus on outputs/outcomes, despite this.

➲ Talk to other professionals and use their expertise, especially where they can point to short cuts (see later on **Networking**).

➲ Don't just keep your learning activities bounded by your profession; many relevant skills and abilities may be gained by looking at other areas of learning. An example would be time management – many professionals are concerned about the time pressures that are upon them, and some of the general management literature might have things to offer in this and related areas. Or someone in another profession may be able to coach you in time management.

2.5 *Internship*

Internships are in a way a form of **apprenticeship**. To a large extent **apprenticeship** has been used for craft-type activity while internship is seen as more linked to professional development for young educationally-qualified people (usually to degree level).

An internship programme is a period of paid or unpaid supervised and structured work experience after the acquisition of a degree or equivalent qualification. It has been especially associated with the medical profession and related fields. Students may be required to serve as interns after they have completed their studies but before they are awarded their professional qualifications or licence to practise.

The main idea is to move from the more theoretical educational studies into practical application and the development of work-related skills. Hence, in one way internships are much like apprenticeships. However, one key difference is that interns join a professional body and then may be expected to engage in **Continuous Professional Development.** Usually a successful **apprenticeship** does not confer professional status on the individual. Also **apprenticeship** is often a combined process of practical (on-the-job) learning and release for college attendance during the period of the apprenticeship; internship is more associated with college attendance occurring before job-based learning.

Examples

Internship programmes vary a great deal between different professions or occupations. As an example, in the United Kingdom, pharmacy graduates must serve a period of internship with a pharmaceutical company, hospital or retail pharmacy before they are admitted to the British Pharmaceutical Society and granted a licence to practise.

Possible benefits

These are similar to the benefits of apprenticeship already discussed. However, there is an important addition and that is that, despite efforts in this direction, undergraduate education continues to be classroom based and detached from live experience. In the medical profession it is particularly important for those intending to gain a professional qualification to get good work based experience. Without it the neophyte professional could do great harm.

Possible limitations

The use of a sequential approach (education before practice) has dangers. New interns may find the application of their degree learning problematic in the hurly-burly of life, for example, in a hospital.

Operating hints

If you are going to have to do an internship (or its equivalent) prior to becoming professionally qualified there may be some important issues to consider. These include:

➲ Choose able, qualified professionals to work under – those who are excellent role models of professional practice.

➲ Make certain that such role models are also able to show you how it is done – someone who is highly effective may not be good at explaining what they do and you may then find it difficult to learn what you need.

➲ Prepare for going into an internship by thinking through what you really need to learn so that you can deliberately put yourself in the way of those learning experiences.

➲ It may be a good idea to write down what your learning goals are so that you can keep track of how you are progressing.

2.6 *Mentoring*

It can be useful to make a distinction between mentoring and coaching. For our purposes here we will take mentoring to mean a strategic approach that is about working with a person over time to support their development. Coaching we see as more tactical. A coach may assist someone to learn a specific skill but not work with the person beyond them learning that skill. (See later on **Coaching**.) Clearly there are overlaps and in many organizations they will talk of coaches doing what we see as the role of a mentor. However, in most people's minds there is a notion that the mentor takes a holistic interest in their mentee and is likely to be involved in addressing career issues, for instance. Also a mentor may not be able to do any coaching. They may have no specific skills that they can pass on – but they can provide support for the person's overall learning by focusing on the mentee as a person and understanding that person's needs and motivations.

Mentoring has become an aspect of development that is more centre stage now. The increased recognition of work based learning has prompted a focus on how to make such learning more effective. This is where mentors can come in. We should note that informal mentoring has a long history. Indeed young people have, throughout history, used adults to provide mentoring support, though it would not usually be labelled as such. The big growth has been in more formal mentoring schemes where individuals are attached to a designated mentor and this person has official organizational backing to carry out such a role.

Examples

An organization had been recruiting graduates but had found that just providing factual information about the business plus attachments to different departments was not working. They instituted a programme where all new graduates had the chance to pair up with a mentor who would meet with them regularly for six to nine months at the very least (and possibly longer). The dropout rate of graduates reduced as a result of the scheme and graduate entrants also said that they liked the arrangement.

In a region of the UK's National Health Service, they decided that they needed to develop potential Chief Executives for hospitals. A group of existing Directors was chosen for the programme and one aspect of it was to provide each person with a mentor. These mentors were often outside the health service and were usually quite senior (even prestigious) people. The use of mentors had mixed results, mainly because some of the mentors did not know what was expected of them.

Possible benefits

☑ Individuals can get support from a more experienced person and help to locate their development in the wider picture, for example, by attending to future career needs.

☑ Mentors are usually outside the normal reporting lines (that is, not the manager of the mentee): hence, they can be a neutral voice with no axe to grind.

☑ Mentoring can be an inexpensive option – often only travel expenses are involved.

☑ Mentees can use the mentor as they wish (provided the mentor is agreeable) – mentees can drive the process, hence making certain that they get relevant support.

☑ Mentoring relationships can evolve to suit the mentee – it is not a fixed process.

Possible limitations

☒ It takes time – mentors may be too busy to do a good job.

☒ Mentors need to be briefed on their role as a minimum – and ideally get proper training for the role – if this does not happen the process may not work well.

☒ Matching mentors and mentees may be difficult – and many mentoring relationships fail because of what people label as 'chemistry'.

☒ People without a designated mentor can feel resentful of someone who has this privilege – this is especially so if the mentor is seen to advance the career of the mentee at the expense of others.

☒ Mentors can sometimes see their role as pushing the mentee inappropriately, that is, the mentee is not able to drive the process.

Operating hints

⮕ If you are looking for a mentor, try to think first of all of what you want from the relationship and then spell that out to a prospective mentor. Clear goals may be important – or if you don't have them, you can be clear to your mentor that that is what you want them to help you with.

⮕ You can have more than one mentor, for example, a female finance manager used her Marketing Director to help her get a better commercial grasp of the business while using a senior female manager in another department to assist her with dealing with the macho male culture in the business.

⮞ A mentoring relationship is unlikely to go on forever – think of moving on, getting another mentor at a different stage in your career.

⮞ Try to get a regular meeting with your mentor – and usually outside the normal workplace.

⮞ Confirm if it is OK to call your mentor outside arranged meetings, for example, if you have a major problem.

⮞ Be sensitive to the fact that your manager may need to be clear about what you are doing with your mentor – and ensure that the process does not undermine your relationship with your manager.

⮞ Don't have unrealistic expectations of the process – mentors usually do not have magic wands to solve all your problems – they may be best used as a neutral sounding board and not as a fixer.

2.7 *Networks and Communities*

In organizations people talk to each other outside the reporting lines indicated on an organization chart. Joe may report to Jane in the hierarchy and be part of a team with Tim, Mike and Caroline, but also spend time communicating with Jim, Anne, Mary and Charlie, who report into other managers. This has long been recognized in the literature and often referred to as 'the informal organization'. We can, though, be a bit more sophisticated than this. In another section we focus on learning in the team and hence through official channels. Here we need to recognize that learning also goes on outside official channels.

The two most used concepts are:

Network and *Community*

The distinction we will make here is between networks as loose connections between people and communities where the connections are closer, possibly longer term and more binding.

Here are dictionary definitions – from the Oxford Concise Dictionary – that indicate how these terms are formally defined:

Network – a group of people who exchange information, contacts and experience for professional or social purposes.

Community – fellowship of interests; a body of people having a religion, a profession, etc. in common (*the immigrant community*); all the people living in a specific locality.

From the latter it is apparent that there are a number of kinds of community. We will emphasize here just three that have importance for learning at work, namely:

- **Communities of Practice** – where people develop community bonding based on common practice. This is most recognizable in professional groupings but the concept has wider applicability.
- **Communities of Location** – this picks up on that aspect of the dictionary definition that refers to people being connected by virtue of place. In work such communities can grow up by virtue of people all working in the same location.
- **Communities of Values** – this kind of community is less written about but has become more important. Here people are linked not by practice or by location but rather through shared values. The dictionary definition refers to religion and this would

be a readily recognizable situation. However, in the work context people can be connected through other shared values. For instance, the three authors of this book are active in the Centre for Self Managed Learning and we find ourselves in a community of like-minded people who also value a particular approach to learning. This informal community includes people in different parts of the world and in different jobs.

Before exploring the use of communities to support learning, we will focus on the use of networks.

Networks

People regularly refer to the process of networking in organizations. Such networking may be to get information, to fix deals or to promote one's career. Here our focus is on learning. Most people use their networks for such purposes, even if they don't recognize it. For instance, getting information from others means that you learn. The issue is to make as certain as possible that you have a network of contacts that really can contribute to your learning.

EXAMPLES

One issue to consider is the reach of your network. If you only network with people who, say, work on the same tasks as you, this may limit your learning options. In our research we found that some people mainly networked with people in their own department or work location. When there was a problem that required wider learning they could be stumped. For example, people in a production area might need to know how the finances of the company worked. If no one in the finance department was in their network then they would struggle. However, those who had made a point of knowing who to talk to in finance could learn what was needed quite quickly.

Of course networks aren't static. In the above example people can add finance staff to their network when they come up with the need to learn something. However, our experience suggests that it's a whole lot easier to make such contacts work if the ground has been prepared earlier.

One development in networking has been the use of the Internet and, inside organizations, intranets. Overall, people are less using snail mail and the phone and the use of email has increased. Given our wide approach to learning, it's clear that email connections between people are a significant source of learning. This can vary from simple requests for information to approaches that are closer to the community model where people collaborate online with an explicit learning agenda as a focus.

POSSIBLE BENEFITS

In working in an organization it's almost impossible not to network, even if you don't use the term for contacts with other people. The issue here is using one's network for learning purposes. Some benefits that people indicated in our research include:

☑ quick and easy answers to specific queries;

☑ low cost, for example, individual emails are almost free;

☑ checking ideas with a number of people;

☑ gaining access to other sources of knowledge – for example, by tapping into other people's networks.

POSSIBLE LIMITATIONS

☒ The information gained can be superficial.

☒ Your network could be limited and provide biased information.

☒ Other people may not fully share knowledge with you.

☒ Skill development may be limited.

☒ If you get something from someone they may expect favours in return.

☒ Email circulation lists can cause information overload – and your time can be wasted sifting through such emailed material – and if your personal email address gets too widely known the dangers of spamming are increased.

OPERATING HINTS

➲ Creating a good network requires conscious effort – for example, collecting business cards and storing information from them; storing email addresses in relevant folders.

➲ It's best to sift through your network regularly and check if all contacts are really relevant – this can mean regular reviewing of your address book, especially with emails.

➲ Note that our focus is on learning so it's worth asking yourself where you can best get the knowledge you need and getting those people into your network.

➲ Give at least as much as you take – sharing your knowledge with others is important, for example, you may read a book that you think others will find valuable and you can tell them about it; you may have found a useful website that you can tell others about; and so on.

Communities

The idea of using a community approach is in part a way of addressing some of the weaknesses of networks. A community implies a closeness of connection which usually allows for more open and deeper communication. Also the skill development dimension becomes more important here – if you are in closer relationships with people then learning new skills becomes easier.

Communities of various kinds exist in the workplace. The most written about are Communities of Practice – often abbreviated as COPs. (Below is a description of COPs.) However, they are not the only kind of community to consider when looking to encourage learning at work. We have indicated above three examples of communities that can help (or hinder) learning.

Communities of Practice

A COP (Community of Practice) is usually made up of people in similar roles who can benefit from providing each other with information, ideas and support. At its simplest a COP is more than a network. However, its defining feature is generally that people in such a community share ideas and information. COPs can then go beyond this because people carrying out similar work and communicating regularly with each other come to share attitudes to work as well as just ideas and information. Hence the label 'community' is attached to such a connected group of people.

Note that COPs are not defined by department/section or by location. It may be that, for instance, HR managers are dispersed through the business and report into the managers of different departments. However, if they share practices and ideas across these departments, they could constitute a Community of Practice. The 'could' means that it does not necessarily happen. The HR managers in question could just focus on working in their own department and not make strong links to their professional colleagues elsewhere in the business.

EXAMPLES

An example was the creation of a COP of salespeople in Allied Domecq's wines and spirits division. Most of the salespeople worked alone out on the road selling the company's products to bars, pubs, clubs and hotels. They came together with their regional manager once a month for a business meeting. But otherwise there was little connection between them. We worked to create a COP which would provide benefits for the salespeople and for the company.

An example will show one change. At a meeting one salesman mentioned to the others about how he had devised a way of showing the value of a particular product to clients. He had been doing this for years – and been very successful with it. The other salespeople were not aware of his technique, but when he shared it with them, they all started using it.

The mark of such a community is that people share a common practice base. In the example mentioned it was selling wines and spirits. Another feature is that COPs emphasize horizontal relationships. They provide the horizontal links and connections that make organizations work. Except that in many cases these links are poorly formed (as in the example of Allied Domecq). Hence the interactions in such COPs require a level of mutual trust so that people are prepared to share ideas, concerns, problems and challenges. However, such social structures can be created more easily once people see the benefits that can derive from them.

In Ericsson we found that the technical specialists tended to work alone a great deal, spending many hours at computer screens. Yet they needed, as a community, to learn a whole range of new things. When we were working there a major issue was the emerging role of new approaches such as broadband. One team found out about a good course on broadband – but it was expensive and lasted a whole week. The idea of all the people going off on this course was not tenable. Yet it was clear that everyone needed increased knowledge and skills in this area. In talking with each other they decided that one person would go on the course and then come back and share the relevant knowledge and skills.

The result of this was that everyone was up to speed yet the cost to the business was relatively low – a very cost-effective solution, which would not have been apparent before we started to create these connections. In what we have said so far we have emphasized knowledge sharing. This is often the starting point for creating such a community. However, the need for mutual support amongst geographically separate practitioners may be another prompt.

USES

Research suggests that people usually see their COP as:

- providing resources for each other – access to expertise, and so on
- facilitating information exchange – quick answers to questions
- making sense of problems – prior to being able to solve them
- sharing tricks and tips
- a forum for developing skills and capabilities
- keeping abreast of the field
- reduced risks – as ideas and approaches can be tested with colleagues
- developing new ways of working
- making work more enjoyable
- increased sense of belonging
- improved learning
- increased confidence in one's role
- enhanced professional reputation.

POSSIBLE BENEFITS

☑ increased innovation

☑ reduced costs

☑ quicker response to changes, for example, in the market, with new technologies

☑ improved quality of decisions

☑ new business opportunities grasped more easily

☑ strengthened quality assurance

☑ makes knowledge management happen

☑ better co-ordination across the business – and hence a more corporate stance to clients/customers

☑ improved morale

☑ reduced staff turnover – people like to share with colleagues and they enjoy the support from others

☑ money and time saved through not 're-inventing the wheel'

☑ easier to recruit as people enjoy working in such environments

☑ ultimately – bottom line pay-off.

POSSIBLE LIMITATIONS

☒ purely inward-looking collaboration between people can leave a COP less in touch with other parts of the organization

☒ a COP can exclude people who are different – the Ku Klux Klan acts as a COP for racist activity – and most people recognize the problem with this

☒ COPs may resist innovation if they become self-sealing entities

☒ it's difficult to form them artificially.

OPERATING HINTS – DEVELOPING COPS

The COP needs to develop the following processes:

➲ discovering how to collaborate effectively

➲ finding out what helps and what hinders useful support

➲ getting to know who is who – and what they offer

➲ dealing with differences – and possible conflicts

➲ developing systems and procedures that allow for 'structured informality'.

There are no easy formulae for creating COPs. The main mode is for people to have time together in ways which allows conversations to occur that get below the surface of everyday pleasantries. And people need to want a COP to exist. Not that they are likely to articulate it in so many words. Rather there often occurs, over time, a realization that a connection which is at a deeper level than a network is valuable.

When a COP is operating effectively, most of the following should be recognizable:

- sustained mutual relationships – not temporary connections only
- rapid flows of information and ideas
- not a need for preambles to conversations – people can get stuck in on the issues as there is a shared language and way of seeing the world – short cuts are common
- quick recognition of problems – easy to analyse a problem and work on it
- people know broadly who is in the COP and who isn't
- people know what others know and/or can do – or if they don't they only need to consult one or two people to find out
- actions that people undertake can be readily understood and assessed
- people trust the information that they get
- coaching of less experienced people happens informally
- levels of interaction vary – some people are more active than others – but that is accepted
- some people may be more central, taking more of a lead – and that is seen as sensible.

2.8 *Qualifications*

This section is about work based learning qualifications. It is not intended to be a guide to particular universities or the awards that they offer but it should provide a framework for thinking through the value of combining work based learning with accreditation and in surveying and questioning what different universities have to offer.

We have focused on university schemes as these continue to have the highest status. However, in various countries there are other options for work based qualifications. For instance, in England, people have been encouraged by employers to do National Vocational Qualifications, which are validated by the Qualifications and Curriculum Authority (QCA). The QCA is an official government body and so the latter has wanted to encourage the use of such qualifications. The problem is that many employers (and employees) have found the process too bureaucratic. Hence there has been a falling off in the numbers of people doing these qualifications whereas university-supported work based learning programmes have been increasing.

Interestingly the UK government has promoted Learndirect to provide online access to learning opportunities. The latter runs 'Learndirect-through-work', which allows individuals to gain qualifications via work based learning. At the time of writing, only universities have been supporting this scheme. The QCA does not provide qualifications via 'Learndirect-through-work'. Hence we will keep our focus on university schemes while recognizing that some individuals might find the 'vocational qualifications' route a useful alternative.

In universities, accreditation is the process of assigning value to learning in terms of the number of academic credit points (a measure of the quantity of learning achieved) and higher education level (a measure of the complexity of the learning achieved). Academic credit points form a common currency in UK universities and increasingly within the European Union and the USA. Credit points can be earned at undergraduate or postgraduate level. These credits can then be cashed in for anything from a basic undergraduate certificate to Masters degree, depending on the level of the credits gained.

Broadly there are four ways in which work based learning is accredited. One of these is Accreditation for Prior Experiential Learning (APEL) which is commonly used to gain exemptions from modules on traditional academic courses. The remaining three are intended to be used specifically within the context of work based learning. One of these is called 'Work Based Learning' and each of the other two takes its name from one of the strategic approaches discussed in this handbook, namely, **Action Learning** and **Self Managed Learning** (SML).

Examples

APEL

Schemes are offered by many universities to enable learners to gain exemption from a proportion of the modules in traditional courses. Typically learners can normally get APEL for up to 60 per cent of the academic credits for an honours degree and up to 50 per cent required for a postgraduate award and up to a number, that is, not all, modules in a course. The measurement is in credit points, for example, at undergraduate level, you might be able to claim up to 240 credits (two thirds of the total required for an honours degree) or at postgraduate level, up to 50 per cent of the total credit value of the programme. The accreditation is wholly retrospective.

Typically the learner is expected to present an APEL claim for each module for which exemption is desired. This takes the form of a portfolio containing the evidence the learner is putting forward to show that they have achieved, through past experience, the quantity and complexity of learning represented in the published learning outcomes of the module concerned. The number of modules for which claims can be made will vary depending on the number of credits assigned to each module. The learner will typically have access to tutorial assistance in creating and submitting their claim, although the amount of assistance given will vary.

WORK BASED LEARNING

These schemes are offered by some universities (for example, see Appendix II on the example of Middlesex University). Like APEL as described above, they enable learners to accumulate credit points at different levels (and might actually include APEL arrangements to accredit past learning). However, where in standard APEL schemes the learner has to translate their real work based learning in the past into a form that demonstrates that they don't need to follow a prescribed academic curriculum now, these schemes are intended to provide learners with the means to accumulate credits from the moment that they begin planning the work based learning they are going to undertake, and to continue to accumulate them through to gaining a named award (where this is desired).

Generally, the modules they contain (and their learning outcomes) assume that the learner will be able to plan and undertake their learning as one or more **projects** and reflect the different stages in the project management process, for example, planning, research/investigatory methods, project development and implementation, and so on. Items for assessment are usually represented by written reports of the work and learning that has been accomplished at different stages, accompanied by written evidence of reflection on the content and process of problem solving and learning (see section on **Reflective Learning**).

Some schemes include the use of 'learning agreements'. These bear some similarity to SML (**Self Managed Learning**) Learning Contracts although with restrictions on the numbers of those who are parties to the agreement (typically the learner, a university tutor and an employer representative) and without the collaborative assessment in the learning group that one would expect to see in an SML programme. Typically these kinds of schemes can cater for individual work based learners and can also be used by the organization in partnership with the university to accredit work based and other learning gained through in-organization programmes.

ACTION LEARNING

The phrase 'action learning' is used quite frequently in descriptions of accredited courses although the extent to which it actually corresponds to the approach covered in the section on **action learning** varies considerably. Where the approach is properly integrated into the course design and operation one would expect to see the use of project work as the main vehicle for pursuing and evaluating the learning, as in the 'work based learning' schemes above.

SELF MANAGED LEARNING

As with action learning, the term 'self managed learning' has become used quite loosely by higher education institutions, and most programmes using this label are likely to be modified versions of the **Self Managed Learning** approach described in this handbook.

Possible benefits

☑ A qualification can provide a clear form of recognition.

☑ It can add considerable rigour to the work based learning process.

☑ It can provide the impetus for achieving more learning than would otherwise be the case.

☑ Writing up learning can be part of the learning process (see the section on **Writing**).

☑ It can increase the depth of learning.

☑ It can bring to consciousness learning that would otherwise remain tacit.

☑ Possessing a qualification can have considerable career benefits.

Possible limitations

☒ It means more work, that is, writing-up that is additional to the work required to do the learning.

☒ Universities' internal processes of assessing and awarding work based learning qualifications (and other forms of qualifications) are surrounded by numerous bureaucratic procedures. The rationale for this is to maintain quality levels at the appropriate level. However, working with these processes and procedures can be irksome, particularly where the bureaucracy doesn't work very efficiently.

☒ Most accrediting and awarding institutions take a very traditional view of what constitutes learning so searching out providers of good work based learning schemes and negotiating the appropriate arrangements takes time and effort.

Operating hints

➲ Opting for qualification programmes is a strategic decision. The minimum time frame for a qualification programme once it is up and running is nine months to a year, to which must be added time for establishing productive partnership arrangements with the university.

➲ Care should be taken in deciding on the university to use – some are more user friendly than others and they need to be tested out.

➲ Consideration should be given to the fact that a minority of people fail to gain the qualification, so you would need to be careful about agreeing to do a qualification if you felt that you would not have the time or capability to carry out the required work.

➲ Most universities leave you very much to your own devices; if you are not someone that copes well on your own it may be valuable to create support structures to assist you, for example, **mentoring** support.

2.9 *Self Managed Learning*

Self Managed Learning (SML) is about individuals managing their own learning. This includes people being given, and taking, responsibility for decisions about:

- what they learn
- how they learn
- when they learn
- where they learn

and most fundamentally

- why they learn.

All of this takes place within the context of organizational needs.

The Self Managed Learning approach provides a structure within which participants decide on their learning goals and pursue them. A typical SML programme begins with a start-up event during which the participants produce a first draft of their Learning Contracts and start working in the Learning Group in which they will be meeting throughout the programme. These two essential elements of Self Managed Learning will be described below.

The descriptions below cover specific aspects of programmes for use in the workplace. Clearly, if your organization does not use this mode of working, what follows may only be of limited interest. However, you might find yourself in the role of influencing decisions about development processes and hence the information in this section could be useful. For instance, in Ericsson the decision to use Self Managed Learning came from line managers not from HR or training – some managers came across the idea and implemented it with their staff.

Learning contract

The learning contract is a strategic learning document and is more than just a fancy name for a 'personal development plan' or an 'action plan'. Such plans often remain no more than wish lists (the equivalent of New Year's resolutions). A learning contract is different because:

- It is a serious written document that is negotiated between the individual and relevant interested parties.
- It is a living document that individuals refer to regularly.

- It covers long- and short-term development needs and spells out a programme to meet these.
- It has measures of achievement built in so that pay-off to the individual and the organization can be monitored.

The way to achieve the above begins with people writing down their answers to five questions. The questions are taken in order and move the person from the past to the present to the future.

1 *Where have I been?* (How has my career progressed? What have I learned from past experiences?)

This question helps the person make sense of their past experiences. The reason for starting with this question is that we are today – any of us – a product of the past. We are 100 per cent created by the past – either we were born this way (the genes) or we had accidents that changed us or we learned to be this way. Whatever the reason it's 100 per cent due to the past. So in order to move on we need to explore where our current capabilities, values, beliefs, and so on, came from. And we may need to modify some of our ingrained habits if we are to move on.

2 *Where am I now?* (What kind of person am I? What are my strengths and weaknesses? What are my guiding values and beliefs?)

This question identifies the person's current situation. The person may have evidence from a range of sources (360° feedback, appraisals, psychometric tests, and so on) to help them address this. Sometimes people want to leap straight into the next question (on goal setting), but getting a secure sense of the present is essential as a baseline for considering the future.

3 *Where do I want to get to?* (What kind of person would I like to be? What strengths can I develop? What weaknesses do I want to address? What are my short- and long-term goals?)

The questions focus now on the future. People often find it useful to specify different kinds of learning goals. For instance, they may identify short-term job problems that indicate a precise narrow learning need. On the other hand, the same person may want to set career goals which imply a broader, longer term orientation.

4 *How will I get there?* (What action is needed for me to progress from where I am to where I'd like to be? What learning do I need to undertake – and how will I do it?)

The answers to this question in essence provide the person's own plan of action and is equivalent to a curriculum (in a traditional educational programme). The learner may draw on a whole range of methods to achieve their goals including even the standard training offerings (for example, workshops, courses, seminars and conferences) as well as coaching and mentoring assistance, learning packages, secondments, projects, and so on. There is nothing that needs to be excluded except on the grounds of cost or organizational policy.

At one level, when the person is pursuing their learning contract it can look like any other development process. The big difference, though, is that the learner will be working to a carefully crafted plan as created in the learning contract. They will not be randomly going off on courses or haphazardly ploughing through learning materials. They will have clearly identified strategic goals and they will be aware that they will need to show progress to those with whom they have entered into the contract.

5 *How will I know if I have arrived?* (How will I demonstrate the achievement of my goals? What will be my measures of achievement? What evidence will I be able to show?)

This last question is vitally important. The learner is contracting to learn against specified goals and they need to show that this has happened (after a period of time – typically six months to a year). This question adds considerable bite to the SML process and is one example of a difference between the learning contract in SML and less rigorous types of learning and development plans.

Learning group

Learners are supported in meeting the goals they set themselves in their learning contract primarily through the learning group. In Self Managed Learning programmes individuals are grouped in 'learning groups' of about five or six persons. The group is the primary place where each person negotiates their learning contract and reports progress on it. The group typically meets every four to six weeks and provides an arena for both support and challenge. Participants comment that the learning group provides a unique, cost-effective forum to push individuals to learn in depth and to solve real business problems at the same time.

Attending a learning group is not like going off on a course: meetings only work on practical issues that have a bearing on the business and the needs of individuals in the group. Indeed, Shell wanted to ensure that the pay-off from the programme, in money terms, was measurably greater than the cost (which did happen). However, most organizations are clear that the major benefits come over time: individuals really do learn to take charge of their own development.

This not only enhances their performance but can reduce training costs. (It's not that training ceases with SML, but rather that it becomes better targeted. In companies such as Allied Domecq – which has used SML extensively – training events were only put on if enough people had the need for them specified in their learning contracts.)

One crucial support factor is the role of the learning group adviser. This person is present in the group to assist it to function effectively. The role may be played by someone in HR or training or an external adviser, but can also be effectively carried out by a good line manager or team leader. The reason for this is that the role is not one of teaching or training but of providing support for the learning group. Such support may at times be in the form of challenges to people to address tough learning needs, so it is not just a cosy facilitative role.

Together, the learning contract and the learning group are the structures which allow participants to identify their important areas of development and to achieve them.

Examples

The Self Managed Learning approach has been used in many contexts since its development in the late 1970s. A representative selection are mentioned below. In-organization programmes have taken place at all levels of organizations, sometimes beginning with the senior management and moving down through the organization and sometimes moving upward. Although most often used for managers, SML has also been especially valued by technical staff, secretaries, administrators, front-line customer service staff and sales people, among others. In consortium programmes, participants of the same level, usually managers or directors, are drawn from different organizations, giving them the benefits of a wider perspective through gaining insight into the workings of other organizations. In qualification programmes, there have been two-year programmes for postgraduate qualifications in management studies, an MBA and an MSc in managing change. The approach has also been used with school-age students.

Possible benefits

☑ In addition to the learning goals that are the focus of participants' attention they also learn how to learn. Because they learn how to manage their own learning, with the supportive structure of the SML programme, they know how to go about learning anything else they wish to in the future.

☑ Within the learning group, participants learn of the experiences of others, often working in different departments in their own organization, and an informal network begins to be established. The SML experience breaks down the silo mentality by exposing participants to the trials and tribulations, aims and intentions of people in areas of the organization about which they may have prior stereotypes and caricatural misperceptions. Similarly, where participants are drawn from different organizations their understanding of how other organizations work can inform their perception of their own organization, as well as offering different perspectives on their own problems.

☑ SML programmes have been used within a single department, or a large organization, in order to enable people to develop into a new role which the organization was requiring of that department. Although everyone would be needing to take on that new role it was, of course, the case that different people needed to learn and develop different things in order to do so. Even where the role was the same for all, a sheep-dip approach would still have been far less effective.

☑ The learning group, where people get to know one another quite well over the course of the programme, can become a supportive context in which to think through issues each is facing and encourage them to take well-thought-through actions to resolve problems. In a way, it is like having your very own think-tank.

☑ The use of questioning, within a support and challenge context, that characterizes a learning group is a useful ability which participants are able to take into their role as coaches and developers of others.

☑ When there are a number of learning groups operating in an organization they provide a strong impetus toward the development of a learning organization. This is sometimes cited as the reason for having an SML programme in that a learning organization is more readily able both to initiate and to respond effectively to change.

☑ Over and above the specific learning goals of a participant in an SML programme there is a marked effect on the individual's level of confidence (based on their knowing they have the ability to learn new things and act in new ways).

☑ SML avoids common limitations of imposed learning such as lack of motivation and lack of transfer of learning. When participants have to identify learning goals which are meaningful to them, they will be motivated to achieve them. Because those goals come out of their day-to-day work context the learning is not separate from their working life but is a part of it, so no transfer is necessary; they simply learn from what they are doing and put that learning into immediate action.

Possible limitations

☒ SML is not a soft option. While the freedom to choose your own goals may be appealing, SML also requires you to take responsibility for pursuing those goals and attaining them. Even identifying what those goals should be can be quite a challenge; nobody is telling you what they should be (as is the case with almost all other contexts from school through to management training) but you are expected to come up with goals that are meaningful to you.

☒ Many people mistake the lack of imposed content within an SML programme to mean the programme is virtually 'empty', and therefore requires little organization. On the contrary, such a programme demands a high level of efficient management and administration which also needs to be flexible and creative in responding to the participants' needs.

☒ It's a lot harder to hide in an SML programme. Nobody can just sit at the back, as it were. They are either engaging with their goals and achieving things or they are seen not to be. It is much harder to go through the motions.

☒ The commitment to learning of senior management can be important. Without it, participants can find their boss demanding they miss learning group meetings to do day-to-day work. In one organization this was avoided because non-attendance could only be sanctioned by Board members, which meant that only the most urgent and crucial task or meeting could take precedence over learning. (At the same time, championing an SML programme provides senior managers with the opportunity to show they have a serious commitment to learning.)

☒ Although organizations often say they want managers to take more initiative, be more decisive, questioning and creative, bosses are still people and they may find it hard to deal with having one of their staff becoming less subservient and more challenging.

⌧ Self Managed Learning, as a capitalized name, must not be mistaken for the phrase 'self-managed learning', which has become popular, though what it means often varies in use. All too often, it gives a veneer of respectability to the message, 'You're on your own, kid', when organizations wish to renege on their responsibility for developing their people. While this gives people the freedom to take control of their learning it offers none of the supportive structures that enables those on SML programmes to make real use of that freedom.

Operating hints

There are books which outline many of the features and facets of SML programmes (see, for example, Cunningham *et al.*, 2000). It is important to consult these as there are too many factors in the operation of such a programme to explore in detail here.

However, there are a few factors which need to be mentioned here:

➲ Although SML programmes all have fundamental processes and structures in common, it is important that the programme is designed to fit the specific needs of the organization. If you want to create an SML programme it needs to be integrated with the culture and style of the organization.

➲ If you are nominated to take part in an SML programme it's important to recognize that it is not the same as a training programme. That may sound obvious but so often participants still expect something like a course. For instance, people are often surprised that most learning is expected to take place through live work contexts – they may still expect material to be delivered.

➲ SML is a strategic approach. Expect to work on a programme over a significant period of time – and hopefully the use of learning contracts may continue beyond the length of a formal programme. Also learning groups often keep in contact, including meeting after the end of a programme.

➲ Preparing to take part in an SML programme is important. This may include clearing any issues with your manager or your work colleagues, such as the fact that you may be trying out new approaches at work or that you will need time to attend learning groups.

2.10 *Team Development*

We deliberately use the term 'team development' here and not 'team building'. Team building is often related to a short-term initiative such as an away day where the team might go off and do some outdoor activities. It may be that people will learn from such an event but it is often just a one shot intervention with little follow through. Our interest here is in people making a long-term commitment to learning to work better in teams. This is essential as teams very rarely have static membership – people come and go and there has to be a recognition of this in any team development strategy.

Our sense of team development is learning activity undertaken in teams and for the benefit of making teams work better. Although there has been more emphasis on team working in recent years, we would say that it is not necessary for everyone to work in a team. If you are not a member of a team but work in other ways, you may still find it valuable to learn 'teamworking' skills as you may in future have to work in such a context. Also what have been identified as teamworking skills tend to have general applicability, for example, getting on with others, developing self awareness and other qualities that have come to be associated with the term 'emotional intelligence'.

One area where there might be a different focus is if you are a team leader rather than just a team member. The growth of interest in teams has been matched by more interest in leadership. However, some organizations have wanted to develop greater 'leadership density'. By this they mean that they want more people to take on leadership roles even if they are not the designated team leader. It is probable that this trend will develop so it may be that you are not a designated leader but you could still benefit from learning leadership capabilities. That being said, it is worth recognizing that formal leaders are usually in a different role because they tend to be accountable for the activities of the team.

Examples

Team development is learning that takes place in the context of a team. The approach recognizes that much learning at work goes on with and through other people. (This issue is picked up in the sections on **Networks** and **Communities of Practice**.) If the team adopts a deliberate strategy of team development it may use many methods described elsewhere in this handbook. These could include:

* The team discusses and agrees individual learning contracts (see **Self Managed Learning**) for team members so that they all have an explicit commitment to development.
* Feedback is promoted in team meetings so that people can learn from each other.

- A learning review takes place after each team meeting.
- Dispersed teams may use computer conferencing to share learning.
- **Mistakes** are used for the team to identify what to learn from them, rather than to scapegoat individuals.
- The team looks at organizational strategies to see what it needs to learn to meet strategic targets.
- People commit to help each other to learn, for example, via informal **coaching**.
- Team members help to induct new people by being open about how the team works and providing support and encouragement for the new person's learning.

These are only some of the things that a good team can do. The main thing is to have team development as an ongoing strategy. It needs to be an ingrained part of the team's culture.

Possible benefits

☑ Individuals learn a range of capabilities that can be used in the team and in other work.

☑ Openness and honesty is developed and allows people to get real learning about how things have to be done.

☑ The team can provide support that would be missing if the person had to learn on their own.

☑ The learning is linked to real needs and is not disconnected from the work of the team.

☑ People enjoy being in a 'learning team'.

Possible limitations

☒ If you are not in a good learning team it can be very frustrating.

☒ The team can close in on itself and become too cosy – and eventually learning is hindered by this.

☒ Some activities take time, for example, learning reviews; in the hurly burly of organizational life there is pressure to dispense with overt learning activities, especially if there is a crisis.

Operating hints

➲ If you are in a team that is not used to overt learning activities, it may be necessary to be circumspect about introducing new ideas – often the best time is when it correlates with some problem. For instance, if there has been a major crisis, it can be useful to ask 'What can we learn from this for the future?'

⮑ If you are the team leader, it is important to model an openness to learning. For instance, if the organization is using **360° feedback** you need to be prepared to talk with your team in a non-defensive way about what has come out of it and to discuss with the team what you might need to learn in order to improve.

⮑ Keeping the focus as strategic is key. It may be that the team goes through phases where little seems to be being learned. However, if the team keeps to the long term and fosters a learning culture it does not matter if there are ups and downs in the process.

⮑ Off-site meetings can be important – but they need to be planned in as part of the ongoing life of the team and not seen as stand-alone events. Having an outside facilitator for such events can be valuable if the facilitator understands the strategic context of off-site meetings.

3 *Tactics for Work Based Learning and Development*

Introduction

In this part we show how particular tactics can be used as part of an overall developmental strategy. We have indicated earlier the distinction we make between strategy and tactics but we will re-iterate some points here in order to provide a clear introduction to this part of the handbook. We are aware that the distinction between strategy and tactics is not always clear cut, but separating approaches to learning in this way does work for us.

The notion of tactics is underutilized and underestimated in the organizational literature. There are numerous texts on strategy in organizations but very few books on tactics. Yet strategies need to be actioned. Tactics provide the bridge between a big picture/long-term strategy and day-to-day action. The basis of the distinction between strategy and tactics is in warfare – strategy is about winning the war and tactics about winning battles. You can win battles but lose the war – but if you lose all your battles you are never going to win the war.

In team sports, tactics may be about winning a game and strategy is about winning the league (or whatever the overall aim is). It is recognized that you may not always win all the games – but if you achieve your strategy you have demonstrated your overall success. However, if you lose too many games you won't win the league – so tactics are important. Such tactics may be about selecting and deploying your team to suit the opposition or practising particular moves in training. Whatever is used it is ultimately about the linkage of tactics to strategy.

In learning and development the same kind of thinking can be applied. For instance, we have suggested that **Continuing Professional Development** is a strategy – it is about long-term commitment to learning by professionals. However, this strategy has to be implemented. In this part of the handbook we cover a number of tactics that might be relevant. For example, you might carry out **projects** as part of your professional development, or use a **secondment** to another organization, or utilize the Internet for dialogue with professional colleagues, or use the organization's **learning resource centre** to get hold of relevant learning materials.

If you are using a **mentor** as part of your development strategy you might find that, from discussions with your mentor, you need to create a **personal development plan** within which to specify learning goals. And from that the mentor might assist you to get some **coaching** around specific skills that you need to develop or they might help you to undertake a **job rotation**. The ideal is for the strategy to drive the tactical choices.

In Part 4 we will indicate methods of learning that can be used to implement your tactical decisions. As in the previous part we have put in **bold** any reference to another section in this handbook so that you can make your own links to other material as you wish.

3.1 *Appraisal and Performance Reviews*

This section is about the potential of Appraisal and Performance Reviews (APR) as a tactic in work based learning. The word 'potential' is used here for a number of reasons associated with the range of ways in which performance appraisal is conducted, not all of which are obviously conducive either to reviewing learning (as distinct from performance) or to setting learning goals. APR is conducted in a variety of ways in different organizations, although formal schemes typically have two elements.

One element is the face-to-face meeting between the appraisee and appraiser, typically the appraisee's line manager, supervisor or team leader. At least one meeting will take place at the end of the defined period for which performance is being reviewed. This is often annually, although the trend seems to be to hold them more frequently.

The other element of many formal APR schemes is the paperwork that accompanies the review meeting. Typically this is comprised of assessment and review forms completed by the appraiser, or by both the appraiser and appraisee, and used in preparation for the meeting and as a vehicle for recording its outcomes. Typically such paperwork includes review forms based on either or both of the following:

- The criteria and methods to be used for making and communicating judgements about performance with, for example, rating scales that represent dimensions of personal qualities, skills or behaviours, deemed by the organization to be associated with effective performance or with the capabilities underpinning it. These methods might include the provision of **360° feedback**.
- Appropriate questions and sufficient white space for qualitative judgements and supporting information to be recorded about the extent to which, over the review period, the individual has achieved performance objectives agreed at the last meeting.

None of these ways of making or communicating judgements need necessarily make any specific references to learning. Typically where a formal APR scheme does consider learning and development it will be through the individual's completion of a **personal development plan**. As noted in that section, there is a poor history of attempts to combine performance and development in the same review meeting. There are a number of possible reasons for this. Despite the fact that a face-to-face conversation can contribute to an individual's **reflective learning,** as part of their developmental review, the climate of trust and openness required is less likely to be achieved when the focus of communication is on judgements about job performance, particularly when these are linked to decisions about rewards.

Another reason is that people's experience of APR often goes no further than complying with the requirements of the system, that is, completing the necessary paperwork and showing that the obligatory meeting has been held. Rather than APR being experienced as a real part of everyday working relationships in the organization, it can become an uncomfortable, time consuming, bureaucratic chore. As surveys have shown, a significant minority of managers would actually rather visit the dentist than carry out an APR meeting!

One way in which some organizations attempt to make APR more significant and relevant to participants is to combine it with **coaching.** That is, to encourage or require appraisers to include **coaching** as part of an APR meeting. Although, potentially, this brings a clearer learning focus to the APR meeting, the remarks above about openness and trust in relation to **personal development plans** are relevant here. Further, as indicated in the **coaching** section, when it is linked directly to judgements about performance in current tasks the appraiser/coach can be tempted to prescribe solutions rather than to assist in learning.

Examples

Well-conducted APR should provide valid, reliable data about an individual's current and prospective performance from which potential learning needs and goals can be derived. In this context APR is often associated with other tactics such as **personal development plans** and **coaching.** However, as indicated above and suggested in the 'Operating Hints' section below, these associations seem to work best when meetings for APR purposes are separated in time from those intended for learning and development purposes. Also, it may well be the case that the coach, or the person who provides assistance with development planning, will be different from the individual's appraiser. People can gain **coaching** from a range of people inside and outside the organization. The same can be the case with development planning, although the individual's immediate line manager, and likely appraiser, does, potentially, have an important role to the extent that they are an immediate and accessible 'representative' of the organization as far as the learner is concerned.

APR can make particular tactical contributions within a number of work based learning strategies. For example, it can be used as a source of performance-related data to identify learning needs and achievements in implementing a **continuous professional development** strategy. In following a **Self Managed Learning** strategy it can be used by learners as one of a number of sources of data to assist them in answering the learning contract question 'Where am I now?', and the data it provides can be used to identify problems that are addressed within an **action learning** frame.

In the light of the evidence about the problems of APR, we have found that appraisee training has a real benefit. In one of the major accountancy firms we ran two-day appraisee workshops which helped appraisees to plan their learning (using the learning contract model outlined in the section on **Self Managed Learning**). This meant that they went into the appraisal meeting well prepared and with an explicit learning focus. The evaluation of these workshops showed that the investment in appraisee training was cost effective – and more so than appraiser training. It is clear that if appraisees can drive the process, then it can work better. And appraisers were happier with this approach. They commented that it took pressure off them to know all the answers and allowed for a real dialogue as opposed to a stilted conversation.

Possible benefits

☑ Performance issues or problems that lead to the identification of learning needs clearly related to organizational concerns can be clarified. You can get a better sense of what the organization is looking for and hence tailor any learning activity to those requirements.

☑ It can be a means to recognize and reward learning that is associated with performance improvement. If your learning in the previous year has helped you to perform better this can be formally recognized and recorded – and it may help your career progression in the organization.

☑ It can provide the context for grounding intended learning in a work context and for promoting work based learning as a contributor to improved effectiveness. You can have an explicit conversation with your manager about how to progress your work based learning.

Possible limitations

☒ The focus on judgements about job performance may limit the openness and trust required to review or plan learning. The extent to which this is a problem is likely to depend a great deal on your relationship with your manager. If you get on well with them the problem will be reduced.

☒ Formal APR processes can become bureaucratic and be seen by both appraisers and appraisees as no more than 'tick box' procedures or 'going through the motions'. Organizations do vary a great deal on this count and you may find that you can work round this if there is some flexibility in the system.

☒ Learning needs that emerge from APR can reduce motivation for learning where they are closely related to lower than expected performance – where, for example, the learning required is seen as no more than remedial.

☒ Our research shows that managers usually do not know about all the learning approaches covered in this handbook. Hence, they tend to play safe and suggest course-based training as the main learning mode and this may distort your learning needs. For instance, if you have difficulty sometimes with contributing in meetings you might be sent on a three-day communication skills course that only covers meeting skills as a tiny part of the curriculum. The rest of the time could be wasted.

☒ In light of the above evidence and the fact that APR takes time, our research suggests that in most organizations it is not cost effective.

Operating hints

(Note: These are written with appraisees in mind. However, appraisers can learn from the process if they focus on the learning aspect of the process, for example, being aware of how the appraisee learns.)

➲ Ensure that there is relevant and valid data to underpin performance judgements and that these show clearly not just *what* has been achieved but also indicate *how* this has been done. You need to prepare well for an appraisal meeting and put time in to work through all the sections in the forms. However, if the forms do not allow you to raise learning needs in an appropriate way, consider how to raise these, for example, by writing a separate addendum to the forms.

➲ As far as the analysis of *how* performance has or will be achieved is concerned, ensure that it provides an accurate picture of all the contributory factors – in particular that it shows that due account has been taken of factors other than your contribution, such as the amount and quality of resources available and the ease or difficulty of the tasks.

➲ Analyse the way you work and its effectiveness, and consider and evaluate alternative routes to the achievement of performance goals, some of which may be unfamiliar and indicate learning needs. You may wish to consult the learning methods covered in this handbook in order to raise the possibility of using some of them for your development.

➲ Ensure that the substance and outcomes of the APR are available to inform any separate, and probably subsequent, use of work based learning tactics and methods such as **personal development plans**.

➲ At the APR meeting, agree whether or not the review will be followed by the use of other work based learning tactics and methods, and ensure that these are planned appropriately. You may want to negotiate resources and time that you can utilize to meet your development goals.

➲ Consider if you want more frequent meetings with your manager in order to discuss your development. As with other items indicated in the above, your manager will not be a mind reader, so you need to ask.

3.2 *Buddying*

'Buddying' relationships are used in a number of organizations to provide peer support, most particularly when there are groups undergoing induction together. Rather than the more amorphous and general support of the group as a whole, buddying uses the pairing of two peers as a way to make the support more concrete and personal.

Frequently, the learning dimension to buddy relationships tends to be ignored or undervalued, with the emphasis usually focusing upon the support element. Within the context of this book, it is the learning potential of buddying which we would like to emphasize.

First entry into a new workplace, and especially first entry into the world of work, can be stressful. Buddying helps people deal with this. Apart from someone to talk to, you also know there is someone looking out for you in this new environment. Where the buddies are both new entrants they can pool what each other is learning about the organization. Their experiences, or the way they make sense of those experiences, will be different even if they are being taken through the same induction. It is the benefit of gaining a different perspective which can be so valuable, especially when you have the opportunity, as with a buddy, to talk through your different perspectives. The result will be a much richer understanding of the organization, and it will be gained much more quickly.

When a new inductee is buddied up with someone already at work in the organization the relationship becomes rather more like a **mentoring** relationship, in that the mentor has knowledge which the mentee can draw upon. However, mentees should not simply be passive recipients of the wisdom of the mentor; they need to take an active approach to learning what is relevant to them, and not assume the mentor is the one who will determine what they need to know, and make sure they know it. (Much that will be found in the **Mentor** section will be pertinent here.) Having a **mentor**, whether it is within the buddy framework or not, is important for graduate entrants in that, on entering the organization, they may not even have an assigned boss; they need someone with experience of the organization to whom they can take their questions.

The very fact that buddies are usually close in age and experience means that people can feel less nervous about asking simple questions and admitting to confusion and perplexity. Additionally, knowing that someone else, in the same situation, is going through much the same experience can lessen the feeling that 'it's just me'.

The buddying concept can be usefully applied throughout organizational life. Nonetheless, it is usually only in the initial entry stage that organizations take responsibility for setting up such schemes. Beyond that, it is up to the individual to seek out that kind of relationship if it is considered valuable. Frequently, people use **networking** as a means to gain some of the benefits of buddying. However, networks tend to be looser and do not provide the kind of feedback on our thinking and our actions which a buddy might be willing to give us.

Organizational tasks and projects have deadlines which assist us in keeping our focus on them, even through the day-to-day distractions and interruptions. Unless one is on a formal programme this is not so for learning and development. Yet there is a similar need to maintain our focus on our learning goals, and a buddy can be particularly valuable here. Going back to the point made above, being accountable to your buddy for continuing to pursue those learning goals can help us stick with our own programme.

Examples

A common induction example is that of a graduate entry group. The newcomers will be paired up so that each person has someone to talk to, someone with whom to share their experiences. Some induction schemes employ buddying to link a newcomer with a person not long in the organization, in other words, new enough to remember what it was like to feel at sea in the new environment.

The concept of buddying is applied in many different areas of life these days, from military units, followers of spiritual practices, those in all manner of 12-step programmes or self-help groups, those with HIV/Aids, and right through to people helping one another keep to dietary or physical exercise regimes. Apart from the advantages of support and having an initial relationship made for you when you are in a new context, and before you have had much chance to build any relationships for yourself, there is, as the above list of such buddying schemes suggests, a tendency for those in buddy relationships to 'stick with the programme', whatever that programme might be.

Possible benefits

☑ The approach is relatively low cost. This means that you are likely to get support from senior people in the organization if you want to create a buddying relationship.

☑ It is quite flexible with buddies meeting as and when it suits them. You can respond to work pressures more easily.

☑ It can be used by anyone and at any level. Although senior managers are less likely to use this approach, due to custom and practice, there is no practical reason why they shouldn't be able to.

☑ You can start to learn how to assist another person to learn and this ability will stand you in good stead for other roles in the organization.

Possible limitations

☒ The buddy relationship does not usually include challenge. Therefore, it tends to be, unnecessarily, limited to the support function of learning relationships (see the discussion of learning groups in **Self Managed Learning**, for the benefits of balancing both the challenge and support function for learning).

☒ There is no guarantee that your buddy knows how to learn. On the contrary, their idea of being helpful may be to give advice, which might have some appeal (of a packaged answer) but carries no inherent learning.

☒ In contrast to a learning group, however good a buddy you have, you are still reliant on the benefits of only one other person's perspective. Also, because there is no requirement to find a way to get on with a number of different people, as with a learning group, whether a buddying relationship works or not is often a matter of whether the chemistry is right. There is less tendency to have to make it right; and more of a tendency to allow the level of chemistry to determine the level of value you will get from the relationship.

☒ Typically, perhaps because the thing that is uppermost is support, buddying relationships lack structure. People are not usually explicit about their learning goals, nor about how they will work together and what they expect to accomplish by doing so. (See the section on **Personal Development Plans** for a useful way to overcome this.)

☒ The fact that buddy relationships are usually set up by organizations for **induction** contexts alone, either induction into the organization or into one of its departments, means that its contribution to an individual's learning and development is, thereby, curtailed by the end of the induction period.

Operating hints

➲ Whether you decide that having a buddy would be useful, or you have 'buddyhood' thrust upon you (in the case of a company scheme), in either case think through what you want from the relationship. That way you will be prepared, when first getting together with your buddy, to talk through with them how you each want to 'play' that relationship.

➲ This means entering into some sort of negotiation, resulting in an explicit agreement about your responsibilities and what each of you can expect from the other. This avoids unrealistic expectations as well as allowing you to bring into the dialogue the things you know about how to learn (from this book, for instance).

➲ Make the contract between you one of supporting each other's learning and development. Decide how you will avoid drifting off into 'war stories' or whinging, and keep the focus on your progressing. One agreement may be to make certain that each person has a chance to talk about their needs with the other person listening and assisting and then to reverse roles.

➲ If you and your buddy get on particularly well there is no harm in a friendship developing, as long as you both recognize that learning will benefit from a more focused and intentional stance (as with any 'task' that friends engage in together).

➲ Agree to a time limit for your buddying. If the context is **induction** that may, of itself, provide a clear end point for the relationship. Even in cases where the buddying relationship has been beneficial and there would appear to be value in continuing it, be explicit about the learning goals you have and about evaluating whether or not you have met them at the end of the period. You can always begin a new period of buddying, for another defined length of time and with another set of clear learning goals.

➲ You may also want to consider having a mentor to complement what you are gaining from the buddy relationship (see **Mentoring**).

➲ You may find that you want to develop the buddy relationship into a learning group, where more of you can support each other.

3.3 *Coaching*

We need to see coaching differently from the way it has been viewed within some organizations in the past, where the word has often carried a remedial rather than a developmental connotation – people needed to be coached because they were not performing well at current tasks. One problem with the remedial approach is that attention is focused on finding and implementing a solution to the immediate performance problem. This can mean that the coach, with potentially greater organizational experience or expertise than the learner, is tempted to take responsibility for prescribing a solution. And if they can't resist the temptation to do that they end up taking responsibility for the individual's learning too.

This issue of responsibility is an important one. Coaching is based on the principle that the individual is responsible for their own learning and that the coach is responsible to them in assisting that learning. The individual's learning will be driven by the real problems or opportunities that they face rather than being pre-determined by prescribed solutions. The problems are real in the sense that they are unique to the learner and defined and owned by them. Assisting them to learn is based more around helpful questioning which stimulates their own thinking, rather than providing them with answers.

The adoption of this principle also means that coaching can be seen as something that is not in the exclusive realm of the training and development department. If learning does not need to be driven by subjects and solutions and coaching has its roots in effective questioning, then coaching can be provided by managers and others across the range of functions in organizations, and not just by trainers and developers.

Of course all this does not mean that the coach is precluded from providing information or suggestions, challenging assumptions, making recommendations, or acting as a resource person. These contributions may be significant in helping the individual to clarify their current situation, to identify what they don't know they don't know, to establish their learning goals, and to evaluate their progress. However, the coach is likely to do these things in response to what they have learned about and from the person they are coaching, rather than by directing them or leading them.

Examples

Coaching can happen at many different times and in different places. There is potentially a whole spectrum of activities in a work context during which one person can provide assistance to another in learning. These can range from the apparently opportunistic to a formally planned series of off-line coaching sessions. For example:

- An individual struggling with a problem associated with a new **project** is able to identify a couple of potential solutions as a result of a short but timely conversation with their manager in the corridor.
- An operational manager who wants to learn more about marketing or finance receives information and ideas in a meeting with a colleague who is a specialist in the field concerned.
- A person new to their role shadows a fellow team member and discusses the meeting with them afterwards. Of the work meetings used in this way, this is the first of a short series in which the person moves progressively from observer to active and effective participant in place of their colleague.
- An individual and their manager may meet on a regular basis over several months to monitor the individual's development, the evidence for which is the achievement of a series of quality improvement targets agreed on during their annual **appraisal** discussion.

Examples like those above show that it is not necessary for someone to adopt or be assigned the label of coach. To the extent that one person is assisting another with their learning, we can consider them to be involved in coaching. However, the effective giving and receiving of this assistance is considerably enhanced if the people involved are aware that they are taking part in a learning process. For instance, the kinds of short and timely conversations illustrated in the first example will happen only if the participants are sufficiently attuned to the possibility that they might occur and sufficiently prepared to engage in them should they do so. So, in order for coaching to operate effectively and coherently, it is very helpful if those involved have shared ideas and expectations about their respective roles, and agreements about the procedures and ground rules that they intend to adopt. (See Operating Hints below.)

Uses

As indicated in the examples, coaching can fruitfully accompany other work based learning approaches such as **projects** or **appraisals**, or lead to or provide a framework within which different methods such as **shadowing** can be used.

Possible benefits

☑ A highly cost-effective approach that does not necessarily require more resources than the time set aside by the coach and the learner.

☑ Can be undertaken in a wide range of circumstances, and at times that are planned and unplanned, as long as the people involved are attuned to the potential of such conversations to enhance learning.

☑ The provider of coaching does not need to be an expert in whatever it is the learner needs to develop.

☑ The things that are learned are of immediate relevance – no sooner are they learned than they are being used.

☑ Encourages and enables learners to take more responsibility for their own development.

Possible limitations

☒ The provider of coaching may lack the perspective towards coaching proposed here and inappropriately adopt the role of 'teacher' or 'instructor'.

☒ Both the coach and the learner may get seduced into attending to immediate task problems rather than the potential of these and other opportunities to provide learning.

☒ Despite their best endeavours, work and other pressures can overwhelm the coach and learner's identification and pursuit of coaching opportunities, particularly if planned off-line coaching sessions are infrequent.

Operating hints

➲ Both coach and learner need to be adept at asking questions and listening.

➲ Even if a formal off-line model of coaching is not going to be used (or is only intended to play a minor part in the coaching relationship) a 'first' meeting between coach and learner is important. The following is offered as a possible agenda to be modified to suit the situation of the particular individuals concerned:

- Clarify the role of the meeting and agree on an agenda.
- Introductions. If the coach and learner don't know each other then sharing information about themselves, their backgrounds and experiences of the organization can be helpful.
- Both should be clear about the division of responsibilities between them and the learner's manager, if the latter is not the coach (see expectations checklist below).
- Ground rules about how they will operate should be discussed and agreed (see ground rules checklist below).
- Both should check if there are any problems to address at that moment.
- The next two meetings should be agreed on at the very least (dates, times, venues).
- Any action points for both individuals should be reviewed.

➲ Expectations about what learners might want and coaches feel able to provide need to be clarified and agreed. Some examples of these are provided below:

- Providing guidance and support.
- Being a role model.
- Assisting in conceptual/theoretical learning.

- Challenging assumptions/mental models.
- Helping to set learning goals.
- Being a source of technical/professional knowledge.
- Being a sounding board for action plans.
- Providing day-to-day advice on problems.
- Listening and questioning.
- Being a resource person.
- Evaluating progress.

➲ Ground Rules. It can be important for the coach and learner to establish some ground rules if they are entering a longer-term coaching relationship. Below is a model list. This can be used to devise a list of ground rules that a coaching pair might want as a basis for discussion and agreement.

- Agree on what can be kept confidential and what may be taken outside the coaching relationship.
- Agree on the frequency of formal off-line meetings.
- Agree on whether there will be informal contact in between formal meetings (for example, phone calls, emails or by other means).
- Agree on a way of involving or keeping informed other relevant people such as the learner's manager (if the coach is not their manager).
- Discussion of the learner's personal life occurs only at their invitation.
- The two parties will not make excessive demands on each other's time (and agree on what this means in practice).
- The learner will use their coach's authority or name only with their consent.
- The learner is in the driving seat: their coach's job is to assist them with their learning.

If you are looking for someone to coach you then you need to consider if a potential coach will be able to work in the way that we have suggested. That is not to say that we expect a coach to do all the things we have outlined above. Rather, we recommend working with a coach who will operate in the spirit of what we have described, for example, that you are in the driving seat as to what happens in coaching sessions.

Another factor to consider is whether you might use a coach internal to the organization or whether you can get support to go outside if there are no suitable internal coaches. The downside for the organization is that they may have to finance an outside coach and you may have to make a good case for that. The more that you have worked out in a rigorous and coherent way what you want to learn, the more likely it is that you could get such support.

A final point is that there is much more that can be said about coaching. It has come to be recognized as almost a sine qua non of effective work based learning. As with other sections in this handbook there is material referenced at the end. We would especially recommend Gallwey (2000) alongside our own collection of materials for developing coaches (Cunningham *et al.*, 1998).

3.4 *Deputizing*

One apparently obvious indicator of someone involved in deputizing is when they hold the title Deputy. However, we are not so much concerned here with roles that are established, titled and rewarded as such in the organization hierarchy (for instance, in the police service, for example, Deputy Chief Constable, or in the education service, for example, Deputy Head Teacher) as we are with those occasions or periods of time when one person deputizes for another without changing their formal title and then returns to their normal job.

Another common use of the term is when one person performs their normal role but does it on behalf of another person who has the same role or a similar one. An example here is when one medical practitioner (who might be employed by a deputizing agency) performs the duties of another as a GP. Here the reasons for deputizing are wholly operational, although this is not to say that the deputizing GP won't have immediate things to learn in the new situation!

One term that is used is that of understudy. It is commonly used in the theatre where an understudy essentially deputizes for an indisposed actor. If the understudy is a novice who is able to learn from the experience, then it fits our use of deputizing here. Another use of the understudy concept is where an organization overtly identifies the successor to a particular manager and this understudy is given specific help to learn the role of the manager who they are eventually to replace. Such help may include a range of approaches such as external training, **mentoring**, developmental **projects**, **secondments**, and so on. The understudy is also likely to do some deputizing and it is this tactic that we focus on here.

Examples

In the context of work based learning someone deputizes for their immediate manager or supervisor in the performance of a part or possibly the whole of the latter's job. For instance, they might chair a series of meetings in the absence of their manager who normally fulfils the role. There is a link here with the learning method **delegating** to the extent that we are concerned with the allocation of work for developmental purposes. However, in the process of deputizing, the 'work' concerned is likely to be greater, both quantitatively and qualitatively, than is the case in delegating. For example, the deputy might perform the whole of the more senior individual's role for a period of time, to cover for their absence on holiday or at another worksite.

These two examples show that in deputizing the deputy will have responsibility, authority and accountability for the activities they are undertaking. However, as the second example also illustrates, there are often very good operational reasons for deputizing, and certainly the individual for whom the person is acting as deputy is likely to want to feel that their deputy is actually fully capable of acting in their absence. If this is the case, and the person is currently fully capable of acting on behalf of their immediate manager and demonstrates this, then alternative tactics that involve whole jobs might be more appropriate, such as **secondments** or **job rotation.**

Possible benefits

☑ You can carry out the whole of the other person's job and therefore learn in a more holistic way what the job is really about.

☑ You can get access to a range of new contacts at a senior level – and learn from such role models.

☑ By being a deputy it legitimates you asking for help in learning the ropes; people around you may not expect you to be perfect so you may learn more easily from any **mistakes** that you make.

☑ You can assess whether you want to go for a promotion or not via an experience of deputizing. It can assist you in reflecting on career choices.

☑ It is relatively low cost – you act on behalf of someone and may indeed save the organization from having to appoint an interim manager.

Possible limitations

☒ You may end up heavily overloaded, especially if you can't find someone to deputize for you.

☒ Others in your peer group may be unhappy if they feel that you have been given preferential treatment – you may have to tread carefully to deal with bruised egos.

☒ You may not be given full responsibility and therefore find that your learning is restricted.

☒ You could just get exploited by the organization if you shoulder too much responsibility.

Operating hints

⮑ Getting support if you are new to deputizing is important. It may be that the organization sees this as a sink-or-swim approach to development. But by being thrown in at the deep end you could drown. It's therefore usually important to set up some kind of support system such as a **buddy**, **mentor** or **coach.**

⮑ You need to continue to reflect on what you are learning and how you can use this when you step back into your usual role.

⮑ As always, having some clear learning goals can help to keep you focused on the learning aspects of the process.

⮑ Ask questions – of the manager for whom you are deputizing, others who have deputized, peers – anyone who can assist you to get a grip on the role.

3.5 *E-learning*

Our focus here is online learning through the Internet or intranet. The term 'e-learning' is used for both online communication (for coaching, tutorials, discussions, dialogues, learning group meetings, and so on) and online access to learning materials (for this aspect see sections on **Computer Based Training** and **Distance Learning and Packages**, which includes CD-ROMs.)

(Aspects of **Video conference / Webcam / Teleconference** are also relevant to this topic.)

The reason we are taking this stance here is that we want to focus, in this section, on the tactical use of online working. We regard websites and online packages as methods that can support learning and they are discussed in Part 4.

One important tactical choice is around the use of 'blended learning'. This notion implies the blending of computer based methods with other methods, such as classroom approaches. Clearly our focus here is more on the integration of online, computer based modes with work based learning. Since much of what is promoted as e-learning is solely the translation of classroom training onto a website, we will not dwell on such approaches here.

For many people the idea of using computers to assist work based learning can seem strange, especially if they are used to the notion that what they find from websites is disconnected from work issues. Our approach is to support the idea that computer connections can enhance work based learning where the learner is using the technology to interact with others. These others may be work colleagues or they may be tutors/trainers who can support the learner.

As with most items in this handbook, a fuller discussion of the interactive use of computers belongs elsewhere. McConnell (2000) shows how computers can support what he calls 'co-operative learning' approaches and his book is probably the best text on this subject.

Examples

The leadership module of the MA in Organization Design and Effectiveness at the Fielding Institute in California was conducted online, after an initial meeting of participants in New Mexico at the start of the programme. Those involved were senior managers and HR professionals living in various parts of the USA as well as Tokyo, Sydney and South Africa. A **Self Managed Learning** approach was employed and people formed into learning groups. Each member posted drafts of their learning contract to their group and developed it in the light of responses from the rest of the group, including the learning group adviser. The module involved undertaking and reporting on research, drawing learnings from the participants' own experiences of leadership and using these to reflect on leadership theory.

Written papers were developed through online interchanges, from initial thoughts all the way to the submitted version.

'Learndirect learning-through-work' was set up in England as an online work based learning route to qualifications. The learner is linked with an educational institution through which they will be able to gain their desired qualification. Interaction between the learner and tutors is designed to be online.

A specific case of this use was Duncan Brown, a 31-year-old designer, who developed a plan for his work based learning and then submitted it online via learndirect learning-through-work. The University of Derby picked it up and Duncan developed a learning contract with the help of tutors. This learning contract included work based projects and he was able to gain a degree through his work based learning. This shows how the technology was mainly a communication tool and not there to impose a curriculum on the learner.

Online coaching has grown, though when coaching is not face-to-face it is more often via the telephone. More common online is the sort of forum represented by HRD Digest. People in the HRD field will post their questions to the site and receive advice from those who have greater familiarity with the area in which they are interested. This can be useful; however, it should be differentiated from coaching, which assists a learner to develop their own answers. Advice often actually discourages learning.

Intranets are used for collaboration between people in different departments or different sites. The value of these depends on how they are being used. While it is desirable to use software that allows group discussion even good old email can be quite effective. For instance, it is possible to create groups of people who can be part of an email discussion which is designed for learning purposes.

Possible benefits

The points below relate to an asynchronous mode of online interaction. By asynchronous we mean that you respond to other people in your own time, as with emails. This is in contrast to chat rooms where the discussion is in real time. The first point under 'Possible limitations' explains why the asynchronous mode is favoured.

☑ People in different countries and time zones can communicate with one another effectively.

☑ You can interact with the group at a time which suits you. You can access what they have posted in the morning or in the night.

☑ You can give even more consideration to what you post to the group, and your responses to what they have posted, than you would be able to do in a live interaction. In a live interaction, the direction of an interaction is often determined by the quick thinkers. They speak first and by the time those who like to think through more are ready to speak the topic has moved on.

☑ More equality. The online environment does not, of itself, indicate race or gender. Those with mobility and hearing problems do not find themselves disadvantaged. Even those with sight problems can use speech translation programmes. So for a number of people there are some distinct advantages over face-to-face interaction.

☑ Continuous development. The process of writing a paper through this mode discourages the sense of finality. When you begin by talking through your initial ideas with your fellow learners, and responding to their challenges and questioning in each subsequent draft, the paper exhibits the development of your thinking. And your thinking has a tendency to continue developing. Thought is less likely to come to a stop when the paper is handed in.

Possible limitations

It must be remembered that most discussions of e-learning concern themselves primarily with what might better be called Internet training. In this regard, the limitations of the training orientation, itself, along with those of **Computer Based Training** apply. As demonstrated below, our interest here is in the Internet as a means of communication for learning purposes, therefore more about people interacting with one another than their interacting with programmed material.

☒ Chat rooms and synchronous modes of interacting are usually not ideal for those in work. Without rapid keyboard skills such interaction can be tedious, frustrating and take a lot of time. Even with the ability to input rapidly, the awareness of someone else waiting on your typing can lead to little more than everyday chat. Asynchronous modes allow time for reflection and thinking through what you want to say and how to express it. This is more appropriate to a learning orientation.

☒ It can be harder to engage in an online learning dialogue without having built up a sense of the person through a face-to-face meeting. It is preferable for a group meeting online to have begun with a face-to-face meeting. Even telephone contact can be helpful in this regard.

☒ Being challenged and becoming defensive. Becoming defensive when we are challenged is a common response. However, it is not helpful to learning. At the same time, challenging questions stimulate learning. It is important, therefore, that you feel those challenging questions are being put for your benefit and are not an attack. This is another reason why it is valuable to have met your fellow learners beforehand. You might not have been able to get to know them well but you will have a sense of them as individuals.

☒ Technology costs money. Although your organization may have already invested in computer facilities it is worth reflecting on Aley's (2002) calculation that for each dollar spent on buying IT an organization will spend anywhere from $4 to $10 making it all work. There is no reason to doubt that his calculations apply in most other countries. If the investment is already there, then online learning can be cost effective. If new hardware and software are required then the costs can be underestimated.

Operating hints

⮡ Learning orientation. Just as in a face-to-face learning meeting, it is important to recognize that learning is the focus. In both cases, the point is not to chat but to learn, and assist others to learn. For your own learning, keep your learning goals in mind. For other people's learning, bear in mind the point above about challenge and defensiveness and ask yourself, 'How is what I want to say going to be helpful for their learning?'

⮡ Be willing to post your first thoughts. This is a very different context from one in which you hand in finished work to a teacher. Your fellow learners will be accompanying you on the journey through which you develop your thinking and your written text. Just as the desire for a polished product can get in the way of writing, it can also get in the way of posting online.

⮡ Give yourself the time to think through your responses to what others are posting. An off-the-cuff response is likely to short change them. Recognize, too, that even in responding you are likely to be learning. In order to respond, you have to think through your own experiences and to organize your own ideas about the topic in order to express them. Responding to fellow learners is not a totally selfless activity.

⮡ Challenge, without attacking. We have said that triggering someone's defensiveness gets in the way of their learning. At the same time, to avoid putting challenging questions to them also gets in the way of their learning. The art of weaving your way between the two is to be clear that your questions are for the learner's benefit, not for your own self-aggrandisement.

3.6 *Job Rotation and Job Swaps*

Job rotation is a phrase used to refer to the planned movement of people between jobs over a period of time and for one or more of a number of different purposes. Basically there are two forms of job rotation. One is within-function rotation and the other is cross-functional rotation. Within-function rotation means rotation between jobs with the same or similar levels of responsibility and within the same operational or functional area. Cross-functional rotation means movement between jobs in different parts of the organization over a period of time. The jobs identified for cross-functional rotation are likely to be arranged in a sequence representing increasing levels of responsibility. Job swaps, as the name suggests, may involve no more than two individuals in different departments or functions, exchanging jobs for a limited period.

Examples

An example of within-function rotation would be when individual members of a permanent work team move between some or all of the jobs covered by the team over a period in order to maintain or improve motivation (by providing variety) or to ensure optimum staffing. Representative of cross-functional rotation is the common arrangement of a planned sequence of job moves as part of a career development scheme. Here, rather than rotating around a number of jobs that are in the same group and closely related to each other, the individual rotates through a number of jobs in different departments, business units or geographical locations. Typically these are chosen and arranged in a series to broaden the individual's experience or to expose them to gradually increasing levels of responsibility. Such schemes are often used with new graduate entrants to an organization who might be expected to spend as much as six to eight months in each of three or four positions over a period of two years or so in preparation for appointment to substantive posts. As well as providing individuals with developmental opportunities, such schemes can also be used by the organization to gather data about their skills, interests and potential to indicate their final placement.

The use of cross-functional rotation schemes with new graduate entrants has a long history in medium-sized to large organizations. They are often accompanied by other arrangements that form part of an induction programme. Also familiar in many organizations are the cross-functional schemes associated with career and management development programmes for staff identified as having potential for senior positions.

Typically job swaps are arranged with the learning of the participants very much in mind. Similarly, cross-functional job rotation is most often associated with an explicit focus on learning and development. Within-function job rotation can also involve learning though. For example, it would certainly be the case with regard to anyone new to the team in the illustration provided above. There may also be learning opportunities for established members of such a team as well. For example, where the team is operating in an environment characterized by frequent changes to roles and responsibilities, or where job rotation is undertaken intentionally to support **team development** initiatives.

There is a good argument for saying that the developmental opportunities and support offered to graduate newcomers and to high-fliers through cross-functional job rotation can and should be offered to established staff at all levels. Potentially, the pay-off for the organization through the contribution of job rotation to the development of individual human capital could be supplemented by its contribution to the development of social capital too. This would be represented by increases in the number and quality of relationships between a much higher proportion of staff at different levels and in different parts of the organization. In practice, however, where this kind of job rotation occurs, the schemes concerned often tend to be smaller scale and much simpler than those for graduate newcomers and high-fliers. They often involve individuals spending no more than a small number of relatively short periods of time each year in another department with which their own has an important working relationship. Such schemes blur the distinctions between job rotation and methods such as attachments and **shadowing**.

Although there is no reason in principle why individual managers should not support and enable cross-functional job rotation for groups of established staff that are bigger and more inclusive than those restricted to new entrants or high-fliers, the demands associated with doing so can be considerable. Where such schemes do not have the benefit of a clear and explicit buy-in at a corporate level, and the resources to match, smaller scale within-function rotation is probably more practical. Here the manager would restrict support for rotation to jobs within the boundaries of their normal sphere of responsibilities. Cross-functional rotation is still possible where the manager can capitalize on their relationships with like-minded colleagues in other departments or locations. However, it is likely to remain restricted to these departments or locations if it does not have corporate sponsorship. In such circumstances, job swaps between individual members of staff in different departments are potentially much easier to organize than cross-functional job rotation. Although the potential development opportunities are comparatively smaller in number and scale, a successful job swap scheme can lay the groundwork for the establishment of cross-functional job rotation.

Possible benefits

☑ If you are a new member of staff, job rotation can be very effective in accelerating your development in the organization.

☑ In general, job rotation can be a rapid learning experience.

☑ The approach is low on direct development costs, though there is a cost if you are moving to an area where you need to be supported by others.

☑ By moving to another part of the organization you can contribute to your new colleagues learning about your area of work.

☑ Job rotation can prevent you getting stale if you are locked into one job for a long time with no chance of promotion.

☑ Career development can be assisted with well-planned job rotation. By getting a real feel for work different from your own you can reflect on career choices that are open to you.

Possible limitations

☒ If the job you rotate into is inappropriate, then the approach can be limited. For instance, if the new role offers little challenge, learning may be quite shallow. On the other hand, if the new role offers too much challenge and is a 'sink or swim' position, then learning is also restricted.

☒ Cross-functional job rotation for selected groups can make considerable demands on the support of the colleagues of participants. This can cause resentment where support is provided for those perceived to be members of a privileged group or to be destined for higher things rather than continuing to work alongside their colleagues. Be careful therefore of alienating others if it seems as though you are getting preferential treatment.

☒ You have to plan for re-entry to your original job – and if this is neglected then you may find the re-adjustment limits the opportunity to utilize any new learning.

Operating hints

➲ In making arrangements for job rotation and job swaps, ensure buy-in both from the managers of the departments, functions or teams within which the jobs to be performed by participants are located and from those who will be the 'temporary' colleagues of participants. Make certain that you stay on top of this – otherwise there could be problems.

➲ The goals of job rotation schemes should be clear and aligned with the organization's business needs at a corporate level. More specifically, the benefits to each individual participant in job rotation or job swaps can be better integrated with the needs of the organization through the use of **personal development plans**. So if you do not have such a document, you need to negotiate this before you proceed.

➲ Consider if you need **mentoring** support so that you can maximize the value of the experience and get appropriate support if you are operating outside your comfort zone.

➲ Learning gained through job swaps can be increased or accelerated by the use of **coaching** from your manager or from an experienced colleague in the host department or group.

➲ Other methods such as attachments or **shadowing** can be combined with job swaps in an appropriate sequence as part of a development programme.

3.7 *Learning Resource Centres*

Essentially, a learning resource centre (LRC) is where an organization keeps those learning resources which are available for use by or loan to members of staff. The location in which such materials are kept varies between a broom closet with a lock on it to a well-appointed, spacious and welcoming facility with helpful staff on hand.

The extent to which LRCs are used also varies wildly. The learning materials which ended up in the locked broom closet had previously been in more august surroundings. But little use was made of the facility and one step at a time, as space was claimed by more pressing needs, the learning material demoted to the broom closet.

As a modern version of a library, an LRC should have links to online search services, computers with Internet access (which is disallowed for office machines in some organizations), and easily accessible learning materials. Availability is an important issue. Some learning materials can be expensive. Yet it is no good having them if they can't be accessed. The possible loss of learning materials also needs to be considered in relation to the cost of people having to find those resources elsewhere or the cost of their being thwarted in their learning. While there can be costs to encouraging learning there are more grievous costs to putting barriers in its way.

Examples

In one hi-tech organization, the learning resource centre was derogatorily nicknamed the Early Learning Centre. It contained a good deal of learning material, though there was rarely anyone in there. There was a member of staff responsible for the LRC, though it was only one of their roles and they were only expected to be there occasionally.

At one residential management institute the LRC was a large space with windows looking out onto green fields and trees. It had a number of comfortable chairs lending it the air and quality of a quiet haven that is traditional to a library. The space was divided by free-standing shelving containing books along with some packages on subjects of common interest to managers. The two staff were well-informed about their stock of materials. They operated computers linked to various search services and were able to obtain books and articles rapidly, which could be posted out to people if they were no longer on the premises. They were also responsive to requests from individuals who were seeking information on a subject but who could not provide book titles or article references. The staff would identify a number of possible source materials and talk them through with the person, ordering what was deemed most worthwhile.

Possible benefits

☑ LRCs are particularly valuable to work based learners. Any kind of learning programme with a fixed curriculum usually includes recommendations for the learning materials considered relevant. When you are pursuing a unique learning programme, one which you have designed yourself for yourself, any relevant learning materials will have to be sought out. A well-functioning LRC is likely to be the first place to call.

☑ An LRC represents a shared source of learning materials. Rather than individuals or departments buying copies of books or packages, which others would not know of, these would be available for the benefit of all.

☑ A pleasant LRC can be a place of retreat. As a contrast to the hustle and bustle of many a workplace it can help you switch modes, into either a more reflective and receptive mode in which to learn or a more concentrated learning focus. While many learning materials can be called up on desktop screens, remaining at your desk is not necessarily the easiest place in which to learn. Some LRCs are also favoured by those needing a bit of peace and quiet in which to write a report.

☑ A staffed LRC can be a valuable resource. When the staff know the materials on offer it makes your evaluation of what is relevant to your own needs so much easier. LRC staff can also be in a position to do much of the searching for sources in your area of interest. As professionals they will be more efficient than if you have to spend your own time doing it.

☑ Information about materials can be passed on. When people are on learning programmes which connect the learners together, as in a **Self Managed Learning** group, they will talk about books and articles or websites they found useful, and the use of the LRC increases.

☑ A thriving LRC is a sign of a learning culture in the organization. When this feeling is absent in the organization, people will feel reluctant to spend time in the LRC as it will be seen only as a place where one would go to skive off.

Possible limitations

There are no inherent limitations to a well-functioning LRC. After all, there is no expectation that it should have exactly the material you want and immediately to hand. The question is whether it can find something relevant to your needs and then obtain it. Seen in this light, the limitations are in relation either to how an LRC is functioning or in how it is viewed within the organization. It is these factors which will be addressed below.

Operating hints

For those setting up LRCs:

⮩ It makes a big difference if you staff an LRC. Many people want quick information and that can only be supplied by someone being available to track it down when it is needed. Additionally, most people will benefit from being able to obtain guidance to the materials available, as well as what can be obtained from other sources. Otherwise you are implicitly presuming that all staff should become knowledgeable in the skills of a learning resource manager.

⮩ As part of developing a learning culture, the LRC should have top management support, together with top management use. If top management doesn't think it needs to learn then the LRC can end up being only for those deemed junior enough to need to learn.

⮩ The status of learning in the organization is also signalled by the LRC being in a prominent location, rather than tucked away somewhere that's not needed for anything else.

⮩ The materials available in the LRC need to reflect the needs of those within the organization. This may seem too obvious to mention but just as a lot of the courses provided by training departments fail to serve the needs of the organization it is far from rare for learning materials to be selected upon similarly wayward grounds.

⮩ One way of ensuring relevance is to link the selection of learning materials to learning goals identified by those within the organization. This is a place where work based learners could take a useful lead.

⮩ It can help to popularize the use of an LRC if it carries newspapers and journals which can be browsed through. Additionally, people can be enticed by having a variety of interesting CD-ROMs and popular items such as language learning materials even where these are not directly relevant to business priorities. An enjoyment of learning is, in itself, something worthwhile to encourage.

For those making use of LRCs:

⮩ Identify your goals. As always it pays to know what you are after. However, the degree to which you need to have refined the kind of information you seek will depend on the abilities of LRC staff to assist you in that process. If you are fortunate, the LRC can be the very place to go to pursue the process of refining your learning goals.

⮩ Browse. Although we are continually advocating being focused in your learning there is also value to being open to unplanned, opportunistic learning. Precisely because an LRC is stocked full of learning materials it can be a great place to browse. A straight line is not always the best path between two points.

➲ Promote the LRC. The more the LRC is valued within the organization the more valuable it will be to you. An LRC which becomes moribund is likely to disappear (into a broom closet). Let your colleagues know the benefits you have found from the LRC. There is another selfish motive for doing this: the more active learners there are in your organization the more stimulating will be the working environment.

➲ Link what you learn to the needs of others. In one organization they had a learning group where all of them wanted to learn from a complex package in the LRC. They agreed that one of their number would go through the package extracting what was relevant to their work needs. That person then came back to the group and shared the relevant knowledge.

3.8 *On-the-job Learning*

On-the-job learning is usually taken to mean learning the job-specific skills and knowledge by doing the job. The learning happens in real time and may be indistinguishable from the performance of the work to which it is intended to contribute. This makes on-the-job learning different from any other work based learning approach. It is not so much a difference in kind as one of degree; the 'degree' being the measure of closeness of the learning activity to the work itself. This means that even if you do not consciously choose any work based learning methods to improve your effectiveness but, in continuing to do your job, demonstrate evidence of such improvement, it would be difficult not to attribute the improvement to on-the-job learning of some kind.

This is a point that we have discussed in Part 1. Even if you do not consciously use any of the other methods covered in this handbook it is difficult to imagine that you would not learn on the job. Few jobs these days are entirely static for long periods. Even if work practices appear not to change, say on a production line, people come and go in work teams and this in itself causes on-the-job learning – you have to learn about a new colleague.

Often, in our research, people would say that they just learned 'from experience'. In making this comment they were indicating the job-based nature of much of their learning. Just doing the tasks needed to perform the job produced learning. However, we were also aware that some people used their on-the-job learning better than others. For instance, they quickly learned from **mistakes** or they sought out feedback on their performance and used such feedback to learn to improve.

Examples

The description above has a number of implications for the work based learner who chooses to improve their on-the-job learning. What this choice actually means is that they attempt to make what happens anyway happen as productively as possible for the benefit of their learning. There are two aspects to this. One is the individual's approach to it. The other is represented by those features of the immediate environment in which the individual works that are likely to have a significant influence on their learning.

THE INDIVIDUAL'S APPROACH

On-the-job learning is more likely to be productive if it is approached purposefully and undertaken consciously. Approaching it purposefully means approaching it with learning goals in mind which have job-performance or other measures of learning achievement associated with them. Undertaking it consciously means regularly taking opportunities to monitor progress against the measures of purpose, but also to reflect in, and on, action (see section on **Reflective Learning**). By these means the learning that is happening, both planned and emergent, can be identified and thought through by the individual, and modifications made to their goals where appropriate. Some people find that keeping a **learning log** is helpful in this context.

IMMEDIATE ENVIRONMENT

The features of individuals' environments that seem to have the greatest impact on their on-the-job learning are their contacts and relationships with others. For example, we can note the importance of contacts with others as sources of relevant information and knowledge (see, for example, the section on **Briefings / Presentations / Demonstrations**). They may be members of established **networks** or new people with whom the individual establishes contact in order to make use of their expertise. Such contacts may also be of value as sources of feedback and as sounding boards in supporting and enabling reflection.

Two potentially valuable sources of contacts of these kinds are integral parts of two work based learning strategies. These are learning groups in **Self Managed Learning** and learning sets in **action learning**. One thing that learning group or learning set membership can provide is a potent combination of support and challenge. Support and challenge seem to be especially important and the individual's manager can be a source of this too. In particular they can provide challenge in the sense of pressure to achieve stretching work-related goals, plus a supportive **coaching** relationship to encourage and enable purposeful and **reflective learning**. **Coaching** can also be provided by colleagues.

Uses

On-the-job learning can be of use both to new and established job holders.

NEW JOB HOLDERS

How much on-the-job learning new job holders will actually need will be a function of the kind and level of job-specific knowledge and skills they already possess compared with those demanded by the job. Someone at the beginning of their working life, or who is making a career change, will probably have the most to learn. However, even if someone has satisfactorily performed a similar job elsewhere and matches the person specification for the role, there will still be things to learn. There is the new department or organization to learn about, with new colleagues, new procedures, and new structures or processes involved, and so on.

ESTABLISHED JOB HOLDERS

Here, the motivation, pressure or trigger for on-the-job learning will be change. This change can be self-initiated if the job holder is purposeful about on-the-job and other forms of learning in the context of their own career and personal development. There may be organizational restructuring manifested in modified job designs and specifications that require learning on the part of individual job holders. Frequent organizational and job changes may be part of a culture of continuous improvement or indicative of an approach to change that encourages innovation and adaptability evidenced in comparatively open boundaries between jobs and high levels of discretionary job content.

Possible benefits

☑ On-the-job-learning can provide you with real-time and just-in-time learning.

☑ By its nature it is flexible and can meet your precise job specific learning needs.

☑ Evidence suggests that people can learn and retain more through doing, and through opportunities to practice.

☑ It is particularly good for developing immediate work-based knowledge and skills, although where conducted purposefully and consciously it can also contribute to your continuing development as an active, self-managing learner.

Possible limitations

☒ On-the-job learning is less likely to be successful in the absence of a supportive immediate work environment.

☒ It may be accompanied by a period of lower than acceptable performance or a higher incidence of mistakes.

☒ If you lock your learning too much into your current work tasks this may limit your career progression. Often career development requires learning that is not related to the current job but is more stretching and which prepares you for different work.

Operating hints

➲ Approach your on-the-job learning purposefully and consciously. The use of learning contracts (see section on **Self Managed Learning**) and **personal development plans** can help you to set goals that orient your day-to-day learning.

➲ Clarify and agree expectations with your immediate manager or supervisor. This can include getting their agreement to your learning goals and to related performance targets and deadlines.

➲ Make connections with colleagues and others as potential sources of expertise and of ideas to challenge your own.

⊃ Try and find a colleague who can take on the role of **coach** and share your learning goals and timetable with them. The person who fulfils this role could be your manager.

⊃ Take planned and ad hoc moments for review and reflection. These can include times when you are not actually engaged directly in job-related activities, such as unproductive meetings, meal breaks when you are alone, travelling and so on.

3.9 *Personal Development Plans*

As the term indicates, a Personal Development Plan (PDP) is a document completed by an individual that details their intentions and actions with regard to their own development. PDPs have become increasingly popular in organizations as perceived demands for staff to become more adaptable, flexible and empowered have grown in response to internal and external organizational change. Moves towards flatter organizational structures and the adoption of ideas about employability rather than security of employment have given credence to the view that individuals should take greater responsibility for their own development. The adoption of PDPs is seen to be in tune with the times. In addition to being a tool to be used by individuals for thinking through and recording their development, completed PDPs can provide a potential source of data about the organization's changing stock of human capital.

In our earlier exploration of the use of planning and organizing one's own learning we raised some concerns about PDPs. While we tend not to use the term in our own work we recognize the idea of PDPs has become the preferred concept in most organizations. To put it on record here, we are, first, concerned that 'Personal' can come to mean disconnected from work or from the organization's strategy. Second, we see too often that these plans stay as interesting plans that do not get actioned. The research that we have conducted shows that PDPs are used patchily and only a few organizations use them well.

A third concern is that the PDP is often very short term. We put it under our tactics heading because it is rarely strategic. This in itself is not necessarily a bad thing. Tactics are important. And in the fast changing world of modern organizations an annual plan is necessary. However, if PDPs are to be used, we would argue that it is a good idea to encapsulate these within a broader strategy. For instance, PDPs often ignore career and other longer term development needs. If the short-term learning planned as part of a PDP is disconnected from longer term plans this can be a disadvantage both for the individual and for the organization.

Allowing for our concerns, we are keen that individuals do set goals and think through their learning and development needs. In the absence of a PDP or a learning contract (see section on **Self Managed Learning**) work based learning is too often seen as a random series of experiences that may provide little coherence for a person's learning. All the methods that are covered in Part 4 may be of little value if they are not integrated into the overall needs of the person and their organization. We therefore offer some guidance to you here on how to get the best from the process. Just because many people and organizations use PDPs badly does not undermine the value of planned learning. It just means that you, the learner, need to manage the process yourself so that you get the maximum value from it.

Examples

Rudimentary versions of PDPs have been associated with traditional training courses for many years, typically at the end of the course under the heading of 'action planning'. To a large extent we can attribute this to the concern of course providers to address the 'transfer problems' discussed in Section 1.2. It might be provocative to note that use of the term 'action planning' suggests that after a course no new learning is required, just action.

There has also been a long tradition of linkages between planning for personal development and appraisal, and for those organizations where there hasn't been this tradition, modifying the appraisal system can be seen as offering an apparently quick and cost-effective means to introducing PDPs. As a tactic for work based learning, **appraisal** is covered elsewhere. We can note here though that the history of combining the two is not a good one on the whole. It is still not uncommon to find that where personal development planning is combined with appraisal, the paperwork that accompanies the process tends to privilege training over work based learning. The standard PDP form in these circumstances may even go so far as to provide the list of courses currently offered by the training department to be ticked as appropriate! Not only is learning then confused with training but appraiser and appraisee may even find themselves using course titles to define initial learning needs.

On the other hand, many organizations now provide more sophisticated PDP forms for the use of their staff. Their precise structures vary, although typically they are designed to cover a couple of areas. The first of these is concerned with where the individual is now. The learner's current role is analysed in terms of skills and knowledge requirements and then the ways in which and extent to which the person matches these are identified. This analysis points up the 'gaps' in the latter and indicates the individual's learning needs. The second area is a plan of the steps to be taken to bridge these learning gaps. Sometimes a third element is added. This is typically some form of **learning log** so that progress in the achievement of intended outcomes, plus any unanticipated learning, can be recorded.

Of course, however sophisticated its design, a PDP is still only a completed form. It is only likely to be of value if what it conveys is grounded in sound diagnosis and, subsequently, when real development actually follows from its implementation.

PDPs AND DIAGNOSIS

It is not often that the process of creating PDPs stands alone. Typically it is associated with other formal methods for managing and developing staff, like **appraisal** for example. Another of the common associations, although in comparatively fewer organizations than is the case with **appraisal**, is with **development centres**. These are covered as a learning method in Part 4 where mention is made of their potential for helping the learner to diagnose their learning needs in some depth. With due attention paid to the operating hints outlined in Part 4, a well-designed **development centre** can make a considerable contribution to the creation of a valid and useable PDP.

Other potential sources of information and analysis for the learner include their manager and colleagues. They are potential sources of feedback in identifying learning needs, for example through **360° feedback**. Further, the learner's manager can be a source of information about broader organizational aims and issues to inform their (the learner's) decisions and can 'represent' the organization in ensuring integration of its needs with those of the learner.

PDPs AND DEVELOPMENT

Despite the confidence that the learner may have in the validity of their plan and the motivation to learn that comes from it (having participated in a **development centre**, for example), it is still only a plan. Even the best laid plans may be no more than wish lists in practice. The individual is much more likely to experience success in implementation and gain real development when they have the support and challenge of others who are significant to them and their learning, and who have been involved in the diagnosis and other aspects of the creation of their plan.

The learner's manager is in a potentially powerful position within the organization to make things happen. Along with the learner's colleagues they can provide **coaching** or **mentoring.** Fellow learners are comrades in a common endeavour and can be involved both in the development of each other's plans and, subsequently, in their periodic review.

Uses

In the context of work based learning, a PDP can be associated with any of the other tactics, and all of the methods, in this handbook. For example, a **secondment** for several months could form a substantial part of an individual's development plan and the PDP would show the rationale for this choice in relation to their learning goals plus, within the framework of the **secondment**, what work based learning methods they were going to use to maximize the learning from it.

Here the PDP comes first and drives the choices of the other tactics (if any) and of the methods. Alternatively, the offer of a **secondment** might present itself first and then prompt the desire on the part of the learner to complete a PDP. Initially this would serve the purpose of testing out the potential value of a **secondment** (or other learning opportunity) on paper prior to accepting or rejecting the offer. If the result of the 'test' was positive, then the next and subsequent iterations in the process of its completion would be for the purpose of maximizing learning. The former of these two sequences is to be recommended. Potential learning opportunities are more likely to be noticed when one already has goals to which they might make a contribution.

Possible benefits

☑ Relevant learning and development is more likely to happen in practice when you are goal directed.

☑ Learning that is planned is more efficient.

☑ Unanticipated learning opportunities are more likely to be seen when you are prepared for them.

☑ The choices of learning methods are more likely to be appropriate following completion of a PDP and their use can be designed and managed to provide a tailored fit with your needs and interests.

☑ Motivation and confidence in taking responsibility for one's own learning can be enhanced.

Possible limitations

☒ The quality of a completed PDP can suffer without timely and relevant diagnostic information from others.

☒ The creation of a valid and useable PDP is particularly difficult to achieve without the active support and agreement of others who are relevant to you in your current role.

☒ The successful implementation of even a well-crafted PDP is not guaranteed without continuing support and challenge from others.

Operating hints

➲ Ensure that there is ready access to relevant and valid diagnostic data in the identification of learning needs.

➲ Ensure that there are opportunities for, potentially, several iterations of the PDP in draft form, to which relevant others in the organization have the opportunity to contribute by way of ideas and information.

➲ In choosing other work based learning tactics, and in determining learning methods, explore and clarify these thoroughly prior to making decisions about which to use. This may involve discussion and agreement with others who will need to provide time or other help with resource implications.

➲ Ensure agreement is reached about learning goals and methods between, for example, you and your manager.

➲ Ensure that clear targets and other 'mileposts' associated with learning goals are agreed between yourself and other interested parties.

➲ Arrange for **coaching** or **mentoring** help where appropriate to cover both the creation and implementation of the PDP.

3.10 *Projects*

Projects are very familiar in some organizations. For example, there are organizations that are predominantly project based. They might be operating in the field of management consultancy or in the creative and media sectors, for instance. They may well have organization-wide matrix structures in place of, or overlaid on, the traditional pyramidal hierarchy and by this means operate extensively with multi-disciplinary project teams in providing services for clients, or for business or product development purposes. Projects and project groups have also come to the fore in many more traditional kinds of organizations over recent years, where they have been associated with organizational change initiatives in, say, business process re-engineering, quality management or culture change. While learning is at the heart of our approach to projects, none of the above examples will necessarily have individual or team learning as their primary or explicit focus. Interestingly, as far as those organizations that are engaged in fashionable organizational change initiatives are concerned, the poor track record of some of these initiatives may well bear witness to this very fact.

Projects are quite often associated with work based learning. For example, they are an important feature of the **action learning** approach. They are also associated with **research.** The activities involved in projects are normally additional to individuals' everyday work but may enable them to pursue their learning by addressing issues of significance to them or their organization. Projects can be investigative by nature or action based. Further, they can be undertaken by individuals or groups. These categories and choices are considered below.

Examples

INVESTIGATIVE PROJECTS

At its simplest, anything that people need to investigate as part of their work based learning can be set up and managed as a project. So, for example, if someone needs to find out more about marketing or finance, or some other function or discipline, they can approach the task by devising a project plan that identifies their goals against a time frame. This will include information about the people or other resources they will access, plus decisions about how, where and when they will do so.

In some cases investigative projects are problem based. The problem may be a real organizational issue that involves accessing existing knowledge, as above, and/or attempting to create knowledge that is new to the organization through the use of social or other research methods and techniques. Although such project work has learning as its main aim, one would normally expect to see an output in the form of a set of recommendations. In this context there may well be a senior person in the organization with an interest in finding a solution and who therefore 'sponsors' the project.

Investigative projects can vary in size, and can expand, particularly if they are other than problem based. Even where they are problem based, without a clear brief from a committed sponsor they may drift. Investigative projects are comparatively low risk, in that the most that is expected are recommendations for action. Further, although additional knowledge may be gained, the process of investigation itself may only provide opportunities for learning that are limited to skills like those of analysis, report writing or making presentations.

ACTION PROJECTS

An action project may involve all that is required for an investigative project but with a big plus. The plus is that the recommendations are followed through into action by the investigator. Alternatively, rather than generating more data prior to action, research evidence already existing in the organization is used and acted upon. The fact that the evidence is there but unused will probably present the greatest learning challenges and opportunities. Rather than being no more than a paper exercise it actually demands that those involved work with the emotional and political challenges of taking action in real life situations. The learning comes from people working in unfamiliar contexts and certainly outside their comfort zones. Although the aim of such projects is action, and thus may not involve the production of a report or presentation, like investigative projects, they must be 'managed' with targets and time scales.

INDIVIDUAL OR GROUP PROJECTS

Investigative projects can be undertaken by individuals or groups. Individual projects are potentially more manageable than group projects, and less likely to expand or become too open-ended. On the other hand, group projects may offer individuals more scope, particularly if the group is multi-disciplinary. This can offer members immediate opportunities to learn about and from each other's area of expertise, plus the potential to develop networks and networking skills. In group projects, though, some people might coast and let others do the work. This is an important consideration in action projects where the learning is going to come from personal accountability for action. This suggests that where learning from action, as distinct from investigation, is the most important thing then individual projects may be the appropriate choice.

There are other ways to influence the distribution of effort in group projects of course. For example, different individuals can be allocated leadership roles in the group at different times. Another potentially effective way is to ensure that for group projects there is someone who acts as adviser to the group; not an expert in the substance of the project but someone who has expertise in helping groups to function effectively in the context of work based learning. This role has similarities to that of the learning set adviser in **action learning** and the learning group adviser in **Self Managed Learning**.

Possible benefits

☑ You may gain increased knowledge that will be highly work related and of direct relevance to your work based learning needs.

☑ Existing tacit knowledge held by experienced people in the organization can be investigated and made explicit for their benefit and for that of the organization.

☑ Problems or issues of significance to the organization can be addressed.

☑ Throughout their involvement as sponsors, senior people can increase their awareness of the value of work based learning and, potentially, develop their ability to enable it in other contexts.

☑ In the process of using projects you can develop your project management skills and, where relevant, basic skills in analysing issues, report writing and presenting.

☑ Action can be taken to solve well-understood problems in the organization if you are prepared to take personal accountability for attempting their resolution.

☑ You can be supported in the type of learning that presents you with opportunities and challenges that take you outside your normal and familiar experiences.

☑ Networking and networking skills can be developed.

Possible limitations

☒ Projects can expand in size or drift in scope.

☒ Despite the immediate benefits to the organization associated with the investigation of a significant issue or problem, it may lose out in the longer term because the project may not present you with learning opportunities that are sufficiently challenging or relevant to your needs.

☒ It is possible for some participants in group projects to contribute less than others while being rewarded equally for the results. If you are in such a group you could find it frustrating.

☒ Reports from investigative projects can end up remaining unread, or presentations forgotten. You may find this disheartening as you could have done work that is not used.

☒ Sponsors of projects can sometimes get so involved in project work, particularly action projects where they are committed to seeing things happen or change, that they limit the project members' freedom and responsibility to learn.

Operating hints

➲ Choose the type of project appropriate for the learning needs that are to be addressed. For example, are your needs concerned with the gaining of knowledge, for which an investigative project may be appropriate, or is the need more to develop abilities associated with taking personal accountability for action or for bringing about change?

➲ If there are a number of you who wish to pursue project work, consider the pros and cons of individual or group projects.

➲ Ensure that where appropriate you can be supported with **coaching** or **mentoring**, especially where it would be more cost effective to learn specific skills this way rather than struggle with the project.

➲ Sponsors can contribute positively to successful project work by ensuring the relevance of project objectives to organizational needs and by providing both pressure and support to ensure timely project completion. However, it is important to ensure that their involvement does not limit your opportunities for learning, for example, by the sponsor exerting undue pressure to achieve tasks at the expense of learning or by levels of involvement that reduce your autonomy or responsibility.

➲ If people are to undertake group projects, consider the need for staffing or outside support such as provided in **action learning** or **Self Managed Learning.**

3.11 *Secondments and Related Approaches*

Secondments

Typically the term secondment refers to the loan of an individual by one organization to another (although it can also refer to situations where someone moves temporarily to another department or function within their own organization). The organizations involved can range from a large commercial or public sector organization to a small voluntary or charitable group. Secondment can take place business to business, business to public sector and vice versa, and business or public sector to voluntary sector. Movement between businesses is much less frequent than between business, government and the voluntary sector.

A secondment can range from as little as 100 hours to as much as two or three years. As far as business and government interchange is concerned, the UK government's Cabinet Office, which promotes and facilitates secondments through the Interchange Unit, prefers secondments lasting from 9 to 12 months. The trend for companies seems to be towards shorter, 100 hour, secondments, often known as attachments. These can be organized in different ways, ranging from one day a week to the whole 100 hours. The idea here is that the secondee gains from taking on a specific **project** clearly designed to meet individual or team needs (see section on **Projects**), rather than from a more in-depth understanding of the host organization's culture.

Some organizations sponsor secondment of their staff alongside a range of other forms of involvement. The government interchange initiative, for example, includes **shadowing** and **mentoring** as well as secondment and attachments. This flexibility is evident too in the links between business firms and organizations in the voluntary sector, where secondment is seen as one among a number of forms of **volunteering** that can be encouraged by employing organizations.

The process of finding host organizations often includes the use of brokers or membership of relevant networks. The Interchange Unit provides these kinds of facilities on behalf of seconding organizations in government with respect to interchange between them and organizations in the business and voluntary sectors. Another example in this context is the Whitehall and Industry Group that promotes better mutual understanding through exchanges of people, ideas and information. There are organizations fulfilling these sorts of functions on behalf of host organizations too. For example, in the voluntary sector, Employees in the Community, which works with the National Centre for Volunteering (see section on **Volunteering**), promotes short-term attachments along with many other kinds of community activity.

Usually secondees keep their existing terms and conditions of employment and the secondment is normally counted as continuous service. Typically the secondee's full salary continues to be paid by their employer, incorporating any normal pay increases during the secondment period. Where the secondment is business to business or business to government, the host organization will usually be invoiced for the cost unless there is an exchange of staff between the organizations concerned. Where the person is being seconded to an organization in the voluntary sector their salary is most likely to be funded by the seconding organization.

Assignments

Some organizations assist people to undertake assignments that take them out of their normal workplace. These are likely to be shorter term than secondments and may also be part time rather than full time. The assignment may be tied to a particular **project** and be narrower in focus than a secondment.

Sabbaticals

We have put sabbaticals under this heading as they also allow a person to move out of their normal setting into another one. Some sabbaticals are very much the same as secondments. Typically a lecturer or professor in a university may go and work in another university or in a company. However, other sabbatical arrangements occur where the person absents themselves from their university to do a piece of research or writing and they may do this at home or in someone else's home. The latter examples are not covered here as they are not so similar to secondments.

Examples

The prevalence and significance of secondments are likely to increase. Opportunities for promotion within organizations have lessened as a result of moves to flatter structures. At the same time working patterns have changed and there is now a greater onus on flexibility. In these circumstances secondment becomes a potentially valuable opportunity for staff development. People can be exposed to a range of activities and situations that are not open to them in the organization in which they are employed. More organizations now have formal policies and processes to encourage and manage secondments and attachments.

The learning gained from secondment can vary enormously depending on the match between the particular capabilities and development needs of the secondee and the scope and features of the role and situation to which they are seconded. For example, in being seconded from a prominent consultancy firm to a large employers' organization, a specialist in corporate finance develops their capabilities in the areas of relationship building, influencing people and productivity. In working as human resources manager in a healthcare company, a deputy head teacher of a secondary school reviews her styles of management and problem solving abilities, **benchmarks** her school's personnel management policies and procedures, and develops her skills in project management and communication.

A secondment from a managerial role in a large life insurance company to a charity involved in helping people with drug problems, presents the secondee with opportunities to learn in such areas as achieving consensus amongst **teams** with different, and strongly held, views; crisis management; working to strict deadlines; and balancing budgets under severe resource constraints. Or, a junior member of a consultancy firm provides pro bono consultancy assistance to a charitable organization and, in working extensively with the charity's board, learns from dealing with challenges and people at a level that they would not normally expect to meet in their client work until later in their career.

Alongside the recognition that secondments are an increasing source of development opportunities for staff, and thus of benefit to seconding organizations, the growth of secondments and attachments to the voluntary sector is part of an increasing trend for business firms to involve themselves more explicitly in social and community affairs.

Possible benefits

☑ A secondment can provide you with opportunities for wider personal and professional development.

☑ It can lead to testing and developing specific skills in situations outside the normal workplace.

☑ Former secondees comment on their increased self-confidence and motivation.

☑ It can present opportunities for exploring future career options.

☑ A secondment can provide you with improved networking within and between the public, private and voluntary sectors.

☑ Former secondees say that a secondment provided them with new perspectives on themselves and on their employing organization/department.

☑ From the organization's perspective it can contribute to the achievement of succession planning goals and, where the secondment is in the voluntary sector, to the public fulfilment of social or community objectives.

Possible limitations

Most of the possible limitations tend to be associated with longer term secondments. For example:

☒ There could be difficulties with the provision of cover for your work while you are on secondment.

☒ You could feel isolated in your role and hence the learning from the situation is reduced.

☒ Performance management issues can occur, particularly where input from the host to normal **appraisal** arrangements is insufficient.

☒ Reintegration into your employing organization is potentially the most difficult aspect of longer term secondments.

Possible limitations associated with short-term or flexible secondments are similar to some of those associated with **volunteering**, particularly if the secondment comes about largely at your initiative and the employing and host organization are unfamiliar with the secondment process.

Operating hints

➲ You should be made aware of secondment arrangements and opportunities. Organizations typically do this through company magazines, events or intranet pages. However, you may need to chase to get a real insight into how your employers see this.

➲ You may need to do some pre-reading about the proposed organization that you will join. Or you may get some oral briefings.

➲ The selection for secondment, whether initiated by you or by your employing organization (for example, in the context of succession planning), should be based on your development needs and goals (see section on **Personal Development Plans**), and the match between these and salient features of the host organization and the opportunity on offer.

➲ A clear agreement should be reached between yourself and your employing organization about whether or not the organization's normal performance management systems or procedures will be applied and, if not, what variations are to be expected.

➲ Appropriate arrangements should be made about covering your work while you are on secondment, maintaining contact to guard against feelings of isolation and arrangements for reintegration once the secondment has finished. Cover, contact and reintegration issues are much less likely to occur with the trend towards shorter term and more flexible secondment arrangements.

➲ A clear agreement should be reached between the organization, the host and yourself about all relevant issues. These can range from the details of economic terms and conditions through to broader concerns related to your secondment role and to your learning goals.

➲ Appropriate arrangements for supporting your learning should be made. These could include **coaching** or **mentoring** provided by the seconding or host organization. If the seconding organization provides support of this kind it can have added benefits in terms of simply maintaining contact to reduce any feelings of isolation on your part.

➲ While on secondment it is important to observe, analyse and note down situations and experiences that you learn from. You may be required to write a report on your return and this will be based on such recorded material.

➲ A clear agreement should be reached with you about reintegration into your organization once the secondment has finished. There are two aspects to this. One is whether, in the case of longer term secondments, you return to your original role or whether, as for Cabinet Office staff, a position is guaranteed but not necessarily your original one. The other aspect is ensuring that the learning gained from the secondment is not lost, whether the secondment is long or short term. This is unlikely to be a problem if, as suggested above, the secondment has been based firmly on a match with your learning needs and goals. Further, if you have had **coaching** or **mentoring** support during the secondment this should help considerably. It can be continued on your return to the organization for a period, specifically to cover your reintegration.

➲ A debriefing session on return to your organization is important. This can help you integrate the various learning experiences that you have had but also confirm your new learning to your manager or the HR department. You may want to use such a debriefing to discuss how your enhanced capabilities can be used in your own organization and therefore how your learning can continue.

4 Methods for Work Based Learning and Development

Introduction

Part 4 is about moving from strategy and tactics into action on specific methods of learning. As we have emphasized, the logical progression is ideally to be clear about strategy and tactics before choosing a particular learning method. For instance, we have come across organizations that think that **360° feedback** or the use of **development centres** is a good idea. However, if they have not prepared for the outcome of such diagnostic activity it can leave the learner high and dry. The person may get lots of useful feedback but if there is no developmental strategy in place then the feedback may not only be wasted but downright harmful. We have come across people in our research who have had negative feedback dumped on them and then had no support for addressing the learning needs identified. This is bad practice and if you are offered such an opportunity, but there is no adequate support afterwards, you would be well advised to consider whether to do it.

The best way to use these methods is, then, within the context of a carefully crafted strategic and tactical framework. For instance, you may have had an **appraisal** or **performance review** from which it is apparent that you will need to develop new capabilities to meet new job goals. You may then find that you want to join a **task group/working party** in order to progress your knowledge. You may also find that **visiting** other organizations will give you useful insights as well as **shadowing** someone who is already fulfilling this role. In some cases you may find that you cannot visit all locations that would be helpful but a **video conference** will suffice. You may even find that you make some **mistakes** in taking on new work but that you can learn from these.

Potentially there are more methods than are covered here but we have concentrated on the ones that come out from our research as being effective or are ones that we have seen used productively in our consultancy work. As with anything we cover, the effectiveness of the approach we mention is often dependent on how it is done. Badly done **360° feedback** is worse than not doing it – and this applies to many of the other methods we outline. Hence it may be useful to have some of the operating hints to hand when considering using any of these methods. Also you may find that you can modify what we have suggested to suit your own circumstances. We certainly do not have a fixed view about how particular learning methods should be used and creative modifications may be desirable.

Again, as with previous parts, you will find that the sections vary in length dependent on how much explanation we felt was necessary. In all cases there is more that can be said about each learning method and we hope that the references and suggested further reading will assist you if you want more information. We have included in this part methods that are borderline work based. For instance, the use of **distance learning** materials or **video/audio tapes** could be seen as not particularly work based. On the other hand, we have seen it argued in organizations in which we work that they *can* be used in the workplace and do not require classroom-based training. So we have said a bit about these methods – but if you feel that they are not sufficiently work based for you, you will no doubt skip these sections.

As in Parts 2 and 3 we have put in **bold** any reference to another section in this handbook so that you can make your own links to other material as you wish.

4.1 *360° Feedback*

In this process an individual and a range of colleagues make their evaluations of the person's abilities. Apart from the person themselves, their manager, peers and direct reports are canvassed for their responses to a questionnaire. (Some 360° processes include customers and/or suppliers also.) The criteria against which evaluations are made can vary but should be those which are considered of importance within the organization and, especially, those considered of importance by the individual.

It may have seemed as if the manager's opinion of you was the only one that mattered. While it may be the case that it is the one most relevant to your fortunes within the organization, the matter is very different if it is development we are interested in. One person's opinion may be swayed by all manner of factors, some having more to do with them than with you. The idea of getting a range of responses, including your own, is to provide a more useful basis for identifying learning and development goals.

The results of 360° feedback can be given in various forms. Rather than all being lumped together, it can be more useful if a manager's responses are identified separately from those of your peers and the peers from those of the people who work for you. It is also valuable to know not only the mean result but also the spread of the responses. Additionally, since 360° feedback deals in interpretations, it can also be helpful to get an interpretation of the interpretation. What do the results mean? It is not always easy to tell. You may want to talk them through with a consultant, coach, mentor, friend, learning group, and so on.

Today, 360° feedback instruments can be completed online, using a site with a password for each individual who is gaining feedback.

Examples

A 360° feedback instrument is only as useful as it is relevant. When using a general 360° questionnaire there are likely to be questions which are not particularly relevant to the individual, and things which are relevant will be absent from the questionnaire. 360° feedback instruments can be categorized as follows:

- Off-the-shelf. There are many general 360° feedback instruments available, most being aimed at managers.
- Sector specific. There are also 360° feedback instruments designed for specific industry sectors such as the health service or local authorities.
- Organization specific. One local authority had identified, through a couple of years of management conferences and chief officer deliberations, those abilities and qualities it required of its senior managers. From this was derived a set of 72 questions, clustered

under five topic headings, to serve as a 360° feedback instrument specific to that organization's needs.

- Individual specific. A consultant working with one senior manager helped the manager identify the precise things on which he wanted feedback, and then devised a 360° feedback instrument to get responses to just those items.

While it may seem that the individual-specific instrument would be the most useful, in being tailored to a given individual, there are other things to be considered. Unless we are working at the very top of an organization, our future within that organization will depend on our 'fit' with what the organization is looking for from its people. This is what an organization-specific 360° feedback instrument is designed to identify. Therefore, whether it is an organization-specific or an individual-specific 360° feedback instrument which is most useful will depend on your purpose. Of course, this may not be a choice you are able to make. If your organization will not fund these more specific modes of 360° feedback then it is a matter of gaining the greatest benefit you can from the more general modes.

Possible benefits

☑ A 360° feedback instrument can provide important information on how you are perceived by your colleagues. This is, obviously, the purpose for which they were created. However, it is a fact which may be forgotten if the process is imposed by the organization and incites resentment.

☑ The results can assist you in identifying areas of development. These can provide the source for creating a set of learning goals in a learning contract (see section on **Self Managed Learning**) or **personal development plan**. Sometimes the results will be confirming thoughts you already had. At other times, they may bring to your notice things to which you hadn't really been paying attention.

☑ When your responses are quite at variance to the responses of others, that will definitely be something to explore. It is not necessarily the case that they are right and you are wrong. A perception is only a perception. However, they clearly need to be taken seriously since a perception can have enormous consequences.

☑ When there is a wide spread of response, meaning that different people see you in quite different ways, it should also be investigated further.

☑ The 360° feedback provides a context for delving deeper into people's perceptions of you. If your manager's responses are separately identified you can talk together about what kinds of observations led to the scores you were given. With those who report to you, and whose scores will be grouped together, it might be a matter of having a group meeting if you want to find out more about their perceptions, or to take the conversation forward to how you might all work together better in the future.

☑ The same instrument, or a sub-set of the questions, can be used later to check on how things have changed subsequent to any development activity you undertake.

Possible limitations

☒ An all-too-general form of 360° feedback instrument may not provide results of any great relevance to the individual.

☒ An individual's response to the results may be to take them as an absolute truth, or to dismiss them out of hand. Neither approach is beneficial in terms of learning.

☒ If you are new to an organization, people might not have had enough experience of you to form a judgement in relation to some or all of the questions.

☒ People are not always prompt in responding to the questionnaire. This can result in your having to do a lot of chasing. As one might expect, this depends a lot on the organization culture, with the process being taken more seriously where learning and development are accorded more importance.

☒ Their development orientation can be undermined if they do not remain confidential. For instance, if someone has the 'bright idea' that 360° feedback could double as a means of appraisal, the focus of attention will shift to one of how to skew the results to look good.

☒ The value of all the feedback depends on the honesty of the respondents. This will not be dependent solely on the honesty of the individuals involved. It will also depend on whether they see you as someone with whom it is safe to be honest. Additionally, the culture of the organization can be influential. In an authoritarian or 'blame' culture it is much less likely that people will be totally candid.

☒ Tick box questionnaires only get answers to the questions asked. There may be other factors that are relevant for you in your development that do not get addressed via a questionnaire.

Operating hints

⮕ Avoid the myth of objectivity. The results of the questionnaire do not represent an objective truth. They are perceptions of you. It can be valuable to explore what it was people were responding to when they gave particular responses. It is important, in doing this, not to put people on the defensive (which would discourage them from being candid in the future). Though there are many ways in which questions can be asked, what you will want to know is the evidence on which they based their response. In other words, the observations they had made of things you have done and said.

⮕ Talk through the results with others. This helps you gain the best value from the process. Any conversation you have about the results has the potential to enable you to learn more about yourself and how you come across.

⮑ Avoid choosing respondents whom you know will give you a good score. Ask people you don't get on that well with, also. Their perceptions may give you some valuable feedback.

⮑ If you are new to an organization it may be best to choose some people from your old organization to respond to the questionnaire. Those in the new organization may not have had enough experience of you to be able to answer all the questions. But where they are able to answer you will be getting a valuable insight into the first impression you have made.

⮑ Questionnaires are not ideal for all purposes. Consider the possibility of interviewing people to get their feedback. Or, if your organization can fund it, get a skilled consultant to interview people on your behalf and then they can feed the results back to you.

⮑ Link your 360° feedback with evidence from other sources. For instance, you may have carried out **psychometric tests** which give a perspective on you – and that perspective may be different from the 360° feedback. A mentor or coach may help you to make sense of any such divergences.

4.2 *Action Reviews*

This section describes the different ways to review live action. The US Army has popularized 'After Action Reviews'. This, as its name implies, is an approach to reviewing what has happened, for example, after a military exercise, with a view to learning from what happened. The US Army has a particular way of doing this, but here we will consider more general approaches.

Also we want to consider the spectrum of situations – which can be identified as follows:

BARs – Before Action Reviews
IARs – In Action Reviews
AARs – After Action Reviews

These three modes are specifically covered here in relation to groups or teams working together. Clearly individuals learn all the time from live action. However, in this section we are looking at group contexts, where learning can be shared.

Examples

Divisions between the different types of Action Review are not all that neat. But let us take the example of a football team to show how each of these processes can be applied.

BAR

This approach to learning is where the team gets together before a match and shares knowledge about the opposition. So, for instance, an experienced defender may tell his less experienced colleagues that the striker they will face tends to go one way and mostly shoot with his left foot. This means that the less experienced are able to learn prior to going out on the pitch. It saves them having to learn this in the action – perhaps with disastrous results.

IAR

Here the learning takes place out on the pitch. Opponents may come up with a new free kick routine that the team has not seen before. They have to learn this in the live action of the game and be ready for it next time their opponents get a free kick.

AAR

This is exemplified by the manager leading a session after a match, in order, for instance, to examine **mistakes**. The aim is to help players learn from their **mistakes** so that they don't repeat them in future matches. Cox (2002) describes the Royal Air Force's Red Arrows aerobatics team and their AAR:

> I sat in on a post-flight briefing. The whole of the performance was videoed and every move (which to the untrained observer was flawless) was examined in detail.
>
> The thing that struck me was the frankness of the analysis and the openness with which all members of the team criticised both themselves and each other. This included the team leader, who pointed out where he had led the formation into a manoeuvre a degree or two adrift of the planned line of approach... There was no covering up, no excuses, no blame. Everyone was expected to assess their own performance, along with that of their colleagues and that of the whole team. Everyone learned, everyone knew what they wanted to do better next time (p. 3).

In the above, learning from mistakes has been emphasized. However, that need not be the sole focus. We can also learn from successes – reviewing why something went well can also assist learning.

Applying this to work in another context, one study showed that teams involved in surgery (consultants, nurses, anaesthetists, and so on) used these approaches. However, the most effective teams seemed to be those that were especially good at learning in action. Something might happen in the operation from which people would learn and even implement a new procedure during the operation.

If we take this example into other work contexts we can see that learning in action is more and more often required. Situations change rapidly and people often do not have time for After Action Reviews. However, we can also see that pre-planning (Before Action Reviews) could be used more. Evidence from project management shows that people sharing their learning prior to setting off on a project is extremely valuable. Project groups that do this have been shown to be more effective than those that dive straight into the action.

Uses

These review processes are of wide applicability. For instance, with **meetings**, it is possible for the person chairing a meeting to ask at the start for suggestions about improving the process of meetings – 'what has the group learned from its previous meeting as to how to work more efficiently?'

It can also be valuable to halt the meeting process to check if things need to be different. 'What have people learned in this meeting that could make it go better?'

And at the end of a meeting it is useful to review how the meeting has gone. This may be not just about the meeting process but also a question of asking individuals what they have gained from the meeting (that is, what they have learned).

Possible benefits

☑ Cost-effective approach that does not require a trainer.

☑ Can be quick and simple.

☑ Can help people to learn to share with others.

☑ Before Action Reviews are especially valuable in avoiding the 're-inventing the wheel' syndrome.

☑ If you take part in such reviews you can raise questions in an open environment that hopefully is not threatening.

Possible limitations

☒ Busy people can see this as an unwarranted interruption to 'real work'.

☒ It requires skilled handling, especially the 'before' and 'after' processes. If it is badly handled it is potentially quite unhelpful.

☒ It can lead to blaming others – and therefore less learning. If you take part in a formal process you may need to look out for the signs of excess blaming.

Operating hints

➲ Anyone running such a process needs to be skilled at asking questions (see section on **Questioning**).

➲ For the before and after processes, it's important to have the whole team there – if people are absent it can hinder the learning.

➲ Before and After Action Reviews are best conducted close to the live event – transfer of learning to the action is hindered by a gap in time.

➲ For learning to occur in the action, there needs to be a good basis of trust in the team/group – hence some pre-work may be necessary to engender that.

➲ A useful process for Before and After Action Reviews is to go round the group and get everyone to have their say. This is especially important if there are dominant personalities in the group who may want to impose their perspectives on the group. Also with less assertive members of the group, going round and asking for each person's views can draw them out.

⊃ If you are a participant rather than the leader of a review meeting you need to be clear about the questions you will raise and any sensitivities there might be if they are seen as too challenging. Also you may want to address questions or comments to specific individuals rather than the whole team.

⊃ For action reviews the team leader/manager can explore learning at three levels. These levels can be seen as three levels of knowledge. They are as follows:

- First Person Learning – using first person pronouns – 'what have *I* learned from previous experience that *I* have found useful'. Also in the plural 'what have *we* learned together in previous experiences that *we* have shared'.
- Second Person Learning – the question would be 'what have *you* learned that I can benefit from', that is, using second person pronouns.
- Third Person Learning is located in reports of general learning – 'what have *others* learned here or in similar situations elsewhere; what has *he/she* learned; what have *they* learned', that is, using third person pronouns.

4.3 *Benchmarking*

Benchmarking is a process in which an organization compares the ways it does things with recognized standards of good or best practice. These standards might be represented by reports or observation of practices in other organizations acknowledged as leaders in their field, and/or with models of best practice such as those provided by the European Foundation for Quality Management. Although benchmarking can generate valuable information about what works well elsewhere and can thus indicate changes that could be made, the application of various data gathering and analysis techniques does not guarantee that best practice will actually be transferred. To do that successfully requires more than just having the knowledge of what will work better. This knowledge has to be applied and lead to changes in practice.

Changes in practice require learning on the part of the people whose practice is under the microscope. Further, there are two kinds of learning to be considered here. One is *adaptive* learning associated with attempting to adapt current practices to match the best elsewhere. In a commercial context this means learning to do as well as your competitors but not necessarily any better. The other kind of learning is that which in a commercial context is intended to give the organization a competitive edge. It is called *generative* learning, where the people involved learn how to create new products, services or ways of doing things.

Broadly there are three aspects to benchmarking. There's benchmarking of overall performance, benchmarking of processes, and what can be called diagnostic benchmarking. These are explained below.

Examples

Performance benchmarking involves each organization in a group from the same economic sector, or field of activity, submitting data associated with different aspects of their activities in order to be able to assess their performance against other organizations or sector averages. For instance, manufacturing companies can make comparisons on the basis of quantitative data about reliability, reject rates or, with regard to human resources, absenteeism levels or turnover rates. In other fields like the public sector, very 'public' performance league tables are now the source of organizational comparisons and some contentious debate – with regard to hospitals, schools and universities, for example.

Process benchmarking involves detailed and in-depth comparative analyses of particular activities associated with how an organization produces its product or provides its service. It can take a lot of time, effort and money to produce useable results. The greater the depth of analysis the more difficult it becomes to be sure that one is comparing like with like. Also, evidence suggests that only a few organizations manage to go beyond the sort of quantitative measures normally associated with performance benchmarking to actually identify best practice. The actual value is more in the third kind of benchmarking, diagnostic benchmarking, that usually precedes the process comparisons.

Diagnostic benchmarking involves gaining a detailed understanding of the organization's own processes in order to identify potential areas for improvement. In combination with the use of comparative measures of performance and processes it can act as a driver to get people inside the organization to reflect on current practices. Potentially this can provide a direct link to **reflective learning** where, through well-informed reflection-on-action, people are able and willing to question some of the basic assumptions and premises underpinning their own practices.

Examples

Benchmarking has been used to promote learning that is both adaptive and generative, at organization, team and individual levels. The outcomes of benchmarking have been used to highlight specific work based learning needs for the individual involved in the activities and practices under review.

As a guide to their own career development, involvement in the process of benchmarking can provide the individual with opportunities for increasing their general business awareness, and their knowledge of cultures and practices in other, comparable, organizations.

Organizational benchmarking models and techniques can offer a valuable metaphor and guide to the work based learner in relation to their own development – in making comparative assessments of their performance and practices and as a stimulus to undertaking their own personal 'diagnostic work'.

Possible benefits

☑ It can contribute to the development of a climate of continuous improvement. If your organization uses benchmarking then it may be easier for you to get support for your own continuous learning.

☑ It can increase awareness of the current 'health' of the organization. This again may give you a better basis to suggest learning needs – for yourself and others.

☑ It can contribute to the analysis of work based learning needs and the identification of learning goals. You can link the diagnostic dimension to decisions about your own learning needs.

☑ It can contribute to tracking improvements as evidence of the achievement of work based learning goals, at organizational, team and individual levels. In this sense it can act as an evaluation process and address questions such as 'Has our investment in learning paid off in terms of improvements in the business?'

Possible limitations

☒ Too great a concern for using 'objective' measures as the only valid ones can lead to resource-intensive activities associated with overcoming inevitable problems of definition, or to only measuring those things that can be easily measured.

☒ Comparative performance measures alone do not indicate how practice could or should be changed, and thus what new learning is required.

☒ Benchmarking by itself does not necessarily lead to the successful implementation of needed changes. Best practice in one organization or context may not be transferable directly to another; it requires learning on the part of those importing the practice into their own environment.

☒ The creation and dissemination of knowledge about best practice may not be sufficient for learning to occur. For instance, you may not be able to get hold of the right information to help you to consider what you personally need to learn.

Operating hints

⮕ Ensure that any organizational benchmarking data about performance or practices is complemented by your own diagnostic work. This will entail undertaking self-assessment against the backdrop of dimensions used in the benchmarking. By doing so you will be better able to:

  • make sense of the data in relation to the specific context in which you work;
  • make informed judgements about the validity and usefulness of the data in relation to your own learning;
  • question the data intelligently where appropriate;
  • use the data to prompt questions about the assumptions you hold that underpin your practice.

⮕ Complement any benchmarking that is undertaken by your organization with your own benchmarking by:

  • keeping up to date with appropriate business, trade or professional journals;
  • making use of your contacts in other comparable organizations, through professional or other networks for example;
  • looking at your or other organizations from a customer's perspective, either by drawing from your own direct experience of that role, or by mentally putting yourself in their shoes.

⮕ Use all the above to help you in identifying specific learning needs and goals, and in choosing the appropriate learning methods.

4.4 *Briefings/ Demonstrations/ Presentations*

In this section we are concerned with face-to-face situations in which a more experienced colleague, or your immediate supervisor or manager, assists you to learn how to perform one or a series of tasks by providing information and/or demonstrating the operations required. There are many different contexts in which tasks can be learned with this kind of assistance. For example, using tools or machinery; managing information using computer or related technology in a range of environments; operating administrative, financial or other organizational procedures; dealing with customers, verbally or in writing, and so on.

Face-to-face assistance of this kind can go hand in hand with **on-the-job learning.** It can be accompanied by **reflective learning**. Where the provider of assistance is your immediate supervisor or manager, it might be an integral part of their **delegation** of tasks and responsibilities. Further it can be supported by **reading** and, tactically, by **coaching**.

Uses

Briefings, demonstrations and presentations can be used in different ways to assist you in your learning. The term 'presentation' is typically associated with the use of audio-visual aids to supplement the verbal transmission of information. In this way words and numbers can be accompanied by images of the operations involved in the form of pictures or diagrams. The use of such aids also means that information can be imparted to large numbers of learners. People may come together at the same time and in the same place for a presentation, or access the information separately and at a distance if it is stored electronically. In some ways a presentation can be thought of as a more elaborate and sophisticated form of briefing. Alternatively, the term 'briefing' may be used as the overarching term to define the information-giving exercise as a whole, and of which one or more presentations may be an integral part.

Whichever of these ways the terms are used, one thing which events entitled 'briefing' or 'presentation' typically have in common is that their main purpose is to *tell* you something rather than to *show* you. A demonstration on the other hand is all about an accomplished performer *showing* you how a task or operation is undertaken. In some cases telling and showing are combined. This could be in the form of a presentation that includes a digitally produced simulation or animation, a video recording of a skilled performance or a live demonstration of the same with a commentary provided by the demonstrator.

One potential advantage of a live demonstration is that you know you are in the presence of the performer and, if you have the opportunity to do so, can question them about the procedures, methods, techniques or behaviours they adopted. A more certain way of gaining and extending on this advantage is actually to sit alongside the performer of the job while the task or operation is being done.

This provides opportunities to watch how these tasks or operations are completed in real time, possibly interspersed with communication with the performer. This is an approach that is similar to **shadowing**, where you accompany someone in order to gain a better understanding of a role to which you aspire. The difference is that, with a demonstration, you would be concerned less with a general understanding of the other person's job as a whole and much more with the detail of specific elements.

In the way we have considered these methods so far, they fall into a pattern comprised of three elements: being told, being shown and actually watching performance in real time. These elements can be seen as lying along a continuum representing the provision of increasing amounts of information. Of the three, sitting alongside the performer has the greatest potential for maximizing the amount and range of different kinds of input. On the other hand, it is likely to make most demands on you, the learner. For example, what is required to perform effectively will not necessarily be explained as systematically as it would in a prepared presentation, where the presenter may intentionally limit or pace what is provided on your behalf. Given that it happens in real time, the speed of performance may well be much faster than it would be in a demonstration, and probably with little or no opportunity to stop the action or repeat particular operations just for your benefit. It requires facility in **observation** and, very probably, **questioning**.

Briefings, presentations and demonstrations can be used to support work based learning of two kinds. On the one hand, there is the learning required in preparation for taking on tasks that are new. These may be associated with a learner's **induction**, or combined with developmental **delegation**. On the other hand, there is the learning gained by someone who is experienced and capable in their current role but who wishes to update the methods, techniques or knowledge that they use in their everyday work, or to develop their flexibility or adaptability.

Example

In some highly effective companies, such as in Japan, the use of briefings and demonstrations by experts is common. The interesting feature of this is that in many other countries HR/training would do a training needs analysis, identify what is needed, spend time for trainers to learn it (or buy them in), design a course and then run training sessions.

The other model is for work groups and teams to identify what they need to learn and if there is expertise in the company they get the expert to come to their team meeting to do a briefing/demonstration and help the team learn what they need. It makes sense to us as a process but many training departments feel threatened by this approach as it does them out of a job.

Possible benefits

☑ Briefings, presentations and demonstrations can accelerate the learning associated with taking on new tasks and roles.

☑ They can provide planned and structured information necessary for you to diagnose your own learning needs.

☑ They can involve colleagues who are experienced in the actual tasks to be learned (rather than training or HR staff), to ensure that the knowledge provided is focused and relevant.

☑ In sharing their knowledge with new colleagues, experienced staff can make their own **on-the-job learning** explicit. This can benefit them in their own development and, where they are open to feedback and **questions** from their audience, highlight potential areas for improvement in their own methods and techniques.

☑ The approach is relatively low cost since we are assuming that the presenter/demonstrator is already in the organization and therefore it does not require paying high fees to an outside consultant or trainer.

Possible limitations

☒ Where briefings and presentations are provided for groups of people it may be difficult for your particular learning needs and interests to be taken into account.

☒ Unless additional arrangements are made, there may be no opportunities for you to practice the skills or behaviours concerned.

☒ The opportunity for you to influence the amount and kind of information provided may well be limited.

Operating hints

⮕ Read any written material associated with what is to be briefed, presented or demonstrated beforehand (for example, manuals, guidance notes, policy statements, protocols or procedures) in order to help you clarify what you need to learn.

⮕ From the above, determine what you want to learn from the presentation or demonstration.

⮕ Take opportunities to question the presenter, demonstrator or performer when what you have heard or seen does not enable you to achieve your learning goals fully.

⊃ Take opportunities to practise what you have heard about or seen as soon after the event as possible.

⊃ If you need to learn a specific technique, see if you can set up an expert to do a briefing. Usually people who are good at something like to show others. Therefore you may find that there is the opportunity for you to be more proactive in this respect, instead of just taking what is on offer.

4.5 *Computer Based Training*

Computer based training (CBT) was developed as a dedicated resource in the days before computers were ubiquitous. The material on the computer could just as well have been in paper form. Often it already was available in paper form. Often, too, it was printed out from the computer and so returned to paper form once again.

Today, CBT programmes can be in your own computer at work or home. This section might fruitfully be read in conjunction with the section in Part 3 on **e-learning**, as we have made a specific case there for the role of e-learning in a work-based context. Also the section on **distance learning and packages** has links to this section.

If CBT is used as a stand-alone approach to training, one could argue that it does not belong in this handbook as it is a training-based approach. However, we are aware that it is possible to orient CBT material more towards a work based approach, so we will say something on that score here (rather than providing a full exposition of all aspects of CBT).

Examples

Obviously, all manner of textual material can be presented on computer. Here, we indicate a few examples where the computer can make an additional contribution.

- Psychometric tests. The scoring of these tests tends to be complex in order to avoid the person being able to second-guess the preferred results. Additionally, the scoring is usually done only by someone trained in the method. All this is avoided when the test is completed on screen. The computer is programmed to complete the scoring and the results are available in an instant.
- Exercises. It is possible to do exercises on the computer which can help you to explore issues from your work context.
- Hypertext environments. These provide learners with the chance to take a more active approach to a text. They can scoot around, on hypertext links, following a particular line of enquiry. Hypertext also facilitates searches for particular items of interest.

Possible benefits

☑ Young people are screen people. While older people may often remain book people, younger people respond more readily to the screen. CBT puts learning in the same context in which they are used to doing so much, including having fun.

☑ Capacity of learning materials. Computers can store an awful lot of material, especially textual material. Consequently, there is no need to restrict CBT to the limitations imposed by publishing paper textbooks. There can be a vast wealth of material for the learner to explore, without the expectation that any one learner would explore all of it. Within the framework set by the programme the learner is free to pursue their own learning trajectory.

☑ Multi-tracking. Many people spend a great deal of time in front of their computers. They are familiar with switching between desktop items, Internet sites, programmes and games. CBT can slot right into this mode of activity, making it more likely that it will be selected than that a textbook would be turned to.

Possible limitations

☒ Training orientation. As the name implies, CBT was developed within a training framework. The programmes carry the assumptions of that orientation, making them less valuable to the self-directed learner. Often they are not all that easy to manoeuvre around if you are not following the path intended by the designer.

☒ Reading on screen. There is evidence that people read slower on screen, making CBT less efficient, in this regard, unless textual material is printed out (which would rather undermine the object of CBT in the first place).

☒ Scrolling. Research has also shown that the majority of people don't like scrolling on a computer. This limits the screen page to what can easily be seen without scrolling, which is considerably less for the average computer screen than an A4 or book page.

☒ Boredom. Many people consider CBT boring. It might be no more boring than a textbook on the same subject, but more is expected of the onscreen environment.

☒ Static. Similarly, CBT presentations are found to be too static for those who are used to much more from their computer screen.

☒ What appeals on screen doesn't fit CBT. The evidence is that what people want on computers is operational whizziness and visual appeal. Applying these criteria to CBT would leave many programmes failing.

Operating hints

➲ Work out goals. First, identify any other routes to the goals for which you are considering CBT. Evaluate their time-efficiency as well as their appeal. Having gone through this process of evaluation enables you either to be more motivated in sticking with the CBT or to be ready to choose an alternative if it proves overly arduous.

⊃ Be selective. There may be a number of CBT programmes for the same subject area. Already being clear on just what you want out of the area enables you to evaluate the available programmes better.

⊃ Get advice. Ask people who have taken the CBT route for recommendations. If your organization has a learning resource person, ask them what responses they have had from learners to the various programmes. They may also have quite a bit of information about the content of each programme, which can aid your evaluation.

⊃ Allow for serendipity. Having said all the above, when you dive into CBT, even with clear goals to pursue, be open to the possibility of coming across things you hadn't expected but which might be valuable to you.

4.6 *Consulting*

An increasing number of specialists over recent years have come to see themselves as consultants providing specialist help to client organizations. This is clearest with specialists who are external to the organizations to which they provide their services and who use the word 'consultant' to describe their role. However, this term is also being used more frequently by internal specialists to describe at least some of their activities. These specialists, in what traditionally would have been seen as service departments, now market themselves internally as consultants to their 'client' colleagues. The human resources function is one where this role change has been very evident. The espoused purpose of such a change is to try to bring the kinds of benefits and standards of customer service associated with external consultancy inside the organization. These benefits and standards are associated with providing specialist advice that more obviously contributes to the bottom line, is better focused and represents more timely responses to colleagues in addressing operational problems.

In principle, any situation within an organization where one person uses their specialist expertise, or their organizational or other experience more generally, to assist a colleague can be seen as an opportunity for consulting. The advantage of adopting this perspective is that it can provide those involved with a framework and language to guide their actions that is different from, and potentially more appropriate than, those that are representative of traditional hierarchical or functional relationships.

This section is concerned with the opportunities for work based learning that are associated with the roles of consultant and client in the process of consulting. In other words, you as a learner may learn from taking on consulting type activities or situations where you look for consulting assistance from others. In this context we are particularly interested in a learning focus and it is important to note that consulting that is merely a mechanistic passing on of knowledge or the production of a standardized report will have less of a learning orientation than a more open process.

Some aspects of the process could be seen as being close to **coaching.** Indeed, the requirements of an internal consultant may be to add a **coaching** dimension to their work. However, our focus here is on the consulting dimension. One way to distinguish consulting from other activities is to consider the classic notion of the consulting process. Consulting is frequently seen as a problem-solving process with six stages.

1   Initial contact between consultant and client. This might include establishing and building a relationship where the two individuals have not had close contact before.
2   Sharing expectations and agreeing a way of working together, including a time frame where appropriate.
3   Information gathering and analysis by the consultant and/or the client for the purposes of:

    (a)   clarifying and diagnosing the problem;
    (b)   generating alternative solutions;
    (c)   formulating proposals.

4   Considering the proposals and deciding to take action.
5   Implementing the decision.
6   Following up the implementation to monitor progress and plan any next steps where appropriate.

Examples

From a work based learning perspective there are benefits to be gained in either the consultant or client role.

CONSULTANT

There are two sources of learning in the consultant role. One is associated with the fact that an effective consultant has first to learn about their client before being in a position to know which aspects of their own expertise will be relevant. This learning should certainly occur while completing the first two stages of the process outlined above. It will also arise to a varying extent in the remaining stages, depending on the degree to which responsibilities and activities are shared between the consultant and the client. The greater the degree of sharing, the greater the opportunity the consultant has to learn about their client and their situation. The anticipated level of sharing will normally have been explored and agreed between the two parties in the second stage of the consulting process.

The other source of learning is associated with the fact that in order to share their knowledge and expertise, the individual in a consultancy role has to be able to draw from their own past on-the-job learning, through reflection, for example (see section on **Reflective Learning**), in order to be able to make their knowledge explicit for themselves and for their client. They need to be conscious of what they know and can do in order to be able to make informed judgements in the consultancy situation. They also need to be able to communicate relevant parts of this knowledge directly to their client. This can benefit them in their own development and, where they are open to learning from the work undertaken with their client, highlight potential areas for improvement in their own knowledge and skills.

CLIENT

The relevance of the client role to the work based learner is most obvious when, in pursuit of their learning, they approach a colleague to gain access to their specialist knowledge and expertise. For example, they might do so in order to resolve a problem; not wanting an 'expert' solution to be handed to them on a plate but rather to be guided through the problem-solving process so that, in time, they learn how to do it themselves. Alternatively, they might be in a position to see their colleague as an 'expert', in the sense that this person could be the provider of something that they, the client, need to know more about and that they think lies in their colleague's area of specialist expertise. The first thing that will need to be done as part of the consultancy is to clarify what is actually needed by the client and to confirm that the consultant is able to provide it.

Possible benefits

☑ If you act in the consultant role you can learn from the person in the client role and from their situation. You can get unique insights that can help you to reflect on your own situation. Dr Johnson once said something like 'You learn so much about your own country by visiting other countries'; the possibilities for reflection on your own world are enhanced by visiting others' worlds.

☑ The person in the consultant role can also learn from the process of making their own work based and other learning explicit and communicable to the client.

☑ The person in the client role can learn through the process of problem solving assisted by the person in the consultant's role, and also directly from the latter's expertise and knowledge.

☑ Organizational issues can be addressed and operational problems resolved without the need to go outside the organization for assistance.

☑ More and better cross-functional relationships can be established and developed.

☑ Networking arrangements and skills can be enhanced.

Possible limitations

☒ Both consultant and client can have unrealistic expectations of each other or of the consulting process. You need to prepare well before using this approach and be clear about your expectations.

☒ There can be confusions and tensions associated with the differences between the roles of the two individuals in a consulting relationship and those on which their normal working relationship is based.

☒ The consulting process itself can demand the possession and application of skills and knowledge that are additional to those associated with the consultant's normal operational role inside the organization. You should assess whether you are sufficiently skilled for the role.

Operating hints

➲ Be sure that you clarify and share your expectations with the person in the other role and that these are clearly represented in a contract between you that covers what you will be consulting about, how you will do so and over what time scale.

➲ Be prepared to find that the consulting process itself is a challenging one and that your learning is likely to include skills and knowledge that are different from those associated with the normal functional or specialist expertise that you bring to your consultant or client role.

➲ A key skill for the consultant role is asking good questions (see section on **Questioning**).

4.7 *Counselling*

Counselling is a one-to-one approach which is useful when the level of emotional distress is getting in the way of functioning.

In terms of dealing with emotional distress there is a spectrum of approaches: counselling, psychotherapy and psychiatry. Counselling and psychotherapy are both learning approaches. Psychiatry tends to follow a biological model and more often leads to the prescription of pharmaceuticals, such as tranquillizers and anti-depressants. The focus of counselling, as with psychotherapy, is on wanting to learn what is leading to the emotional distress and what can be done about it. A counsellor is a professional both in listening and in asking questions. They use both these modes in helping us to unravel the tangle of thoughts and feelings which are assailing us when we are in distress.

Examples

- A person may be feeling bullied by either co-workers or a boss.
- Family issues may be impacting on work.
- Someone recently bereaved may be attempting to tough it out but finding themselves frequently distracted.
- Taking on a challenging new role can lead to feelings of anxiety and vulnerability at the same time as removing a previous support network.

In all of these examples an individual might go to a trained counsellor for help. The counsellor may be employed in the organization or they may be part of an Employee Assistance Programme where outside counsellors are available to employees, often on the telephone.

Possible benefits

☑ Many people experience a benefit simply from being able to talk through how they feel. Often it is only with someone who is outside their family, social or work relationships that they feel able to unburden themselves fully. When distressed, we often don't want to worry those close to us by fully expressing what we are feeling. The tendency is to censor ourselves somewhat. This is unnecessary when talking to a counsellor.

☑ The confidentiality of a counselling relationship, similarly, means we need not be concerned about repercussions from revealing what we might feel are weaknesses.

☑ Help in thinking through the issue. It is well-known that as our emotional distress increases, our ability to think straight decreases. This frequently leads us into repetitive loops of thoughts and feelings which cycle around without leading to any exit. That is a state in which it is helpful to have someone on the outside to aid you in bringing some organization to your thoughts, as well as in allowing your feelings to have their say.

☑ Recognition that our distress is quite normal. Sometimes our emotions can surprise us, hitting us like a wave that knocks our legs out from under us. We might have prepared ourselves for the death of an ailing parent only to find ourselves swept away in a confusing welter of thoughts and feelings when it actually happens. We can feel completely at sea when this occurs. It may be the first time such feelings have happened to us, especially as our upbringing has often taught us to keep a tight grip on our feelings. Talking to a counsellor, whose profession brings them a greater understanding of the world of emotions, can help us regain our feet.

☑ Learning to deal with distress. Apart from the immediate benefits, which were the reason for seeing a counsellor, you have learnt something for the future. While the exact same situation may never happen in the future, there may well be other causes of distress. Knowing you have been able to weather the storm in this instance will be very reassuring for the future. Also, you are likely to have learnt something, both from the experience and from how the counsellor helped you through it, that you will be able to bring to bear in any future occurrence.

☑ Increasing sensitivity to others. Emotional distress in others is often ignored on the grounds that it is personal and has no place in the working world. To continue the previous point, having been through the experience of navigating an emotional storm yourself is likely to make you more sensitive to others being buffeted by similar circumstances. You might be able to offer a kind word of reassurance or, without intruding on them, let them know you are ready to assist them should they wish it. At the very least, you will be more understanding of the impact it might have on their performance.

Possible limitations

☒ Acceptability. The biggest limitation is the feeling that there is something shameful about going to see a counsellor. This is a combination of past societal norms and unfamiliarity, for counselling is still a fairly recent profession.

☒ Difficulty talking about our emotions. The causes of the previous limitation also mean we are often not all that familiar with our emotions and also reluctant to talk about them. Our reluctance to talk about our emotions has a lot to do with the notion that we should keep a 'stiff upper lip'. This can lead to emotions being cut off, not only from expression but also from our conscious awareness. Previously, this stance was associated with men but many women have felt obliged to adhere to male norms in order to advance in organizational life and can be even more loath to allow any hint of emotionality. Fortunately, the professional expertise of the counsellor will usually allow us to get in touch with the emotions which may be troubling us.

☒ Precisely because the counsellor is a professional of the emotional life, we may be less convinced of the normality of what we are experiencing than if we were to hear it from a group of colleagues. Obviously, this possibility would only be open where we felt able to trust a group with personal matters, and where we could be confident of confidentiality being maintained.

☒ There may be no counsellor immediately available. Most smaller organizations, for instance, provide no counselling support. However, it can be possible, in some circumstances, to go via your GP to get counselling support provided outside work.

☒ Counselling can be overdone. While there is now strong research evidence to suggest that effective, timely and organized counselling is of value, the notion that all seemingly distressing situations require a counsellor is not a valid conclusion. People vary and what is distressing to one person may not be to another. This has been the case with large-scale disasters such as air or rail crashes. Some survivors of such experiences find that they have the resources to deal with it while others do need counselling support. To provide counselling to everyone is not only wasteful but inappropriate.

Operating hints

⮊ Consider that there is a level at which what is most personal is also most universal. Good and bad things happen to good and bad people alike. If others around you haven't felt the same things they have felt something similar, or know someone who has.

⮊ If you get the chance to choose your own counsellor, you should feel free to ask them about their professional qualifications and expertise. These days most counsellors have had good training but not all of them will have the expertise that you may require.

⮊ It can be important to recognize the professional expertise of the counsellor. Because their expertise is of the emotional world, their manner and style is likely to be quite different from that of your own working environment. That makes it no less worthy of respect. At the same time, while they might have mastery of what are considered the 'soft skills' they may not always be that soft. Alongside their supportiveness they might also be quite challenging. They may require you to become aware of your emotions, including those you would rather ignore, and expect you to wrestle with problems you find much more difficult to deal with than your everyday work tasks.

⮊ Give yourself time for thinking. While counselling sessions might be the most obvious focus of activity, it is not necessarily the case that everything will be resolved in the sessions. Make a point of taking time alone, perhaps walking in a park or countryside or sitting in a garden, to turn over the things that were said and came up in the sessions.

It is not so much the focused problem-solving mode of thinking that is required here. It is more a contemplative mode, bringing the relevant thoughts and feelings to mind, without rushing to resolve them; more a matter of allowing them to drift into the part of our mind which is below the level of our conscious awareness. It is from here that insights and resolutions, whether of minor or major import, are likely to pop unexpectedly into consciousness, often while our attention is engaged on some other matter.

4.8 *Critical Friend*

The term 'critical friend', and the approach associated with it, has tended to be mainly restricted to the public sector and especially education. Our research suggests that the idea could have wider applicability. In the context of this handbook we will focus on the learning dimension of this role. In this respect a 'critical friend' is someone who is outside one's team or project group who can be called in to comment on what is going on. The 'critical' part is associated with the notion that the person will critique the work of the team or individuals in it. The 'friend' part is around the notion that the person is assisting with a review of work from the position of a friend rather than, say, a detached auditor or assessor. The critical friend is there to help the team learn from and improve on its practice.

One way this approach works well is where one person in a team acts as a critical friend to another team and one of that team returns the favour. This can ensure a level of mutuality and a sensible trade-off in terms of time. However, many people are quite happy to take on the role without this reciprocity. The external examiner system in UK universities works at its best when the external examiner acts as a critical friend, that is, they want the course to succeed and are prepared to raise issues about improvement from this basis (as opposed to being destructive or apathetic). In the case of external examiners they do get a small fee for doing the work – but the fee is too small for it to be the main reason people take on the role. However, payment for the critical friend role might be necessary.

From the description above, it may be apparent that a critical friend can be added to methods such as **action reviews**, for example, in order to spice them up and get an external perspective. This is especially useful where a team becomes too used to doing rather bland reviews and the learning is rather superficial.

Examples

The authors of this book each act as external examiners to postgraduate programmes. In this capacity we see our role as a critical friend. We will raise concerns about the programme operation, design and procedures but we will see our role as working with the internal staff team so that they can learn from this and make changes, as needed. We have meetings with staff teams which are very much in the **dialogue** mode – we do not see our role as purely criticizing but rather as part of a learning and improvement process.

One of the authors was involved in setting up a new project which was seen by others in the organization as high risk. One senior female indicated to us her 'misgivings'. We labelled her 'Miss Givings' (this was not meant in a nasty way!) and invited her to a team meeting to tell us in more detail what her concerns were. This proved very successful as we were able to engage in a **dialogue** with her which did not get members of our team on the defensive. In true dialogue fashion we held the project idea at a distance and joined with her in kicking around the concerns.

Given the success of this, we set up a regular 'Miss Givings'/misgivings session each month where we asked for people who had misgivings about our work to come and talk with us about their concerns. We learned a lot from these sessions as they allowed both us and the visitor to get beyond the water cooler/corridor conversations into a deeper understanding of the issues.

Possible benefits

☑ Stimulus to open up issues that might not be aired – if you are in a team which uses a critical friend, there is the opportunity to encourage the person to help the team think of new areas for learning.

☑ At a personal level you might specifically ask the critical friend to comment on your own learning agenda. As they are outside the normal team relationships they can be a useful neutral voice.

☑ If you trade-off with another team then there is no financial cost.

☑ Critical friends can enjoy the role and learn from it – you might find that volunteering to take on this role gives you new insights into how another team works.

Possible limitations

☒ The role is not an accepted one in many organizations – it could therefore be difficult to set up.

☒ Critical friends are most use when they are insightful and careful in their observations – a person who is just critical from a position of not knowing the full information can be a real nuisance.

☒ You might find that you and/or your colleagues become too defensive or too closed – and therefore minimize learning.

☒ It takes a bit of time to set up and make it work.

Operating hints

➲ Ideally a critical friend might work with you over a period of time – if this is not possible then a one-off session could need a lot of pre-briefing for the critical friend.

➲ Selecting the right critical friend is crucial – they must genuinely be interested in what you are doing and be interpersonally skilled, for example, in asking good questions.

⊃ The critical friend needs to know that you have listened to their views even if you don't act on all of them – otherwise it is a bit demoralizing to play the role.

⊃ After a critical friend has visited it can be important to have a separate team debrief in order to confirm the learning from the event.

4.9 *Delegation*

Delegation involves one person entrusting responsibility and authority to another. Typically the individuals concerned include someone in a managerial or supervisory role who, while retaining accountability, delegates responsibility and authority to someone else, who reports to them, to accomplish one or more tasks. There are a number of reasons why the delegation of responsibility and authority is involved when it comes to the allocation of work inside an organization. For instance, dispersed geographical location can mean that those working out in the field will need to have sufficient delegated authority from the centre in order to maintain organizational efficiency. More frequently, many managers see delegation from the point of view of optimizing the use of their time. Delegation of those tasks that can be completed just as effectively by their staff provides the manager with time that they feel can be used more profitably elsewhere.

Neither of these reasons necessarily includes fostering the learning and development of those to whom the work is delegated, at least not explicitly. Where it is explicitly for this purpose, we can call it Developmental Delegation. The examples above fall more into the category of Performance Delegation. The two kinds of delegation are defined below, although in practice they are not mutually exclusive.

Examples

Developmental Delegation refers to the allocation of work by a manager to an individual member of their staff who is *not* currently 100 per cent capable of accomplishing it effectively – with the specific purpose of providing them with opportunities to learn how to do so. Although the work may be routine to the manager, or to the individual's colleagues, it may be unfamiliar or challenging to the person to whom it is delegated. It need not necessarily be 'routine' work though and could constitute a new initiative or project. In this case, there is the potential for learning both for experienced people and for those who are new to the field or organization concerned.

Our simple rule for managers considering delegation is that if someone else is likely to be able to carry out the work 80 per cent as well as you, then you should consider delegating and providing appropriate coaching and remaining support for the other 20 per cent. If the person can't do the work 80 per cent as well as you then you may need to consider using other methods in this handbook to develop them first, for example, **shadowing**, **coaching** or the use of **task groups**.

Performance Delegation refers to the assignment of tasks to individuals who are generally fully capable of accomplishing them effectively and who take responsibility for the outcomes. The explicit purpose here is maintaining or improving current performance. The performance of the delegated tasks themselves might be the major concern. For example, they might require specialist knowledge and fall into the province of but one individual. Alternatively, the performance of the delegating manager might be the overriding concern. Here the delegation of routine tasks might be for the purpose of freeing up the manager to concentrate on more important or demanding priorities.

Where work is assigned for developmental purposes, the person delegating the tasks will typically take responsibility for the outcomes until the individual to whom the tasks have been delegated is judged to be proficient. In this case, what begins as Developmental Delegation becomes Performance Delegation. Conversely, Performance Delegation can become Developmental when the process is followed within a framework of continuous improvement, where all tasks, including those that are very familiar or routine, are examined for their improvement potential. This in turn demands that even highly experienced staff be open to work based learning.

Clearly, where it is developmental in nature and purpose, delegation can be used for work based learning. The potential range of skills that can be learned will be bounded by the actual requirements of the responsibilities and tasks that are delegated. Of course, what is developmental in the eyes of the person delegating the tasks might not match the perspective of the individual to whom they are delegated. This implies that such delegation works best when it is achieved through joint diagnosis and decision making, and with continuing support for the person taking on the delegated tasks. This in turn requires that you, the work based learner, are clear in your own mind about what it is you want to learn. This will better enable you to shape the tasks that are eventually delegated to you.

As noted above, Performance Delegation can also be, or become, Developmental in the context of continuous improvement. Such a culture is not always present of course. However, just as clarity about learning needs and goals can help in Developmental Delegation, so it can if you are faced with delegation without this focus. By clarifying your own learning goals before and during the delegation process you will be better attuned to identifying potential learning opportunities in whatever work is delegated.

Possible benefits

☑ It can be a direct source of on-the-job learning (see section on **On-the-job Learning**).

☑ It can provide you with a real-time test of your promotion potential.

☑ By enabling a better use of time and other resources, more space can be created for further work based learning activities for the person doing the delegating.

☑ It can contribute to a culture of continuous improvement.

Possible limitations

☒ The person who has the authority to delegate may be reluctant to do so. For example, they may feel a sense of loss about letting go of what they enjoy, that it's too risky or that it's easier to continue doing it themselves.

☒ It can lead to an overload of work and associated pressures if it is merely an addition to current responsibilities and tasks.

☒ It might be accompanied by insufficient support and **coaching** from your manager.

☒ It might not attract the appropriate material or other forms of recognition.

Operating Hints

➲ Clarify your own learning goals and consider the match between these and potential delegation opportunities.

➲ Be clear about and communicate your expectations and goals to your manager – be prepared to negotiate these or the delegated tasks as appropriate.

➲ Find out about the bigger picture – determine what is important about the delegated tasks in relation to group or organizational performance goals as well as to your own learning.

➲ Ensure that you have an agreement with your manager about review dates and targets, in developmental and performance terms.

➲ Prepare for review meetings by undertaking a self-appraisal, and identify areas for feedback that are particularly pertinent to the achievement of agreed learning goals (see sections on **Appraisal** and on **Coaching**).

If you are the person considering delegating because, among other things, it will give you a chance to develop, consider such things as:

• identifying where your focus needs to be now;
• identifying an appropriate person to take on the task (preferably one for whom it will be developmental);
• identifying, through negotiation, the **coaching** and development they require (some of which may come from others);
• learning to deal with the emotional strain of handing over responsibility for tasks for which you remain accountable;
• having to deal with giving up areas of comfortable and confident expertise for areas less familiar.

4.10 *Development Centres*

(This is addressed to a person who has been invited or nominated to attend a development centre provided in their organization.)

The specific purpose and design of development centres varies, as can their duration – from a part of a day to several days in length. They typically contain mixtures of exercises similar to those encountered on training courses, such as in-tray exercises, group exercises and presentations, plus, in some cases, psychometric tests. Like exercises on training courses, these activities are intended to simulate the sort of events or situations encountered by participants in their work. However, they are likely to be run less flexibly than on a training course – a development centre is usually a pretty intensive event run to a tight and fixed timetable. Things are arranged in this 'standardized' way in order that the data generated can be deemed to be valid.

The exercises are intended to generate behavioural and other data by and about participants, gathered by trained observers, and of use to the participants and to organizational decision makers. Each exercise will have been designed to measure particular skills or abilities and each skill dimension will be measurable by more than one exercise. At the end of, and possibly during, the development centre the interpreted data will be fed back to participants verbally, one-to-one, and possibly also in written summary form.

Examples

What are today called development centres grew out of assessment centres, which were originally used in the armed forces for officer selection. As the title suggests, the primary purpose of an assessment centre is to measure the potential of participants to perform in one or more designated roles. From the perspective of those running such a centre the data generated is for decision-making purposes, for example, which of the candidates attending the centre fits the specification for the posts in question?

Feedback to participants may be no more than a 'yes' or 'no' decision some time after the event. Such feedback is of little use to participants for development purposes, whether or not they have got the job, and, in addition, can give rise to negative emotional reactions on the part of those who have not been selected. In fact, one of the stimuli for the growth of development centres was the highlighting of this issue. It was recognized that more was needed than merely communicating the selection decision to a candidate and, further, that data gathered for selection decision making was also of potential value for learning and development purposes.

Development centres currently in use in organizations can range from 'off-the-shelf' packages through to those designed specifically for the organization concerned. In the case of the latter, this involves a lot of work on the organization's part to identify the dimensions that are to be measured in the centre. Then someone has to design from scratch, or at least tailor, the exercises that will be used to elicit the behaviour most likely to be representative of the dimensions concerned. In addition, a well-run centre will be staffed by observers who are already practised in their roles and fully conversant with the dimensions used.

Like assessment centres, the dimensions may be based on the analysis of one, or a small number, of target roles in the organization, and on the criteria that are used to judge effectiveness in these roles. However, from the work based learner's perspective, this does not mean that their subsequent development has to be directed only towards the particular roles used in the initial 'target' analysis.

Clearly a well-designed and well-run development centre is, potentially, a powerful source of data to help work based learners in diagnosing their learning needs. It can be used by those new to the process of planning their work based learning, in effect giving them a head start. It can also be used by those who are more familiar with the process. Here the learner might see the data generated as something to compare and contrast with on-the-job evidence they have already gathered. This will require preparation on their part assisted by information from those running the centre.

If you are to take part in a development centre you may want to get details on its objectives, structure and design. It could be important to know, for instance, if data collected in the development centre will be put on record in the organization. Or, will the data on you be given to you and not recorded elsewhere? You may also want to know how the feedback from the centre will be organized.

Those providing feedback to participants in a development centre can be of considerable assistance to learners in helping them to make sense of the data. First they need to be as conversant with the dimensions, and as practised in their role, as the centre's observers.

Further, they should be willing and able to go beyond their immediate task and assist the learner to place the feedback in context. The 'context' here can mean the learner's current work situation and role and the implications the feedback has for effectiveness and learning now as well as in, and for, the future. As to the future, the learner can be helped to decide whether the possible career futures represented by the target roles and their associated dimensions are still attractive to them. More creatively, they can be assisted by the feedback provider to map a number of possible futures, similar to or different from those related to the target roles or dimensions.

As an alternative to the above, some organizations have provided development centres of a more general nature and allowed anyone to volunteer to attend. This has, in some cases, meant that, say, a secretary has gone through a development centre and discovered that with a bit of development they could take on a managerial role. In the case of these centres, the exercises may have to be designed with a level of robustness that would not be required in a role-specific centre.

As indicated above, a development centre is not in itself intended to be a work based learning method. In this handbook it is viewed as a method of gathering and interpreting data for use in making strategic and tactical decisions about work based learning and then for choosing and planning the appropriate methods. In practice, in some development centres, exercises and feedback processes are designed and scheduled more explicitly as learning events. For example, the centre provider might work with a model of experiential learning in which feedback in early exercises is intended to prompt and encourage participants to behave in later exercises in ways that are different from the ways they would have behaved had they not received the feedback. In other words, the boundary line between development centre and training course becomes blurred, taking us away from the focus of this handbook.

More importantly, perhaps, it can mean that development centres can become less developmental from a work based learning perspective if the 'blurring' leads to confusion about the status of feedback received at any point. The onus is then on the work based learner to be clear in their own mind what they wish to gain from their participation, for example, mapping and diagnostic work as a prelude to work based learning.

Possible benefits

☑ Can provide a potentially wide range and depth of diagnostic feedback.

☑ Can be a learning event in itself.

☑ Potentially low-risk situation for performance/experimentation (as with any well-designed simulation).

☑ Getting oneself noticed.

☑ Can start the process of career development (diagnosis) or provide one source of evidence of achievement of learning goals.

☑ It can give data that can be compared with other information, for example, from **appraisals** or from **360° feedback**.

☑ Material from a development centre can be fed back to one's manager in order to get support for other development experiences.

Possible limitations

☒ Over-reliance on the diagnostic data generated (that is, it's not necessarily the whole truth about the person).

☒ Lack of integration with other data.

☒ Blurring of the distinctions between development centre and training course.

☒ Typically development centres 'fail' when they don't provide adequate pre- and post-centre support, and this is by no means uncommon.

☒ Poor design of the centre such that the data is not of a good quality, for example, might give a distorted view of your strengths and weaknesses.

☒ It takes time to do it well. And given that you need skilled observers to make it work it can be low on cost effectiveness. (This has meant that some organizations have stopped running development centres.)

☒ It can be emotionally draining, especially where the development centre is designed to take a tough and challenging approach. Many people say that a development centre is no fun at all.

Operating hints

➲ Prepare for the centre by getting hold of information about its purpose, rationale and design and consider the implications of these for your own needs, particularly if there are no formal pre-centre briefing events or other discussions with development centre staff.

➲ Involve your line manager in preparing for and debriefing the event.

➲ Decide what you want to use the centre for. It's your career that people are impacting on so the more that you are proactive the better – even to the extent that you might, after due consideration, decide that you don't want to go through with such an event.

➲ Adopt a learning orientation during the event. Consider what learning lessons you can take from the exercises that you have to undertake.

➲ If opportunities for **coaching** or **mentoring** assistance are made available to you, take advantage of them.

➲ If there are no post-event support mechanisms like **coaching** laid on, can you involve your line manager in such a role or, if this is not appropriate, is there a work colleague participating in the centre who would be prepared to collaborate with you in 'peer' coaching?

4.11 *Dialogue*

Dialogue is an exchange, a conversation, through which people learn together. In this it differs from three other 'Ds', namely Direction, Debate and **Discussion**. We can begin to define it by looking at what it is not, by looking at the other forms of verbal interaction. Direction is the mode of a command and control culture; it is one-way communication and is rarely open to the ideas, thoughts or feelings of the other person; it is a 'just do it my way' message. Debate is an exchange in which different views of a topic are aired and argued; it is not about learning from the other participants but more a matter of convincing them of your own point of view. Essentially, it is a matter of winning, the verbal equivalent of battle. **Discussion** is an exchange of views, ideas and information; things might be learnt and this learning is usually more of a knowledge acquisition kind.

The point about dialogue, as we are using the term here, is that the parties to the dialogue are all open to learning, open to having their own thoughts and opinions changed by what they learn from others. The same may be so of some discussions; the difference is that a dialogue is focused on that learning possibility, so it digs in on things and attempts to get to the bottom of them. The fact that values and beliefs may be open to question and change in a dialogue usually makes it a quite different process from a discussion.

Examples

Dialogue can crop up in everyday life when people come together and are genuinely interested in what each other has to say. It can be delightful. Here, though, we are looking at how this mode of communication can be brought about intentionally, for learning purposes. Dialogue is the preferred mode within learning groups (see the section on **Self Managed Learning**).

In political and conflictual situations, we talk about people having a dialogue when they are really communicating with one another (not merely mouthing slogans). Peter Senge in *The Fifth Discipline* advocates the use of a mode of dialogue (stemming from the work of physicist, David Bohm) as contributing to the development of a learning organization. It is to be drawn on for many types of **meeting**, whether creative, planning or conflictual.

Possible benefits

☑ David Bohm's idea was that dialogue should allow people to hold their ideas and opinions as if suspended in space before them; that they should be able to examine them, without being caught up in an identification with them.

☑ It is within dialogue that our ideas can come into question. Suspended in front of us, as it were, they are ripe for examination. What is this belief really saying? What evidence do we have for it? What might we expect its consequences to be? How does it compare with someone else's idea? What are the benefits and limitations of this other idea? Are there any areas of commonality between the ideas?

☑ When participants to a dialogue are able to enter into the notion of putting an idea forward, as if into the space between them, everyone can approach the idea without a feeling of ownership, and examine it along with the others without fear of feeling attacked.

☑ Within a dialogue, people become open to change. Rigidities of thinking can become more malleable, perhaps with the realization that the other participants have no agenda to force change upon them, which they don't have to defend against.

Possible limitations

☒ Dialogue is not a familiar mode in our culture. (Bohm drew his ideas of it in part from the Native American context.) Consequently, it is all too easy for us to fall back into feeling attacked, and then becoming defensive, when one of our ideas is being questioned.

☒ Dialogue tends to happen most readily in a reflective mood, and a reflective mood is not the most appropriate for all situations.

☒ As with a mode such as 'brainstorming', it can take a group a while to get into the dialogue mode, though this can happen more readily the more often it is done.

☒ Dialogue requires a disinterested (not an uninterested) stance. The only agenda is that there be learning, not that anyone changes their ideas, their opinions, their behaviour. That will happen, if it happens, only when an individual is ready to do so.

Operating hints

⮕ In one sense, dialogue is very simple. Yet, it is all too easy for us to feel that when someone is questioning one of our ideas or opinions they are putting us on the spot. It can be uncomfortable. We tend to feel we are our ideas. If someone attacks our ideas they are attacking us.

⮕ From a different perspective, we might recognize that most of our ideas are not our original creation, they are put together from the ideas and experiences of others. We decide to believe them but this does not, in itself, make them any more right or real than any other ideas. Having a **questioning** approach to our own ideas is much more appropriate; after all, if they are not defensible, surely, we would not want to continue believing in them.

➲ Dialogue in groups often requires the slowing down of interactions. Often in discussions people are thinking of what to say while another person is speaking. Hence they may lose the full import of what is being said. One technique is to suggest that there should be a five second gap between each contribution. This means that a person can be listened to in full and the next speaker can reflect on what they have heard before making their own response.

4.12 *Discussion*

Discussing a subject is one way to learn more about it. This means that discussion is an aspect of knowledge management; it brings into the open the tacit knowledge around a subject. A discussion is often a context in which people will think aloud.

Examples

Discussion will often take place in **meetings**, when things are to be decided and, especially, when there are differences of opinion on what should be decided. A water-cooler conversation often becomes a discussion. It may not begin with any particular focus but simply drifts from pleasantries into a specific subject, work related or not.

Discussions can be set up deliberately, and operated somewhat in the vein of a brainstorm, with different ideas being thrown out and then batted around a bit as their value is assessed.

Possible benefits

☑ Sharing of ideas and information can benefit the organization, as is emphasized in the fact that this is the basis of knowledge management. Discussion is the most prevalent form in which this takes place in organizations.

☑ Beyond sharing knowledge, discussions can lead to the creation of new knowledge.

☑ Discussions, being informal (when they are formal they become something else), allow for the exploration of ideas and perspectives which people would be unlikely to state formally as they have not been thought through sufficiently. Often these ideas are a product of the discussion; one person says something which stimulates an idea for another, and so on.

☑ As they are so ubiquitous, finding value in discussions, and valuable ways to use discussions can make a profound difference to the culture of an organization.

Possible limitations

☒ Precisely because discussion impinges in so many areas of organizational life, its potential is likely to be ignored.

☒ Many discussions simply re-hash old opinions, rather than rehearsing new ideas.

☒ Discussions can easily take on the character of debates, where entrenched positions battle it out. A debate is not about sharing ideas or learning, it is about winning the argument. When this happens learning tends to stop. Holding to rigid positions leaves no room for learning. When you *know*, you don't tend to learn. To avoid rigidity, and debate, discussions can benefit from facilitation or chairing.

☒ A discussion only requires a topic, it does not require that the topic be 'owned' by anyone. It can remain a bit distant and 'out there', rather than carrying the emotional investment of a person or persons for whom it has real significance. Therefore, discussion can float around and may never be grounded in the concrete; it may never lead to choices and actions. It is also liable to conversational drift which can take it skittering off along the surface in any direction.

Operating hints

➲ Recognize the potential of discussion for sharing knowledge.

➲ Steer discussions in a useful direction; at the very least so that they concern things in which you have an interest.

➲ Introduce topics into discussions about which you wish to learn more.

➲ Instigate discussions. You can do this formally, for instance, as part of a regular departmental **meeting**. You can invite people to put forward topics about which they wish to learn more. By **questioning** and through maintaining the focus on a given topic, a discussion can become a fruitful context for learning.

➲ By recognizing the ubiquity of discussions within organizations, and learning how to use them for developmental ends, you can bring about a change in the culture of your organization or department. Discussion can take on the qualities of **dialogue**.

4.13 *Distance Learning and Packages/ CD-ROMs*

Distance learning was originally conceived of as written materials that would allow learning to take place outside the classroom. Today it is no longer a novel concept that learning can take place outside a formal educational context. Nonetheless, distance learning materials and packages can provide a rich resource for those who are taking charge of their own learning.

The origin of distance learning and, later, packages, lies in correspondence courses. These were established to deal with the needs of people who were already employed but wished to obtain professional qualifications. Being unable to attend a college course the learner would receive materials by post, work their way through them and return them for marking. Thus the name 'correspondence course'. Qualifications gained in this manner never achieved the status, with employers, that was given to college education. However, there were a number of studies which found that many learners preferred this mode to their experiences of formal education. They could follow the course in their own time and didn't have to sit through lectures trying to identify what were the important points to remember. It was as if they were being sent a set of lecture notes with the relative importance of different elements being highlighted for them.

Correspondence courses became distance learning as other media and means of interaction with tutors were developed. Packages combine mixes of media: written, audiotapes, videotapes and floppy disks, though without involving enrolment with a qualifying body, nor contact with tutors. These kinds of materials are in the process of changing their form due to developments in IT. Now, computer advances in multi-media presentation mean they can be found on CD-ROMs.

In one way such packages and materials are not work based. They may be just a fancy way of packaging standard material and may be quite disconnected from work. However, there are some packages that explicitly encourage and support a link to work experience. For instance, they may contain exercises that you can use directly in your work. Clearly, our emphasis here is on the latter.

Examples

The founding of the Open University gave a tremendous boost to the practice of distance learning. It also opened up a wider range of subjects which could be studied in this manner. The result was that a much wider range of people took up a much wider range of learning.

CD-ROMs are being produced with all manner of educational aims. Some are designed to satisfy a desire to increase general knowledge, others to develop professional abilities. It is to be expected that more and more learning resources will become available in the form of CD-ROMs and also through dedicated providers on the Internet.

Possible benefits

☑ Saves time as learners do not have to travel to classroom-based courses.

☑ Can be done anytime. The learner chooses when to pursue their learning, and they are not tied to the availability of tutors and colleges.

☑ Can be done anywhere. No requirement to attend a specific location. People can work on the materials wherever they choose.

☑ Easy to use. This is especially so of print materials. These require no special technology and are the most flexible medium we have.

☑ Learners are free of the distractions of a college environment. There is always more going on in a college than the lectures and tutorials. Getting involved in other activities, along with socializing, can take up a lot of time.

☑ Employers do not have to give time off work to those who are pursuing professional qualifications.

☑ More learner-friendly. For many of the reasons given above, the learner has more freedom in how they go about their learning. If the materials are well-produced they will highlight the crucial points to be remembered and will help the learner make sense of the subject area, rather than leave the learner to wade through an undifferentiated mass of material.

Possible limitations

☒ Learners are constrained by the materials. Although the learner has freedom in terms of when and where they learn they will, nonetheless, be faced with a pre-determined learning path. They will be expected to follow a laid-down sequence in their journey through the subject area, just as they would were they attending a college or university. Often, therefore, the materials are not conducive to work based learning as they are detached from an individual's work life.

☒ Materials lay down the way to learn. Because distance learning materials and packages are designed to be approached in a certain way, no alternative 'laws' of learning are explored. Even where there are different media, the materials are unlikely to lead to other modes of learning such as **coaching** or **apprenticeship**.

☒ Learners are isolated. You are on your own. There may be no one with whom to share your learning journey. Motivation is, consequently, a problem and many people never complete the course or package. In response to this, the Open University has mixed distance learning with face-to-face contact as, for instance, in their summer schools.

☒ Social learning is absent. While the extra-curricula activities of a college or university can be time-consuming, the learning can be important. There are many journalists, playwrights, performers and politicians who first took up those activities while studying something completely different. The benefits of developing what are called 'social skills' is also not to be ignored.

☒ Technological constraints. As more and more distance learning material shifts to CD-ROM format, while the learner can use them anytime they cannot use them anywhere. They are tied to their computer. Consequently, some of the earlier benefits of distance learning are being lost, even while the quality of presentation of the materials increases.

☒ Materials are standardized. As with textbooks, distance learning materials can only be designed for the average learner. They cannot respond to the individual learner as another person could, for instance, in **coaching**.

☒ Learning for stock. As with the formal education courses which were their inspiration, distance learning follows a warehouse metaphor of learning. Learning is not in direct response to a need made evident in the workplace. The assumption is that what is being learnt will be useful at some point in the future, at which time it can be pulled off the shelf and put into action. However, the lack of direct relevance and the consequent lack of impression on memory means that, when the time comes, the shelf may be bare.

Operating hints

Although distance learning materials and packages are often worked on in the workplace, their use is not specifically work based learning. However, they can be used within a work based framework.

➲ Know your learning goals. Approach any such materials with a clear knowledge of what you want to gain from them.

➲ Try to influence the purchasers of such material to make certain that what is bought is consonant with a work based approach to learning and development. Some packages help the individual to reflect on and utilize work experience. These are usually to be preferred over those materials that are more general or more abstract.

➲ Establish relevance. Your learning goals fulfil this function, in the first instance. Check out what is contained in the materials and, perhaps, talk to other people who have used them.

⊃ Be selective. While such materials have a pathway designed into them which the learner is expected to take, this does not have to be followed. Strike out on your own path, based on your learning goals, and use the materials for your own purposes.

4.14 *Induction*

The term 'induction' is primarily applied to the process of an individual joining an organization as a new entrant. From the individual's perspective, the fact that they are entering a context that is new to them means induction is largely if not wholly to do with their learning. In order for the learning not to be overwhelming though, or at best only ad hoc or haphazard, it does need to be planned and organized in some way.

As a secondary issue, some organizations will talk of induction into a new role even if the person is already an employee. The same basic principle applies, namely, that the main focus is on learning to carry out the new role.

Induction is a vehicle for developing:

- your knowledge about the substance of your new role;
- your relationships with the key people who will make up the community that you are joining;
- your understanding of the wider organizational context.

Of these three domains, the first, the substance of your role, is the one in which you are most likely to feel confident that you can get up to speed pretty quickly, given that during your recruitment hopefully you will have been successfully matched with the person specification for the role concerned. However, even if you were a perfect match on the basis of your qualifications and experience, it is worth remembering that the successful application of any skills and knowledge is to a considerable extent context specific. What induction provides is the opportunity to gain a much better sense of the new context and its demands, and at a manageable pace. In this way induction is both a process of work based learning in itself and, at the same time, an opportunity for active data gathering related to future work based learning needs and goals.

Examples

Most people are familiar with the notion of an induction course. This will probably be a formal affair lasting from as little as part of a day to several days over a period of weeks. Typically it is provided for groups of new entrants to medium-sized or large organizations. The course is likely to include presentations from various people about the organization itself, its history, products and services, and about company benefits and other terms and conditions of employment.

Planning and organizing learning during induction will not necessarily be associated with the provision of a course, for a number of reasons. For example, the organization might be small and have neither the resources nor numbers of new entrants to enable or warrant the provision of a formal course. In this case the induction is likely to be largely work based out of necessity. It is also likely to need a considerable measure of self-management on the part of the new entrant. There may be a modicum of support provided through face-to-face encounters with key, but busy, people, combined with access to relevant written material. This scenario might also apply in larger, better resourced organizations too, when we consider that the need for induction is not something that arises only for new entrants to the organization. It is also associated with movements within the organization. Induction becomes relevant whenever someone takes on a new role, particularly if this is in a different section, department or location, or when new projects or procedures are introduced.

An induction programme can be provided that is primarily work based, using a combination of methods drawn from those covered in this handbook and designed in consultation with the new entrant prior to taking up their new role. Where a programme is provided that is course based the new entrant does not have to respond passively, however. They can choose to approach and participate in events from an active work based learning perspective. This means that they have to be clear about what they need to learn, how, and from whom. Being thus well prepared, they should be in a much better position to identify opportunities to take supplementary or compensatory actions where required.

Possible benefits

☑ It can provide the means to gain considerable knowledge and understanding in a relatively short space of time and in an organized manner.

☑ It can ensure that you are sufficiently well informed about the new organization or role to feel welcomed, and secure in your knowledge of where you fit in.

☑ It can provide you with the satisfaction of being a potential catalyst for change in contributing fresh ideas and perspectives drawn from your experience elsewhere.

☑ It can provide a positive motivational effect for existing staff who have been involved in assisting you in your learning.

☑ Through induction a balance can be established between the challenges of the new and the provision of support.

Possible limitations

☒ The very fact that you are new might mean that you quickly get handed an objective or task that has been shelved for quite a while and is now strangely a massive priority.

☒ There can often be a mismatch between expectation and reality (the new role might have been over/under sold).

☒ What organizations offer in the way of induction is often woefully inadequate. Usually little recognition is given to the emotional stress of entering a new context, or a new role.

☒ Our research confirms Wenger's (1998) and others, in that people say they learn *what* the work is about on a course but that they learn the reality of *how* to carry out their role through work based methods. Therefore it is important to put your focus on the work context.

☒ No matter how much research you do to determine the cultural characteristics of your new organization, you are bound to get some surprises.

☒ You may well feel pressure to make one of your major priorities the immediate demonstration of your own or your function's credibility.

Operating hints

➲ Develop your understanding of the strategy of the organization, in particular those features that have a direct bearing on how your contribution is measured.

➲ Be open about your learning needs. You may have covered up weaknesses during the selection process. Now is the time to admit to them, as people will be more forgiving of lack of knowledge or skills when you are new than when you are fully into the role. If you try to cover up weaknesses you may get found out later – and that will almost certainly be more damaging to you then.

➲ Ask, ask, ask. When you are new you can ask all sorts of seemingly basic or naïve questions – and this is the best way to learn.

➲ Develop your understanding of your colleagues, for example, if they are supposed to work as a team, do they? Is the place rife with organizational politics?

➲ Identify your interpersonal, management or leadership style and how it can be used most effectively in the 'new' culture.

➲ Identify the people who will be your allies and start to develop a relationship with them.

➲ Determine your first actions quite early. Prepare for entry to your new work team or department and first try to understand them and their needs so that you can relate to them appropriately.

➲ Map out your 100-day plan (or some such similar strategy). After your initial induction phase there will still be a period required for fully understanding all the nuances of the work context.

⮑ Get to know your colleagues and/or your staff and their strengths as well as areas for development. Also find out who can be trusted and who can't, who knows things that can help you, and so on.

⮑ Keep close to your manager, learn to understand the person as well as you can, and assess what assistance, such as **coaching** support, your manager can offer you.

⮑ Create early successes – even relatively superficial ones. This can give you confidence that you are applying what you are learning and it gives you a basis to build on – thus making further learning easier.

⮑ Regularly review where you are at (10 days in, 50 days in, 100 days in, and so on). Are you learning what you really need to be successful?

⮑ Consider if you need other support. For example, can you **buddy** up with another new recruit? Can you get the support of a **mentor** (some organizations automatically offer this to new recruits)?

4.15 *Interviewing*

Interviewing can be seen as a research method which can be used to find out what someone does. For instance, it can be used to find out more about a role, in the same way **shadowing** can, though here the person is talking 'about' what they do, rather than you observing them actually doing it. In the context of work based learning, interviewing people in roles or situations that you want to learn about can be very cost effective.

Examples

As a result of a learning programme, senior managers in one accountancy and consulting firm went out and interviewed CEOs of other companies. They brought together what they had gained and pooled their findings as part of their exploration of what it takes to lead an organization.

In **mentoring** relationships, which involve an active mentee, they will often informally interview their mentor on both the politics of the organization and on the level of role at which the mentor works.

Possible benefits

☑ Interviewing can be a very time-efficient way of finding out information, though the quality of the information and the efficiency with which it is derived depend upon the abilities of the interviewer.

☑ It is a flexible mode, spanning the spectrum between a formal interview and popping in the odd question when you have the opportunity. For this reason it is worth considering developing the ability. (Much of the section on **Questioning** may be useful here.)

☑ In contrast to (metaphorically) sitting at someone's feet, when interviewing them you can draw out from them information they would not previously have made explicit. In other words, your questions can guide them to aspects of their experience of which they were not previously aware. This returns us to the point that questions are the engine of introspection.

☑ Often senior people, when asked to make a presentation about their work, will tidy up the realities of their working life. However, in an informal interview where the interviewer is interested in learning, they are more likely to tell it like it is.

Possible limitations

⊠ While interviewing can be time-efficient, it does also take time. Often much of that time is spent setting up the interview and preparing for it.

⊠ The people you want to interview might refuse. Being on a learning programme which is recognized within the organization can be very helpful in gaining access.

⊠ You have to sift through the information you were given. If it was a formal interview you may have it tape recorded (to bypass the vicissitudes of memory) but are now faced with an overabundance of material of which to make sense.

⊠ One interview gives you a research sample of one. While it, potentially, gives you a considerable depth of understanding it may be unwise to generalize from one person's point of view. Of course, it depends what you want to know. In the case of the managers who wanted to know what was involved in leading an organization, one case would have been insufficient; however, if you want to know how *your* CEO leads *your* organization, a sample of one is quite sufficient.

Operating hints

➲ It is important to know what it is you want to know. Hence the importance of preparation. It is also important to know how to find it out. Hence the importance of **questioning**. Finally, it is important to know whether you have found out what you wanted to find out. Hence the importance of being able to assess the information you are being given even while you are receiving it; to know afterward can be too late.

➲ It is beneficial to work with others, in that they can help you think through your questions beforehand and assist you in making sense of the information, and its significance, afterwards.

➲ Even while your attention is on what you want to know, and on getting it, you need also to attend to the comfort of the interviewee. These are not separate aims or incompatible claims on your attention. The extent to which you put your interviewee at ease is the extent to which the interview proceeds with ease. We have all experienced how, in a situation that discomforts us, it can be difficult to think straight.

4.16 *Learning Logs*

A learning log is usually a record of the learning activities you have undertaken and what you have got out of them. It can have a broader focus and include all you learn, whether that be through activities intentionally undertaken for learning purpose or any other activity. Often people may not call their written notes a learning log. In history there is evidence that successful scientists such as Darwin, Edison, Faraday and Newton kept journals and other records that clearly assisted their learning.

A simple format for a learning log would be to write down first the experience from which you learnt, then the conclusions that led you to the things you learnt from it. Finally, what that suggests for future learning activity.

Learning is not a finite activity. There is not only so much learning to be had from any particular activity or incident or conversation or page of a book or whatever. We may have had the experience of gaining more from a book, for instance, on subsequent readings than we did on the first time. We didn't squeeze out all the learning that first time through. We never can. Learning is not like that. It is of infinite scope. Artists, for instance, are learning as they are painting. They don't simply learn to paint and then do what they have learnt, learning nothing more. Each painting, by an artist, is a learning experience. There is always more learning, and a learning log, by bringing our attention to learning, can be a way for us to enhance and amplify our learning.

One particularly recommended approach is learning from **mistakes**. By recording what happened as soon as possible after the incident, your learning log can assist you in learning from events that did not go well. For instance, a presentation that was not well received could be recorded in a learning log and ideas for the future can be captured. For example, you may have tried to speak without sufficient notes and you may therefore have learned that in future you should make better notes before the presentation. **Writing** it down may ensure that you are less likely to forget what you learned.

Examples

- People on **qualification** courses undertaken through universities are sometimes encouraged to keep a learning log and to use that as evidence for assessment.
- People have kept learning logs so that they can use the material to discuss in an **appraisal** interview.
- Some people have used a learning log more like a diary (or as part of a diary) so that they can link this to **reflective learning** processes.

Possible benefits

☑ It encourages you to reflect on what you have learnt. In the process, you can find you are learning more, and perhaps making connections to other areas of relevance.

☑ It makes your learning explicit. Rather than having a vague feeling that you are learning, the need to complete the log forces you to become explicit about what that learning consists of. In the process, what is called tacit learning, the kind of learning we don't consciously know about, can be turned into explicit learning.

☑ It brings your attention to learning continually. Our thoughts and actions follow our attention. Consequently, the more our attention is on learning the more we are going to learn. We can certainly learn without being at all conscious of what we have learnt, but being aware of our learning adds yet another level of learning.

☑ As long as we are not too narrow about its purpose, a learning log will make us aware of what we learn even when learning is not our main intention. Our everyday activities can be a rich source of opportunistic learning (also called incidental learning). We have not set out to learn, in the sense of undertaking a specific learning activity, yet we are learning. And through becoming aware of what we are learning we give it an added dimension of depth. Our thoughts can now play around the incident, in just the way we do when considering more intentional learning. As a result our learning can multiply.

☑ The very process of writing something down increases the involvement of our mind-body. That is why we are less likely to forget items on a shopping list if we have written them down, even if we then mislay the piece of paper. In this way, writing about it in a log helps to keep the learning alive.

☑ A practical advantage of a learning log is that it can be evidence used toward a qualification, especially one by work based learning.

Possible limitations

☒ It takes time to log the learning, over and above doing whatever it was you learnt from. As a requirement of some qualification programmes it is often felt to be an unwelcome chore. It can also seem mechanistic and tedious.

☒ For those to whom learning something means integrating it within one's self, it often feels that there is no point to then go on to log it.

☒ Even if you have logged items seriously, the effort of going back over many pages of notes can seem time not well spent.

☒ If you don't have a **personal development plan**, or equivalent, the logged learning can be quite random and disconnected – and it may be less easy to see any pattern in it.

Operating hints

➲ If you have to keep a learning log, experiment with ways of making it useful to you. If there is an external purpose for keeping the log, such as a qualification requirement, fulfil whatever the requirements are. Then explore ways of doing that which gives you added benefit. This may simply mean doing it in a slightly different way than you were, or it may mean extending it beyond the requirements, in order to make it useful to you.

➲ If keeping a learning log is a matter of choice, do it as you wish and when you wish. Don't make it a burden for yourself. At the same time, you may find it worthwhile to experiment with different ways of using the log, simply in order to get the most out of it.

➲ Make certain that you give time to review what you have written so that you can get value from the process.

4.17 'Management By Walking About' or 'Managing By Wandering Around'

Although this idea seems to be similar to a manager having an open door policy, it is actually intended to be contrasted with it. Yes, a manager may have an open door policy, but unless you go in and they are there, you don't see them. With Management By Walking About, or, Managing By Wandering Around (MBWA) they come to you. The idea is to have managers out and about in the workplace, so their presence is felt and they maintain contact with the workforce.

To an extent, the name is a misnomer. It is not about walking up and down. Sauntering would be more appropriate: moving slowly, looking about and observing. It is about being present, approachable, and finding opportunities for contact. As the name implies, this is something for managers to do. (When other people do it they are often seen as sloping off.)

It is a learning approach. The questions in your mind will be: 'How's it going here?' and 'What should we do to change things?'

Example

Typically a manager will establish this as part of their style of working – they will habitually walk the floor in order to talk to people and observe what they are doing. One manager in our research found that he talked with the people on the way from the lift to his office but missed casual conversations with those who were not part of his route to his office. As he started to realize that he only had a partial sense of the people who worked for him, he made a conscious effort to wander around the other areas of the office at some time in the day so that he could have the same casual conversations with other staff.

Possible benefits

☑ The benefit that should come out of this is maintaining contact with the workforce. Other benefits are the benefits that accrue from this. For instance, the manager can tell the atmosphere of the workplace, can solve things before they become problems, can operate as an assistant to those directly involved in the production or service and make their work easier.

☑ Such a manager can also create a culture where everyone is working together, doing this by encouraging a sense of belonging and letting people know their work is appreciated. Much of it is about treating other people as people.

☑ If you are a manager you will find that you can learn a great deal through informal wandering of this nature.

Possible limitations

☒ People may feel they are being spied on, that you are checking up on them.

☒ If you approach this with a punitive mind set, you are not going to learn much. You would simply bring about the circumstances which would reinforce the perspective you already had.

Operating hints

➲ Do it regularly. Initially, if you have not conducted yourself in this way, or you are taking over from someone who didn't, people might be sceptical or outright suspicious about your motives. Consequently, you need to give it time for the contact to develop.

➲ Recognize that your initial purpose is to make contact with the people who work for you, and the purpose of that is to find out how people do their work and to discover how you can help them do it better.

➲ MBWA is almost a goal-free mode of learning – the aim is usually to just learn from whatever happens. Therefore it is important to see this as an open-minded approach to learning.

4.18 *Meetings*

Most organizations have a lot of meetings. Many of the decisions within the organization are made in those meetings or, at least, get ratified in them. Therefore, this is a context in which the organizational dynamics and politics play out. How you play the meeting, and how others play the meeting can provide a basis for learning.

Examples

Regular meetings, ones which you are obliged to attend, can be approached from a learning perspective. Over and above what can be learnt, this orientation also makes them a lot more interesting. In the case of meetings you would like to join, you can ask your manager. That could be a very appealing request if your manager sees it as meaning they will no longer have to attend. It can provide you with insight into an area or level of the organization not previously available to you.

One manager recognized he wasn't influential at a regular meeting he attended. Wishing to become more influential, he brought a learning orientation to bear on these meetings. He observed carefully to discover who was influential, and what they did and said to be influential. In his context, he discovered the crucial factors were the timing of an intervention and less what was said than how it was said. He was able to apply what he learnt and make his own interventions more influential.

Possible benefits

☑ Insight into how the organization operates. If you wish to operate in that organization it can be worth paying attention to what happens in its meetings. Organizational politics feature in most organizations and meetings are often the public forum where political moves are played out. You can learn from this.

☑ You can identify the different perspectives people bring to the topics and decisions under discussion.

☑ Learning which approaches work, and with whom, in that organization.

☑ If you wish to influence what happens in the organization, being able to influence meetings can be a very important step. In general you can assess your own interpersonal skills in such contexts – and such assessments may influence your own learning goals.

☑ You can gain much by **listening** to others and by asking **questions**.

Possible limitations

Many people have regular meetings they are required to attend. Since they are going to be there anyway it makes sense to learn something as well. However, there can be downsides to focusing on learning from a meeting.

☒ Putting your attention on learning can distract you from the content of the meeting. Thus it is best to use regular meetings, where you are very familiar with the content, as your learning venue.

☒ Time and energy required. Meetings can stack up against one another. You need time to recover from one, and to prepare for another. If they are not sufficiently spaced out you have less chance to reflect on what you are learning.

Operating hints

⮑ Preparation with a view to learning from a meeting is different from preparing to present something at a meeting. Be clear about what you want to observe – for instance, how people influence one another.

⮑ Identify instances when people attempt to influence others, and notice whether or not it works. Analyse the difference between the interventions which work and those that don't. You may find a range of different approaches work in a particular meeting. Do they all have something in common or are they effective because they are a match of the style of intervention and the individual? Analysing what doesn't work can help to highlight what does work.

⮑ Once you have learnt through **observation** and analysis, it is a matter of learning how to put into practice the patterns you have identified. It makes sense to try this out in situations where there is not a lot at stake (only because when there is a lot at stake there is a tendency to be more nervous about trying new behaviour).

⮑ The content of a lot of regular meetings does not always grab one's interest. Taking a learning approach, for instance, setting yourself the task to work out how the different people think, predicting their reactions and finding out how to interact effectively with them, can bring an almost endless fascination to such meetings.

4.19 *Mistakes*

We might not like making them but mistakes do happen. When they do, a lot can be learnt from analysing them.

The very fact that we talk about learning through trial and error suggests that the error part is not going to be eradicated, unless at the expense of learning. There is also our recognition of the need to take risks. Risks would not be risks if there were not a significant likelihood of them going wrong – of making a mistake.

We should put effort into avoiding mistakes, but not at the expense of attempting to accomplish our various goals. If we act, there will be mistakes. The question becomes one of how we respond to making a mistake.

Blaming ourselves, or blaming others, does not encourage us. In fact, it is anti-learning. If we, or our department, or our organization has made a mistake then we might as well get what we can out of it – the learning. Pearn *et al.* (1998) talk of moving from a 'Blame Culture' to a 'Gain Culture' to exemplify this notion – and they argue that this shift takes us away from a culture of cover ups and denial into one of gaining learning from mistakes.

Examples

There is a sense in which there is no such thing as a 'mistake'. We all know the common sense meaning of the word but, in essence, a mistake is a mistake because someone wishes to call it so. If an action was taken and it did not lead to the intended result, was it a mistake if it failed in its aim due to circumstances which were unforeseeable? In other words, was it a mistake if you could not have avoided it? And what if the circumstances were not unforeseeable but only unforeseen? Then there is, potentially, something to learn. If so, perhaps that is where the focus should be put, and castigating ourselves or others will only get in the way of our being able to accept and integrate the lesson. So let us look at examples of what might be considered mistakes, but look at them in a slightly different way.

- A scientific experiment is undertaken. The expected results are not found. The experiment is a failure. Or is it? It is something to learn from. Science is all about learning from what you do. That is why experiments are done. When the expected results are not arrived at, and the experimental procedures are, on examination, found to be sound, then something very significant may have been found. Indeed, many scientific breakthroughs have resulted from just such an upshot.
- A management institute launches a new course. The uptake is insufficient to run it. Has the course failed? Or did the institution have a valuable market research finding – and at very low cost.

- A manufacturing company launches a creative new high-end product to market at the same time the stock market takes a nose dive. Did the product fail? It didn't sell, but that doesn't mean it wouldn't sell under more favourable circumstances, or if it could be produced for a mass market at a much cheaper price, and so on.
- Akio Morita, who created the Sony company, launched his business by trying to sell a tape recorder in the Japanese market. Having failed to get sufficient buyers he went away to explore why this had happened and what he could learn from the initial failure. The rest, as they say, is history.

Possible benefits

Apart from the learning that is available through mistakes there is one other benefit. This is that action is taken and things are done. Nothing can be done, save it be done against a backdrop of (potential) mistakes. There is no such thing as a sure thing. The Catch 22 of it is that doing nothing might avoid your making a mistake, but doing nothing can be the biggest mistake of all.

☑ Avoids pretentions to omnipotence. Mistakes are a reminder that our control of any situation, even of ourselves, is never absolute. Even if our own efforts are impeccable we can still be felled by the fickle finger of fate.

☑ Learning from mistakes. In order to learn effectively from what has proven to be a mistake, that is, to achieve 20/20 hindsight, you can pose questions in relation to various aspects of the situation. For example:

- Where did the mistake occur?
- When did it occur?
- What did you do? (If possible, try to capture your words and actions at the time.)
- How did you feel about what happened at the time?
- Exactly what were the consequences that made you think of it as a mistake?
- What did you learn?

☑ These questions can be supplemented by the following (in order to delve more clearly into the issues):

- Was it possible to foresee what happened? (If the situation was not obviously beyond your control, like a meteor falling from the sky, for instance, it is better to assume it could have been foreseen and to figure out how you could have foreseen it.)
- Were you clear about your goal? Or was there more than one goal? And were any of the goals in conflict with one another?
- Were you clear about the consequences, and how to deal with them, if the goal was not achieved by your intended actions?
- Were you clear how you would know whether the goals were achieved? Did you have ways to maintain the action on-track between its initiation and its achievement? Did you have secondary operations if what you were doing was not achieving what was expected?

- What justification did you have for thinking your actions would be appropriate to achieving the goal? Had you thought through other, untoward, consequences they could have?
- Had you made sufficient contingency plans for those parts of the process which might be vulnerable to adverse circumstances?
- Were you relying on other people and/or machinery? What basis did you have for relying upon them? Had you given sufficient thought to the possibility of their failing you in the process?
- What unrecognized assumptions had you made?
- What were the signals that could have let you know things were going awry?

Possible limitations

☒ The biggest limitation of mistakes is that fear of them might stop us from going forward. That is why it is important to reconsider mistakes, recognize that they cannot be completely avoided and to gain their benefits. That is, learn from them.

☒ They can be costly. While some mistakes are the cause of no more than dented pride, others can have more serious consequences for ourselves and others. This is why we should make every attempt to avoid mistakes, short of allowing fear of them to shackle our endeavours.

Operating hints

➲ Face your mistakes head on. You can't learn from them if you deny to yourself that they happened. Blaming others, for instance, does not allow you to learn much. If you deny your mistakes to others, this can also get in the way of learning from them. Additionally, if you are found out you will be distrusted more than for simply making a mistake.

➲ Apply the kind of questioning illustrated in the 'Possible benefits' section to assist you in figuring out exactly what happened. Those questions can take you beyond identifying the source of what went wrong in that they can alert you to other vulnerabilities which had been present, even though these were not the cause of the problem on this occasion.

➲ What kinds of mistakes do you make? The following categories are worth considering when analysing your mistakes (they are taken from Pearn *et al.*, 1998):

SETTING GOALS
Do you find that you are working with unclear or competing goals, or not agreeing goals with others?

INFORMATION HANDLING
Do you get overwhelmed by the amount of information, and as a result feel unable to act or decide?

Do you find that you work on the basis of assumptions and generalizations that are not tested?

Do you concentrate on only a narrow or small part of the available or potentially available information?

Have you acted without due regard for consequences or side-effects;

Have you been too concerned with the present and not anticipated the future outcomes of your actions?

TAKING ACTION

Do you act too quickly in response to either internal or external pressures?

Do you find it difficult to act on the basis of gut feel or intuition?

MONITORING

Do you find it difficult to monitor what you are doing – and therefore are not able to take corrective action along the way?

Are you poor at reflecting on actions taken, or considering underlying causes of failure or success?

The kind of analysis we have been mentioning should give a basis for planning your further development, for example, through the writing of a **personal development plan** or through discussion with a **coach** or **mentor**.

⮑ Learning from a mistake makes it easier to be compassionate toward yourself and any others who contributed to the mistake. Self-blame is unlikely to be beneficial either to you or to anyone else.

⮑ There will be times when you want to keep your mistakes (and the learning from them) to yourself. For instance, in highly politicized environments the admission of a mistake can be used against you. Not all people in organizations are going to be sympathetic to your mistakes – there are unpleasant people around who will use any admission of weakness as a lever to get at you.

4.20 *Observation/ Listening*

Those who look and listen well, learn well. An example of this principle in action runs alongside our frequent emphasis on the importance of asking **questions**. There is little point to asking them if you don't listen.

Observation is the way to find out what's going on. It's the way for us to draw our own conclusions about a situation. Without it we are condemned to the second-hand ideas of others. We can't use our own experience as a touchstone if we haven't noticed that experience.

Examples

It is difficult to think of an interpersonal situation which wouldn't be an opportunity to observe and listen. Here are a few categories of such situations just to give a flavour for the ubiquity of application for this method.

- Meetings. A tremendous amount can be learnt at **meetings** just through looking and listening.
- If there is a role you aspire to, make a point of observing others who have that role. Your observations will allow you to identify some of the abilities or qualities you might need to develop for taking on that role.
- Interviews are an important place in which to bring your observation skills to bear. This is a context where you want to find out about the other person. It is not so easy to do if you are the one who is talking all the time. Or simply if you don't pay attention to the other person.
- A very concrete example is Bill Gates who is renowned for reading up on a place during his flight, looking around a lot when he lands and bombarding people with questions. He also listens to what they say.
- A common example in the training literature is 'Sitting by Nellie'. This approach was given its name because newcomers to a task, for example on a production line, were told to 'Sit by Nellie' and learn from her. Nellie was the archetypal old hand who knew how to do the job well and the new recruit was expected to absorb Nellie's skills by observing her for some considerable time. The approach has gained disrepute in training circles as observing Nellie may not give you the full flavour of the tasks involved and, as new recruits might be told to sit by Nellie for many hours, it was seen as a very wasteful activity which could easily bore the new recruit. However, the best Nellies can explain their work well and help a newcomer to learn from the observation period, so long as it is not too protracted.

Possible benefits

The benefits are, in a sense, the very benefits we gain through having eyes and ears, though more so. To only use our eyes, for instance, to avoid bumping into things would be a rather limited use of the faculty of sight. At the other extreme, there are people who are so perceptive that those they meet feel they are almost psychic. We are advising against operating at the lower end of that range. To elaborate on a rather obvious point:

- ☑ You get to find out what is going on around you.

- ☑ You get to find out more about the people you are interacting with.

- ☑ Your world becomes richer when there is more of it that is in your awareness.

- ☑ There are a lot of things which can't easily be learnt from books. They need to be learnt from observation or from people; and learnt from people by observing them and listening to them.

- ☑ It is a very cheap way of learning. And you are already carrying the equipment.

Possible limitations

- ☒ It is hard to imagine situations where it is not a good idea to know what's going on. Admittedly, it might not always be pleasant. That is why people ignore things or try to pretend them away. But this is rarely a very useful strategy, and is often disastrous.

- ☒ Prolonged imposed observation can become boring and less useful for learning (see the example above of 'Sitting by Nellie').

Operating hints

- ➲ Find a learning focus. Simply looking and listening brings no more than a general increase in awareness of what is going on around you. For learning, it is more effective to have a focus for your observations. One way to think about such a focus is that it is a question you are asking yourself. For instance, in a meeting you might be asking yourself, 'What is it about the way she makes her point that gets everyone's attention?'

- ➲ Follow the wry principle that since we have two eyes and two ears but only one mouth we should look and listen four times as much as we speak.

- ➲ As with developing any skill, it may be helpful to set yourself tasks. Observe someone, or some facet of behaviour, for a while. Then either pass to some other focus, or let your concentration relax. Even when practising, though, it is still better if you have a focus, a question in mind, something you want to know about. It provides motivation and keeps it real; after all, those are the very reasons for being good at observing.

4.21 *Peer Review*

Peer review can take place on a one-to-one basis or in a group. It can focus specifically on learning, or on aspects of activities or performance with which individual or collective learning is associated. (In this section we are concerned with the use of peer review for learning purposes.)

Those involved might be close working colleagues, such as the members of a work group or team. If so, peer review may be undertaken formally and on a regular basis (to monitor and improve group performance as a part of quality management arrangements, for example) or more sporadically (to address unanticipated problems or opportunities, for instance). Our view is that such meetings need to have an explicit learning focus. If, for instance, a review meeting is held because there have been problems, the **dialogue** needs to be around 'what can we learn from this' and not about apportioning blame.

Peer reviews can also be undertaken by those who do not normally work closely together. They might work in different parts of the same organization, or in different organizations, but have shared interests and ties through membership of the same occupational networks, professional bodies or trade unions. Here, peer review is likely to be part of individuals' **Continuing Professional Development** or intended to contribute to more effective knowledge management in their field of expertise.

Peer review can be conducted face to face or mediated by a range of communication technologies – from the telephone through to the use of ICT to video conferencing. Whichever media are used, peer review is intended to be a process of mutual exchange and support, so it is important that those involved are aware of the need for good **questioning** and **listening**, see themselves as equals, and value each other's opinions and views.

Examples

As indicated above, peer review can be used in two different ways. One way is where peers review something that, together, they have actually done, created or experienced. The other is where individuals who do not work together join in reviewing their separate accomplishments or experiences.

The latter use is closest to the origin of the phrase 'peer review'. This is in the establishment of referee systems in the first scientific journals in Europe in the seventeenth and eighteenth centuries. Peer review is now a well-established system for judging whether or not a paper submitted to an academic journal is worthy of publication in the eyes of the author's peers in the particular academic community of which they are a member. It is also a means by which authors can gain feedback from their peers on what they have produced. In addition, peer review of this kind is used more generally in such communities to assess the quality of work and to aid decision making in recruitment and selection and in apportioning funding for research.

In the work based learning context, written material to be peer reviewed might include pre-publication drafts of articles or papers. It may also include the review of documents such as task or project reports. This might be because report writing is the focus of the learning. Alternatively, the primary focus might be on reviewing the tasks, activities or project that the report is about.

Where the primary focus is on tasks and activities (whether or not these are represented in the form of written reports), peer review can complement **action reviews** undertaken by all the members of a working group or team plus their leader or supervisor (see section on **Action Reviews**). Where the focus of peer review extends beyond immediate operational tasks and activities to **project** work then it can be linked closely with learning at a tactical level (see section on **Projects**).

Possible benefits

☑ It can be a readily available means for those who work closely together to learn from each other. They are 'in the know' and therefore the very people to have informed and relevant views from which to learn.

☑ It can be an opportunity for individuals, who would otherwise remain isolated, to engage with others in providing mutual support for learning. In this case you might find it valuable to have new perspectives on things that you are working on. Where this process is formalized it becomes closest to a learning group (see section on **Self Managed Learning**).

☑ It can be a way of capturing, creating and disseminating knowledge in teams, organizations or wider occupational or professional communities. You can share knowledge and you can get access to new knowledge from others.

☑ It can be a means of maintaining and improving quality standards. This is best achieved by keeping the orientation on learning. It may be important to avoid mechanistic analyses where learning issues are avoided.

☑ It can contribute to the development of more collaborative and productive relationships in groups, organizations and **networks**. You can benefit from the support of colleagues.

☑ Peer review can be highly cost effective if people are prepared to listen to each other and provide mutual support.

Possible limitations

☒ Opportunities for peer review can be missed where individuals or groups are under severe time or task pressures. You need to evaluate if this is going to be a feasible option.

☒ Peer review amongst those who work closely together can lead to scapegoating rather than individual or collective learning, particularly where it is triggered by crises or mistakes.

☒ It can be a complex and demanding process, particularly in a group context, and might require facilitation at least initially.

☒ Those undertaking peer reviews who do not normally work closely together, and are without a shared history, may make erroneous assumptions about each other's situations and needs.

☒ Peer review in academic circles (in order to get a paper published in a journal) can focus too much on the need to get published and prospective authors may avoid valuable learning from peers who have undertaken a review of a paper.

Operating hints

⮑ Where the peer review takes place in a work group or team and focuses on reviewing the learning from collective efforts, the contributions and achievements of all individuals should be recognized. You may be able to play a role in assisting in this if you find that others neglect this aspect of the review.

⮑ When mistakes that are the result of collective efforts are being reviewed by the members of the work group concerned they should avoid apportioning blame to individual members. You need to consider how you will approach and best deal with such situations.

⮑ With respect to peer review in a work group or team where the focus is on deriving learning from the group's normal operational activities, also refer to the operating hints provided for **action reviews**.

⮑ When undertaking peer review with those with whom you do not have close working relationships, be prepared to invest time in establishing shared, and clear, understanding of your respective roles and circumstances.

⮑ Prepare well for review sessions. This can include undertaking and recording your own reflections on your learning (see section on **Reflective Learning**). These might be related to work you have already completed in pursuit of, or towards the creation of, a **personal development plan**.

⮑ Where, in a group, the focus is on reviewing individuals' learning, be prepared to devote attention to each person in turn. In this way what is reviewed can be determined and owned by each individual.

⮑ Don't use peer review with your own work colleagues if there are internal conflicts in the team or if people are jockeying for position. Instead look to create a group of people from outside your team.

4.22 *Psychometric Tests, Instruments and Checklists*

This section looks at the use of 'tests' designed for people to gather information about themselves: their personal characteristics, qualities, interests, abilities, values or motives. The range of tests available now is huge. Note that we have used the word 'test' here although many suppliers of such materials emphasize that they do not provide tests, as the latter term is associated with right/wrong answers and with negative feelings from people doing them. Hence we have mentioned two other terms in the title, namely 'instruments' and 'checklists'. Note also that the most popular 'test' used in organizations is called the 'Myers-Briggs Type Inventory' (MBTI for short), that is, it does not claim to be a test in its title.

Examples

At one extreme of the continuum of tests are the quizzes about 'your personality' published in popular newspapers and magazines and on the Internet. These are usually presented without any serious purpose and so questions as to their accuracy, relevance or objectivity are rarely of concern to either designer or user. Typically this lack of serious purpose is signalled by the aspect of personality measured (for example, what kind of 'lover', or 'partner' or 'driver' are you?) and the way in which the data is gathered and analysed. Data generation and analysis is usually accomplished quickly by the person attempting the quiz, in response to a small number of questions associated with a simple, and explicit, interpretive framework.

At the other extreme are psychometric tests. These will have been carefully designed and trialled to measure aspects of attainment, aptitude or personality. They are administered under strictly controlled conditions by a person trained to do so. This person continues to follow a strict protocol in scoring and interpreting the results. In addition, the results achieved by an individual are compared with a representative sample of people who have completed the test before, so that a psychologist or human resources person can decide how the individual compares to others – are they average, above or below, and by how much? All these characteristics are intended to ensure that the results are objective, valid (that is, the test actually measures what it sets out to measure), reliable (that is, the test continues to measure the same thing with no marked differences over time, except, that is, for an attainment test where you will expect to measure what has been learnt), and fair (that is, that any differences shown between people are not the result of the way the test is designed).

At various points between these two extremes are a large number of tests, instruments and checklists that have serious purposes as far as people at work are concerned. They include questionnaires that conform to the characteristics of psychometric tests outlined above and are designed to measure aspects of personality in a work context. These have become popular with those providers of training courses and development centres who have been trained to administer and interpret them. Similarly, psychometric tests that measure job interests or preferences have attracted a growing interest from human resources staff and consultants in the contexts of career management and outplacement consultancy.

There are any number of instruments that do not pretend to be psychometric tests but have the advantage of more open user-access and potentially less dependence on the need for expert interpretation (unless they are under copyright to consultancy firms and associated with branded approaches to training or development). These include well-known instruments to measure styles of learning, styles or modes of conflict handling, team roles, and so on. Then there are the many instruments and checklists that appear in published self-help management development manuals and to which purchasers have full access for their own use, plus those of a similar kind that appear in training packages and from which purchasers can make and distribute photocopies for development purposes.

Apart from tests designed specifically to measure attainments, most tests, instruments and checklists are best used for initial diagnostic work, rather than as an integral part of the learning process. They can help explain past experience and decisions, and assist in identifying past learning that informs the present. They can provide data about current strengths and weaknesses, and identify possible future work roles or activities that can be matched to the user's interests and aspirations.

Different kinds of test are appropriate for gathering data about different capabilities or characteristics. For example, personality tests are useful in identifying personal qualities such as flexibility, independence, decisiveness, initiative, energy, resilience; or in highlighting potential interpersonal learning related to things like impact, persuasiveness or openness. Reasoning tests can measure abilities in analysis, problem solving or attention to detail. Personality, ability or interest questionnaires can provide data about a range of managerial or organizational abilities such as leadership, project management, empowerment, and so on.

Possible benefits

☑ Can provide insights into aspects of your abilities, attitudes and personality of which you were unaware. This can stimulate you to identify learning needs.

☑ Can provide focused feedback along with a conceptual/theoretical framework.

☑ Can be helpful strategically by providing information for career development.

☑ Can be an enjoyable and stimulating method for some people.

☑ Can provide unbiased feedback.

☑ Can enable you to make more accurate comparative judgements about yourself.

☑ They are usually relatively low on time taken to complete – although analysis and feedback on the more complex tests can be time consuming.

Possible limitations

☒ Over-reliance on tests can mean the user is less open to, or discounts, everyday informal feedback from others.

☒ The answers provided may be assumed to be the whole truth about you. Tests do not provide truths – only perspectives from the point of view of that test.

☒ Some tests are quite expensive to use.

☒ The nature of the feedback, or the test's conceptual framework, may make it difficult to integrate the data with that from other sources.

☒ Some tests are very boring to do.

☒ Popular tests such as Myers-Briggs and FIRO-B have been overused so that you might end up doing one of these popular tests on more than one occasion.

☒ Some tests are poorly created and have low usefulness – yet it can be difficult to identify them beforehand.

☒ We have observed some psychologists mis-using the material and implying that, for instance, the test is providing objective and unchangeable evidence. This has meant that some people have not pursued careers that might have been open to them because they were told that the tests showed that they were unsuitable for such careers.

Operating hints

⮩ Use tests as a stimulus for further data gathering and not as the only data source.

⮩ Compare test results with other feedback and information.

⮩ If the test results are analysed by someone else, go back to the analyst with any questions.

⮩ If possible, go back to the instrument itself and think through the reasons for your answers.

⮩ Complete more than one instrument measuring the aspects in which you are interested and compare and contrast the results.

⮩ Consult people with expertise (for example, in HR/personnel) in order to get guidance on the most appropriate tests for you.

4.23 *Questioning, Asking*

It may seem that there is nothing to be said about the need to ask and to question if we are to learn. As a concept it is blindingly obvious. Yet, culturally, we are not very good at asking, whether it be asking for help, asking for advice, or asking how to do something. It is as if we feel an inhibition, as if we are supposed to know everything we need to know and to be able to do everything without help. Or that by asking we may be taking up someone else's time inappropriately.

There is a similar inhibition to asking questions. Particularly, to asking a lot of questions. We allow ourselves one or two questions, when we are feeling bold, but may get concerned lest a sustained sequence of questions be experienced as the dreaded 'third degree'. Yet questions are the royal road to learning.

Examples

Asking and questioning are such ubiquitous components of learning that it is hard to identify when they would not be useful. Essentially, they are useful when you want something or when you want to find out something. The 'something' may be direct help with a project, or it may be help in making sense of some procedure or system within the organization. Precisely because there is not a finite amount of learning in any one situation or text, questions can continue forever. The overarching question, then, is what do you want to know; for questions will take you there, be it something internal to yourself or in your external environment.

Possible benefits

☑ If we don't ask, people aren't to know that we want their help. In fact, even if they feel we do they may be inhibited from offering it unless we ask. In that sense, our asking provides them with the opportunity of offering their help.

☑ Questions are the motor of the mind. When we ask them, either of ourselves or others, they start the motor running and slip the mind into gear. Therefore, questions stimulate our interest and curiosity, both of which are prerequisites for effective learning.

☑ Much of the process of thinking things through is carried on by asking ourselves questions. If this does not immediately seem obvious, simply wonder to yourself what questions might be implicit when you last thought something through.

☑ A lot of the language used in work contexts is mid-level language. That is to say, it is not abstract, theoretical or generalized nor is it very specific, nitty-gritty, down-to-earth or concrete. Typically, it is somewhere in the middle. This means that it is almost always lacking in specificity. That leaves a lot of gaps in our understanding. All too often, we fill those gaps with assumptions. Assumptions, though, are dangerous. Making incorrect assumptions can lead, quite literally, to disaster, while asking questions dissolves assumptions.

☑ To take an example of the problem of unspecific language, you may be asked to lead a team. But what exactly is 'leading'? And what is a 'team'? We have sometimes asked these questions of a team and received as many definitions as there are people in the team. The terms are not specific. So if you are asked to lead a team, you may want to ask such questions as 'How should I lead this team?' 'What do you expect of me?' 'What would be the measure of a good team?' And so on – hopefully you can see that there are many important questions to ask here.

☑ Questions are not only useful for the person asking them. As you will recognize if you think of times when people have questioned you, this can often take your own thinking further and, in the process, reveal where you are not that clear yourself on what you mean. (Not everyone, of course, delights in having their ignorance revealed to them, so delicacy and diplomacy is often required.)

Possible limitations

☒ Limitations in this area are only found when you have received clear signals that people are not willing to help and/or are threatened by questions. In such cases, rare though they are, asking or questioning are unlikely to lead to any useful learning. Other than such situations, they are almost always likely to lead to your gaining more learning than you had at the point of asking or questioning. The more likely limitation is your own discomfort with asking or questioning, and this is best dealt with as soon as possible because it is keeping you from a considerable resource.

☒ As we have seen, there are some people who are not comfortable with being questioned. Any questioning is taken as criticism. Pop a few questions and they react like it's the Spanish Inquisition. For such people, you need to find a way to frame your questions so they will find them acceptable. Sometimes it is possible to observe how others deal with these individuals, or to ask others how they are best approached. Typically, the most important thing is to make yourself non-threatening to them. If they feel confident that you are not a threat to them they are more likely to be open to your questions.

☒ As we saw above, questions can be felt as an attack. If the person feels their ideas are being questioned (and this leads them to feel their worth as a person is being questioned), then the questioner needs to soften the question. This can easily be done by softening voice tonality, by framing the question as an exploration, by engaging with the person so they are aware of the sincerity of your interest before any question is put, and so on. People seem to pick things up subliminally, so, in a similar vein to what was said above, the best way to avoid their defensiveness is to ensure that you really do have no hidden agenda concerning their answer. If your question really is genuine it is much more likely to be experienced as such than if you attempt to make it appear to be disinterested.

Operating hints

Social conversation is not about gaining precise information. Much of it is about making contact and oiling the social wheels. So there are very many contexts in which it would be inappropriate to be pressing forward your questions. But our focus is on the context of learning and vague generalities will rarely serve us here. It is specifics, detail and clarity of information that we want.

➲ If you feel inhibited about asking for help, recognize that this is the case, and that it is a common feeling. Think about how it is best for you to approach the person. It may be that you want to make it easy for them to refuse what you are asking without embarrassment. It can be considerate to do so, but it is also important to be sure that they are aware that you are asking. A request for help which is too wrapped up in cotton wool may not be understood as a request for help. Remember that it is up to the other person to decide for themselves whether to agree to your request, it is not your place to decide beforehand that they won't.

➲ There are two sides to questioning: developing the ability to ask good questions, and knowing whether or not you have got an answer to them. The point is that no matter how good our question there is no guarantee the person will answer it well. Usually, they will give an answer, but it is not necessarily an answer to what you wanted to know. Thus, there is the need for being clear about what information you can expect to get from your question and being able to identify whether or not you got it. Many questioners operate as if all they have to do is ask their questions, and it is only later they realize the responses they elicited didn't provide the desired information. Best to know this at the time.

➲ There is an additional benefit to being sensitive to whether or not your questions brought you the information you wanted. It enables you to evaluate the effectiveness of your questions and, in turn, to develop your ability to generate better questions. As we indicated earlier, questions set the mind's motor running. They not only set the motor running, they set the direction in which the vehicle goes. In which direction do your questions take the person? Recognizing that we may be getting answers to the questions we asked, not to what we thought we were asking, can help us refine our questioning.

➲ Since assumptions can be the enemy of learning it is important to be able to identify when you are unwarranted in making them. One way to find out is to attempt to make what someone is saying into a movie. If their words, and only their words (without adding any of your own assumptions about what they might *really* mean) were to be a movie, would it be clear what was going on, and would the implications and consequences of what was going on be clear? If not, it is a signal that questions need asking.

⮑   While you are asking your questions, allow the other person's words to fill in details on your internal screen. Then which details you have and which you don't have will lead you to your next question. What kinds of things are you likely to want to know about? The big two are:

- What is important here?
- What do I need to do about it?

Often the answers you are given will need specifying, to bring more detail into the image. You may need to ask such clarifying questions as:

- What does that mean?
- How would you know if you had it (if it was there, if it were done properly, and so on)?

Plus the questions that go for the nitty gritty detail:

- What, specifically?
- How, specifically?

It is not that these questions would be asked only once; they are asked as often as is necessary to derive a clear picture, or at least one that is clear enough for your purposes.

4.24 *Reading*

For most of us reading is something we cannot do without in our everyday lives, inside or outside work. In a work context, many people are expected to read large quantities of written material ranging from short memos and emails to long reports. Here we would also like to look at the contribution that reading books or articles can make to work based learning. Given that many people would say they receive far more emails and reports than they are able to deal with effectively in the time available, the prospects for undertaking additional reading for learning purposes might look bleak.

It is fine to be selective about the books and articles we choose to read, particularly if time is short. We can also be selective about how much of a particular book or article we read and in what order. Usually it is only a work of fiction that we would expect to read from beginning to end and in that order. The non-fiction books or articles we choose to read, how much of each, and in what order, will depend on the use to which we want to put the information or knowledge that we expect to gain.

It may seem surprising to mention reading as work based learning. Many people's experience of educational settings predisposes them to think of reading non-fiction books as a detached academic study. We recognize that this can be so. What we are interested in here is the fact that many people do find that a textbook in their area of interest is valuable in supporting their work based learning. They may, for instance, wander into a **learning resource centre** and happen upon a book that will help them with a work problem.

We do accept, though, that most of the reading from which people will learn will be reports, emails, letters, memos and the like. In what follows we have deliberately used book/article reading as the example. However, we would suggest that many of the points we raise, especially under 'Operating Hints', apply to the reading of lengthy reports. If we don't learn something from a report what is its use to us? The learning may be a simple addition of some new information or about the views of the report writer. However, some reports give new insights into complex situations or cause the reader to reflect on their own values and beliefs. All of this is about learning. And it's clear from our research that some people are much better at extracting the relevant learning from a particular report than are others. Poor readers often miss the key messages of a report or even misunderstand it. Good readers are quickly able to grasp the main learning points.

In some programmes that we have run for managers they have suggested doing a speed reading course in order to improve their reading ability. Our stance would be that such a course could help but that often it is not about reading quicker but reading better. It is usually a quality issue not a quantity one. Simply reading more pages of text may not be the answer. In the Operating Hints section we use book reading as the context for developing a good reading strategy.

Examples

Basically there are two uses for reading in this context. One is for the reader to gain a detailed and comprehensive understanding of a report, book or article – to know in depth what the author wants to tell them and why. The other is to find answers to their own questions about particular facts, definitions, theories, methods or techniques and so on, in which they are interested. A number of suggestions about reading selectively with both uses in mind are provided in the Operating Hints section below.

Possible benefits

☑ We have to read, so learning to read well is a valuable skill. And the skill can be applied to reports, books and articles.

☑ Books and articles can provide unparalleled, and in some cases the only, access to relevant information, and knowledge.

☑ Given that reading only requires a text, it can be undertaken at times and places that are most convenient to the reader and without the need for other resources. Many people in our research commented that they used long train journeys or flights as a way of catching up on reading.

Possible limitations

☒ Where the learning desired is associated with changes or improvements in the person's practice, reading is unlikely to be sufficient on its own.

☒ The prospect of sustained periods of reading can be off-putting to some people.

☒ With the overload of emails for many people they find that they overdose on reading junk material, for example, attachments that are only sent for information – and do not provide useful information. In some work settings it has become a major problem that people email each other rather than talk face to face or on the phone. This is creating an unhealthy balance in communication modes.

Operating hints (with a focus on book reading)

The hints are grouped under three headings: Previewing the text prior to reading it; Reading the text itself, and then, as a check, Reviewing what has been read. The Previewing phase begins at the point where the book is in the reader's possession. The beginning of this phase can be brought forward to include the point when the reader need not even have a particular text in mind. In this case, previewing can start with the reader first deciding what kind of book they are looking for. They might frame a number of questions to which they wish to find answers. Once they have identified some keywords from their questions, they are in a position to consult library catalogues for the titles of books, or to access written material through Internet search engines or other sources.

PREVIEWING

➲ Previewing does not take a lot of time and can save time. With appropriate modifications it can be applied to reports, articles in magazines and journals too.

➲ Look at the publisher's description to check what the book is about, who it has been written for and what it says about the author(s).

➲ In order to consider the scope of the book and the approach taken, look at the table of contents and the way it is organized. In the same way look at the preface, or introduction, and some of the summaries, tables and diagrams, if provided.

➲ See if any of your keywords are shown in the index and, if so, read one or two paragraphs to see how the information or ideas are presented.

➲ If the book looks promising, scan or skim one or two pages of interest. Read quickly and don't be concerned about missing the odd phrase.

➲ Now, decide whether or not the book is what you are looking for and, if so, whether certain parts are more important than others, or whether you need to read the whole of it. Remember that you are not required to read everything in the book or even to read the parts in the order in which they appear. (This handbook is a good example of this – we would be surprised if most people read every section in the order they have been placed in the text. Skip around the sections as it suits you.)

READING

➲ You only need to read in detail those parts that you feel you have to. You can leave the remainder, or scan or skim other parts if you are not sure. One trick to remember is that journalistic writers often introduce each paragraph with a sentence that indicates what the rest of the paragraph is about. Hence reading the first sentence of each paragraph can help you to pick just those bits of the text that are really important to you.

➲ As you read keep in mind the questions that brought you to the book. These will depend on your purpose. For example, are you reading in order to explore the background to something, or to gain particular kinds of knowledge important to your work or in other ways to inform your reflections on your own or others' actions (see section on **Reflective Learning**).

➲ Whatever your purpose, question what you are reading. For example:

- If the text is not just description, what is the main argument?
- Does the writer take a particular standpoint?
- What assumptions is the writer making?

- Who are they attempting to persuade?
- How do other writers, or you, argue differently?

⮕ To help you remember and understand what you are reading use Post-It® notes to highlight points in the text or, *as long as the book belongs to you*, make notes in the margin or use a highlighter pen.

⮕ At intervals put the book aside and recall what you have read and make notes. This might be at the end of a section or, if the material is detailed or complicated, at the end of a paragraph.

REVIEW

Go back over your notes, in combination with skimming or scanning the text, to ensure that you have achieved your purpose. Where there are gaps in your understanding re-read the relevant parts of the book.

4.25 *Reflective Learning*

Reflective learning can come from reflection-in-action or reflection-on-action. That is, we can reflect on what is happening while it is happening (the 'in action' variety) or we can make time after an event or experience to reflect on it (the 'after action' variety).

Reflection-in-action is real-time reflection that can lead to immediate changes in behaviour in the situation. Where those undertaking it are experienced practitioners in a field, this often amounts to the application of very familiar, internalized, systems of rules, such that it appears to be an almost automatic process where judgements are grounded in intuitive familiarity with what's going on.

Reflection-on-action is reflection undertaken at some distance from the action, both metaphorically and in reality, for example, through post-event reviews, briefing **discussions** about the immediate future, or through planning in relation to the longer term in team **meetings**. Reflective learning 'after the action' comes through people stepping back from their experiences to think through what is happening; literally or metaphorically, even if only momentarily. One view is that there can be no learning without reflection, bringing to mind the old adage about the person whose twenty years' experience of their field is actually just the same year repeated twenty times. Reflective learning is not the experience itself. Discovering or creating new meaning or understanding is the product of reflective learning. This may lead to new actions or the further development or application of ideas.

Example

One successful director in our research commented that he was able to stand above events while they were happening and modify his behaviour accordingly. Hence he was learning. However, he was also very good at reflecting on an experience some time after it had occurred and wondering why certain things had happened. This allowed him to consider if he would do things differently next time he might be faced with the same situation.

The ability he showed is not common. He could do both the 'in action' and 'after action' reflection. And he was good at acting on his reflections. Indeed, being able to do this was a key part of his success.

Uses

Reflective learning can be used to produce three kinds of knowledge: practical, theoretical and transformative.

PRACTICAL KNOWLEDGE

With the appropriate balance of reflection in and on action, reflective learning is used to make explicit, develop or change the rules, or 'rules of thumb', accompanying skilled performance. This learning often happens amongst peers when reflecting on actions taken individually or collectively in the actual situations concerned. This may be done formally in specially convened meetings or informally as part of everyday conversations in the peer community (see the section on **Communities of Practice**). The learning can usually be articulated to some extent when needed, say when required by new or novice community members. It will often take the form of stories or anecdotes but it may also be communicated more formally, possibly in writing, and informed by theoretical knowledge.

THEORETICAL KNOWLEDGE

Here reflective learning is used to make an explicit link to theories and ideas. For example, it may be that a period of reflection leads you to doubt some existing assumptions about how the work should be done. One example from our research was a manager who had the theoretical assumption that money, status and other material factors were the major ways in which people could be motivated. With some lively young people joining his team he found that his assumptions did not work. They were keen to get support for their development and were more interested in their career progression than immediate financial rewards. After losing some good people he reflected on why this had happened and revised his theory of motivation.

TRANSFORMATIVE KNOWLEDGE

Here reflective learning is very much about the reorganization or reconstruction of understanding, or of the meaning of experience. What is familiar is recast or reframed, or practitioners focus on aspects of the situation previously ignored. Thus practice can be transformed. For example, in problem-solving situations those involved will go beyond the resolution of an immediate problem to begin **questioning** why the problem concerned keeps recurring (to which the answer may be insufficient reflective learning of course!). Alternatively, transformative knowledge comes from questioning the basic assumptions and premises underpinning the practice itself. This is very much the province of reflection-on-action, probably conducted away from the situation itself. However, it is likely to have been driven by a build up of frustration associated with the lack of success achieved with the usual processes of reflection-in-action, on-the-job, or because the situation confronted is entirely new or uncertain.

Possible benefits

☑ It can bring to attention those things of which the person is unaware.

☑ It can make a major contribution to continuous improvement initiatives in the organization or, individually, to continuous professional development.

☑ It can identify and map the gaps between what the individual or group intends to do (and probably espouses) and what they actually do in practice.

☑ Particularly when achieved with others, it can highlight the biases and errors in the individual's perceptions of reality, or challenge those elements of their reasoning that are closed and self-confirming.

Possible limitations

☒ Reflective learning can be of poor quality, and possibly no more than the product of 'jumping to conclusions', if there is a significant bias towards action.

☒ A significant bias towards reflection can lead to procrastination rather than the improvement of practice.

☒ It can be difficult to develop or apply in organizations that lack a tradition of reviews or 'think-tank' procedures, as in 'blame cultures', or where the culture is one characterized by an excessively fast pace or short-term thinking.

Operating hints

➲ Actively take time to reflect, and record your thoughts in a **learning log** or diary if it helps.

➲ Make use of opportunities for **action reviews** and **peer review**.

➲ Avoid debating points with peers or others; reflective learning does not thrive in adversarial relationships. **Dialogue** works best.

➲ Be open to feedback, and to making your assumptions explicit, in the knowledge that reflective learning often arises when what is taken for granted is questioned.

➲ Take opportunities to brief others about areas of work with which you are very familiar to assist them in their learning. One pay-off for you is that you can increase your own reflective learning by needing to make explicit and critically examine your own everyday 'rules of thumb'.

4.26 *Repertory Grid Method – Understanding Your World*

The repertory grid technique is based on the work of the American psychologist, George Kelly, and was formulated by those working with his Personal Construct Theory (see Stewart *et al.*, 1981). In this section we will show you a simplified exercise based on this work as it is very difficult to describe it without a practical example.

This exercise is a structured way to help you identify how you see the world. Typically, the focus for the exercise is somewhat smaller than the world itself. It might be a particular role, say, that of a manager or leader. We can have all sorts of thoughts and feelings about such roles without being clear what they are or having them mapped out in any accessible way. This exercise helps you get what's currently in your head out onto paper.

Although it appears to be based on other people it is actually an exercise to get you to outline ways in which you see the world, since your views of others are *your* views, and only those. The exercise can be used for diagnostic purposes since you can rate yourself against the criteria that you identify.

Examples

The following simplified structure for the exercise (Figure 4 overleaf) can be used for a variety of issues and is the same no matter what the subject is upon which you are focusing. As an example, we will take the subject of leadership. (When doing the exercise it is important that you pick a role to which you aspire.) The purpose of the exercise is to draw out from you the key values, capabilities and attributes you feel are important in a leader.

This exercise has been used by us in a number of organizations as part of the diagnostic work at the start of a **Self Managed Learning** programme.

Possible benefits

☑ The process helps you squeeze all the juice out of the differences between the people you identify.

1   Think of two people you know who best exemplify effective leadership. They should ideally be people you have personally seen perform in this role. They might be from work or they might be people from other contexts, for example, sport. Write down their names below.

A _____

B _____

2   Think of two people who demonstrate the opposite of best practice. Again it is desirable that you have direct experience of their leadership activities. Write down their names below.

C _____

D _____

3   Now compare A and B with C. How are A and B similar and also different from C? Note down any key values, capabilities and attributes that come to mind in distinguishing A and B from C.

4   Now compare A and B with D and repeat the procedure above in step 3.

5   Now compare A with C and D and repeat the procedure above.

6   Finally compare B with C and D and repeat as above.

7   Now write down the key factors from all the above in a list in approximate order of importance. (NB The list does not have to be exactly in order of importance but some idea of which things are more important than others would be of value.)

8   Additional step. It can be interesting to have friends or colleagues do the same exercise, and then to compare what you come up with. In talking through their list with them you might decide you would like to add some to your list.

9   Further additional step. Whether or not you have done step 8, you might like to score yourself on a scale of 1 to 5 (1 = low, 5 = high) in relation to each of the factors on your list. Given how you have scored yourself, note down what you intend to do (a) to maximize the use of your major strengths, (b) to address any areas where you feel development will be important.

Figure 4   Simplified repertory grid structure

☑ It makes your thinking more concrete and less abstract. It teases out the constructs (thoughts and beliefs) you actually have, and live out of, rather than having you think about leadership in the abstract.

☑ It is your list. The list is derived from your own thinking. You might add to it, through talking with others about what they have put on their lists, but even then you only add what you decide is important. This makes the results of greater value than a list in some text on leadership.

☑ Having derived your list you can then use it to check against those leaders you see in action. This can enrich your sense of what those key values, capabilities and attributes are all about.

☑ Being able to make a self-assessment of the key values, capabilities and attributes in relation to a role you wish to take on will provide a good basis for defining your learning and development goals.

Possible limitations

☒ It is necessary to have some experience of people who have the role you are interested in. Of course, if you have not had that experience you should do some research on the role before you decide whether or not you would like to fill it yourself at some point.

☒ If used for diagnostic purposes you need to remember that it is just your perspective. You might find that you are missing a great deal in the way that you have analysed this material.

Operating hints

⮩ The exercise, though it seems a bit unusual at first, is fairly straightforward. It is necessary to think about the implications of what the exercise brings out. There is little point in deriving your list and then simply leaving it at that. If this is a role you want, the things you consider important are the things you would want to develop.

⮩ Some people might find they are not able to draw out many items for their list. This might mean that, in their experience, there are very few crucial factors. On the other hand, it might reveal to them that they need more direct **observation** of people in the role. In this case their senses will have been sharpened by doing the exercise and their observations will be the richer for it.

⮩ It can be useful to compare your list with those in standard texts. This might enrich your thinking.

4.27 *Research*

Research is normally associated with the work of scientists, technologists or other specialists in organizations, who may well be employed full-time in this activity.

In this context we are using the notion of research in its broad meaning of 'careful search', that is, research that is more systematic and organized than ordinary (less careful) 'searching'. Research is about finding out things in an orderly way and in many ways all research can be seen as learning – someone finds out something that they may not have known before. The kind of learning we are dealing with in this instance is more associated with knowledge acquisition – research helps us to know things better – but it may also involve skill acquisition and, with major breakthroughs, cause a paradigm shift (with associated attitudinal change).

Although our interest here is in seeing research as potentially within the scope of all in relation to their learning, expert and non-expert alike, it may be helpful to outline and examine some of the approaches and methods that expert researchers use in order to assess their relevance to work based learning.

In the world of work, the word research brings to mind those organizations where long-term success is dependent on discovering new products or processes and where significant numbers of people are employed as specialist researchers. Those in the pharmaceutical sector are obvious examples. In this sector research can cover the full panoply of scientific approaches and methods, ranging from laboratory experiments through to controlled field trials of new drugs. This can be seen as *applied* research in that it is undertaken with very practical, and commercial, outcomes in mind. It is underpinned by the work of other scientists in other institutions though, such as universities and research institutes, who are conducting more fundamental, *pure*, research that is undertaken to develop theoretical understanding, without the same concurrent pressure to apply it to practical ends such as discovering, inventing or developing marketable products.

Of course lots of organizations in other sectors employ people with research roles or who undertake research from time to time. In this context, market research is one well-known function in many medium-sized and large organizations. This uses social research methods such as questionnaire studies and focus groups to investigate customers' preferences. Similar methods are adopted by private and government agencies specializing in opinion surveys for measuring staff attitudes in other organizations or, in society more generally, changing political preferences or general social trends.

In a lot of these cases the researchers use *quantitative* methods. That is, they attempt to describe the broad pattern of what's going on by coding and counting a limited range of data gathered from a comparatively large number of people. Where the researcher wishes to understand the sources of people's views or experiences in much greater depth they are likely to use data generated from interviews or focus groups. These are examples of *qualitative* methods where the questions posed are more open ended and where each of a comparatively small number of people can provide a lot of data that will eventually take the form of, say, verbatim transcripts of conversations with the researcher, or the researcher's detailed notes of their discussions or observations.

Examples

Most people actually spend quite a lot of time trying to make better sense of their day-to-day experiences inside and outside work or to find ways of improving the effectiveness of what they do or to increase their knowledge in areas relevant to their work. Using research to achieve these kinds of aims inside your own organization might encompass the adoption of some of the methods noted above but possibly on a more limited scale. It will certainly mean adopting a research approach, in the sense of being clear about what it is you want to find out or to develop, and systematically undertaking some investigatory or development work. This should lead you to a better understanding than would otherwise be the case and can fruitfully accompany the use of **reflective learning**.

Seeing your research as applied research and holding very practical outcomes in mind fits well with the use of **projects** at a tactical level. One form of applied research project that is commonly used in organizations is the evaluation of programmes or processes, such as the introduction of new technology or a departmental reorganization.

Linking applied research to change, through evaluation, points to another related approach. Rather than following the change, through researching on it, this approach is based on the idea that research should lead to change and that change should be incorporated into the research process itself. The approach is called *action research* and proposes that if we want to understand anything better we should start by attempting to change it. The relationship between change and increased understanding or learning links action research with **action learning** where, in a small group (the learning set), individuals can be helped to use action research methods to pursue their learning. Some action research can involve active collaboration between the action researcher and their research subjects, with the aim of increasing shared understanding – and can result in their operating as 'co-researchers'.

Possible benefits

☑ Your understanding of areas of relevance to your learning can be accelerated, broadened and deepened through research.

☑ In undertaking research in your own organization, you can capitalize on your existing knowledge of the organization to obtain richer or more relevant data than would be the case if you were an outsider.

☑ Depending on the approach adopted, there can be an increase in shared understanding with colleagues.

☑ Research can be highly practical and directly associated with changes and improvements in work or other organizational processes.

Possible limitations

☒ There can be disadvantages associated with conducting research in your own organization, such as accepting taken-for-granted views rather than challenging them sufficiently, or assuming too much and not probing as deeply as you could.

☒ You may experience tensions and conflicts between your research activities and your normal work role.

☒ Depending on the approach you adopt, you may find that your research activities put some strain on your established work relationships by setting you apart from your colleagues.

☒ There may be difficulties associated with the normal politics of the organization; if your research challenges organizational norms, for example, or if you are intending to gather data from your direct reports.

Operating hints

➲ Consider the kinds of research that you could undertake, and the methods available, in order to make informed choices appropriate to your needs.

➲ Consider any ethical questions that may arise and abide by any procedures associated with these in your organization. These questions could be related to how you intend to use the data you generate, or about issues of confidentiality or access to the data, and so on.

➲ Use your existing knowledge of the organization to help you clarify the questions you wish to address in your research, to map your existing understanding and to identify potential sources of support. At the same time, subject this knowledge to rigorous reflection to ensure that you are not making untenable assumptions or jumping to conclusions.

➲ It is worth consulting standard texts on research methods as there is a real skill in designing a questionnaire or conducting a focus group. Poorly conducted research not only limits your learning but also can be a nuisance in leading others to erroneous conclusions.

4.28 *Shadowing*

Shadowing is a good way to get an inside perspective on someone else's role, and one to which you might aspire. The sense we have of another role is frequently built up by a combination of assumption and observation. This can result in an image of the role which is at variance to the reality of the role. Shadowing can provide some of the experiential texture of the role.

The essence of shadowing is following someone around during their normal work. The shadowing is usually for a minimum of a day but may last longer. Here's a quote from Charles Handy (2000) to exemplify how the process worked for him as a new manager in Shell. He describes being posted to an office in Kuala Lumpur and being allowed to shadow his manager for a month as his **induction** into the office. His manager is quoted as saying:

> You will learn more about this business from watching me for a month than by sitting next to some other Nelly, and I will learn too from having to explain to you what is going on and why I did what I did. Feel free, when we are alone, to ask me any questions that are on your mind. And one thing – keep a diary with our impressions, lessons learned, resolutions made. That will serve as your report on the month – except that I don't want to see it, it will be your report to yourself.

Handy commented: 'It was a fascinating month. I watched a union negotiation, the sacking of a sales manager for dishonesty, the planning of a new refinery – and many other smaller things. I also learned, could not fail to learn, some important lessons in management, the biggest of which was the thrill of being trusted' (p. 166).

There are typically three modes of shadowing:

- Shadowing someone in a role to which you might aspire, as in the Charles Handy example above.
- Mutual shadowing, where two peers take it in turns to shadow one another for a day, learning how the other operates in the same role.
- Being shadowed (overlaps with the category above), where someone in a **coaching** role will, after the shadowing process, feedback and talk through their observations and assist you in devising ways to develop where you feel the need to.

Examples

What jumps to mind at the thought of 'shadowing' is the typical situation of shadowing someone who is in a role to which you aspire. Such an instance, in one organization, was a receptionist shadowing someone who works on estates. The receptionist thought, for various reasons, that she might like such a job and so spent a day with the estate worker as she went about her business. The receptionist gained an inside sense of what the job involved and was able to identify what she would need to learn and develop in order to be ready to take it on.

Also very familiar is the process of shadowing someone who is doing the same kind of job, though perhaps in a different organization. This is usefully done by managers, in that there are elements of managing which remain the same regardless of the organizational context in which they take place. However, that context, and the fact that this is another person, mean that a lot can be learnt. In the process, a mirror is held up to how one manages in one's own organization.

Local authorities have sometimes been creative in pairing people together for mutual shadowing. For instance, a social worker was paired with a housing manager. This provided each with a great deal of beneficial understanding of the approach taken by professionals in quite different domains and yet whose work impinged on one another within their local authority. Such an understanding can make a huge difference to interactions between those departments, as too in general meetings where they are both represented.

Bringing in a consultant or **coach** to shadow you is a lot less common – though, with the growth of the internal consultant role in many organizations, it could become more prevalent. One of the ironies of learning is that, generally speaking, those who are good at learning, value it, and those who value it are good at it. Consequently, the kind of people who would seek out, or agree to, being shadowed in this way are those who are the better learners. Nonetheless, it does mean that they will be in a position to make best use of the experience. The focus here is purely on development. A case in point is a senior manager who had been on a learning programme and gained from having made a number of changes in the way he functioned within his department, stretching himself into a more strategic role while delegating many of his former responsibilities to others in his team. He recognized the benefits of this, both for the department and for the team, who also recognized the benefits to themselves. However, he thought there was further he could go. The idea of being shadowed was put to him as a way of obtaining a neutral, disinterested perspective and, despite some trepidation, he took it up. The result was that he became aware of other areas for development at the same time as gaining confidence that the differences he had already put in place were solidly there.

Possible benefits

☑ We can have goals and ideas about what we would like to do, with only the most sketchy understanding of the reality of the job. It is important to gain as rich an understanding as possible and, preferably, an understanding from the inside. That is to say, an understanding which is 'up close and personal' rather than factual and objective, but at arm's length. Shadowing helps us get right up close to the role in its moment-to-moment lived reality. This avoids one chasing after a fantasy or living in a 'the grass is greener' phenomenon. For example, many aspire to senior manager positions. However, after having got close to the lived experience of those roles a number have re-arranged their priorities and put aside such ambitions.

☑ Where the purpose of shadowing is to learn how others do a similar role there is valuable learning. As well as all that might be picked up from how the other person does the role, you will find yourself questioning the way you do it, too. Since **questioning**, whether explicit or implicit, is the motor that powers learning, the benefits of this mode of shadowing can be immense. They are amplified if the shadowing is mutual. Not only are questions raised in your own mind about how you do the job, they are asked, and answers are required, by someone else. This is a lot harder to ignore.

☑ Being shadowed provides you with the perceptions of another on your daily activity, and also their questions on your intentions at various points can assist you in becoming aware of many aspects of your thinking and behaviour that were not previously available for investigation. When the person doing the shadowing is a **consultant** or **coach**, the contract between you means that the whole process is for your learning (it is not that the **coach** wants to know about your role for their own sake). Consequently, the benefits are amplified. The **observations** are being made by a skilled pair of eyes and ears and by someone who should know how to draw out the value of **questioning** various aspects of your work patterns.

Possible limitations

☒ The necessary time and co-ordination of diaries are limiting factors. For instance, a period needs to be chosen which provides a relevant range of typical activities.

☒ It is not always possible to find someone who is in a relevant role and who is prepared to be shadowed.

☒ The tendency is to focus on the observation of the person's activities and it is important to remember the necessity to have sufficient time to debrief, so as to find out the person's intentions for different points in your observations.

☒ It is important to stay away from actually doing the work involved. A limitation that came up in our research was where the person doing the shadowing was pulled in to assist with menial tasks, hence reducing the learning opportunities from observing the manager concerned.

Operating hints

➲ Record what the person actually does, not your interpretations of what they are doing. For example, a seemingly casual coffee-machine conversation may, in the mind of the person you are shadowing, have been stacked with intentions. If it is recorded as social conversation while waiting for the coffee (or worse, not recorded at all) it may well not seem worth asking about.

➲ It is better to shadow people or roles with which you can see a clear connection. The fairly common-sense principle of Near–Far transfer suggests that there is less to be gained the more remote from your own concerns is the role you are shadowing. Although the role of the receptionist and the estate worker may seem far from one another, there was a clear connection to the receptionist's ambitions. Another way to look at this point is that there should be a concrete purpose to the shadowing. In organizations, or on learning programmes, where shadowing is a frequent occurrence it may be best set aside until such a purpose emerges.

➲ Prepare for the shadowing period by thinking through what you want to know about and how you will record your observations. You can always practice by imagining yourself shadowing as you observe a colleague and think through, or write down, your observation records. Once again, decide how you will go about asking about the observations you have made. Would you go through the day chronologically, which can make it easier for the person to recall things, or group your observations into themes where the exploration might lead to a greater depth of response? Where will the debrief take place, will there be a need to avoid interruptions, and so on?

➲ It is best to shadow someone who is relatively experienced in their role. They may not be the best practitioner but they will have absorbed the work.

4.29 *Tapes – Videotapes/ Audiotapes/DVD*

Many learning resources are available on videotape and audiotapes and, increasingly, on DVD. We will treat them together as alternatives to learning materials in text form.

There is a cross-over between learning materials in these forms and those on **CD-ROMs**. As yet, Internet video is usually not of high enough quality to be included, though when it is much the same considerations will apply.

(This section deals with professionally marketed and manufactured audio-visual materials. It will have some points in common with the section on **distance learning and packages**. See also the section on **video feedback** which deals with making your own videos for learning purposes.)

As with sections such as those on **computer based training** and **distance learning and packages**, we are here focusing on the relevance to work based learning. As such these sections could be regarded as more peripheral as they are mostly associated with off-the-job learning and also with more of a training orientation. However, we want to mention such pre-created material for the sake of completeness and because it can link in with a work based learning programme.

Examples

A busy salesperson, who has a great deal of driving to do, uses their time in the car to listen to audio tapes that are related to the sales process. A manager who has to make a presentation goes to the **learning resource centre** to watch a video tape on presentation skills as part of preparing for the presentation.

Possible benefits

☑ Audio-visual culture. In the past, Western culture could have been characterized as a culture of the book. It was through writings that knowledge came down to us and it was through books that it was maintained, developed and created in our own time. However, today we are very much more of an audio-visual culture. Much of our information is gained from TV programmes. The preference of the majority of people is to switch on the TV rather than take up a book. Consequently, material provided in audio-visual form meets this situation more readily, is more familiar as a mode of input and is, therefore, more readily accepted by us.

☑ Audiotape flexibility. Audiotapes are cheap to produce and to reproduce, and easy to listen to. The Walkman has freed us from having to sit around our home hi-fi. We can take our sound system with us, so we can learn from audiotapes while jogging, going shopping, driving in the car, walking in the countryside, lying on the beach, and so on. Audiotapes can turn many a dead time, like waiting in line, into a learning time.

☑ DVD advantages. DVD adds to the benefits of videotape. A DVD can carry much more material than a videotape. The facility to play DVDs is becoming a computer standard. The same material can be approached in more than one way. Just as DVDs of films also often carry commentary on the film by director and actors, a filmed sequence of learning material can be enriched by bringing different perspectives on the action to the viewer's attention.

Possible limitations

☒ Audiotapes. While audiotapes are far more flexible in their usage than videotapes or DVDs, people miss the visual. Apart from when listening to music, we are used to seeing the people whom we hear speaking.

☒ Videotapes and DVDs. While audiotapes are more flexible means of input than books, videotapes and DVDs are less flexible than books. You have to have a sizable hunk of technology with you to see them.

☒ Time inefficient. Although we may respond favourably to audio-visual input it is often not an efficient way of conveying information. This can be noticed in TV documentaries which strain to find a visual that complements what they are conveying; even when they do it, it rarely adds to the programme. A written article on the topic could be scanned and the information gained in a fraction of the time. This is also the case with much of the videotape and DVD learning material.

☒ Inability to scan. One of the great advantages of written material is that it is easy to scan. You can pick up an article or a book and flick through it, dipping in as you wish, to get the information you want or to decide whether it is worth more of your time. This is very difficult to do with audio-visual material. The fast forward button can help but usually tapes/DVDs take as long to listen to or to watch no matter what you want from them. In that sense, you have to live the time of the audiotape or videotape programme. With written material you do not have the same time constraint.

☒ Entertainment is not the same as learning. A tendency with audio-visual material, precisely because it is so associated, in the minds of both its makers and its viewers, with broadcast TV, is to attempt to make it entertaining. While it is true that pleasure and laughter can increase one's openness for learning (just as distress can close it down) it is not the case that what is a source of entertainment is necessarily a source of learning. You can find you have spent an entertaining hour watching a supposedly educational videotape and having gained no more than if you had simply been indiscriminately watching TV.

☒ Disconnected from organizational realities. We are constantly stretched to find material that is going to support work based learning. Too often tapes and DVDs are detached from real work. Even case study material will be about another organization than the learner's and therefore usually less relevant.

Operating hints

➲ Identify learning goals. The very appeal of audio-visual material can undermine our discrimination. Because the form is so acceptable, fitting right alongside our viewing of TV programmes or our listening to the radio in the car, we far more readily watch or listen, even when it is not warranted.

➲ Evaluate the likely benefit. Consider whether the same information can be more effectively gained in another way, and whether it really justifies the time of listening or watching.

➲ Get recommendations. But be careful to distinguish between people's enjoyment of the material and what they actually gained from it.

➲ If your organization has a learning resource person they may be helpful in identifying worthwhile materials. Recognize, however, that they, too, and those viewers from whom they had responses, may have been seduced by the entertainment value of a particular item.

4.30 *Task Groups/ Working Parties/ Committees/ Steering Groups – Temporary Groups*

The common factor among these types of groupings is that they are brought together for a specific purpose. In this they differ from those teams or work groups which you are part of in everyday work. Although the time-scales of such groups will differ, membership in them and the existence of the groups themselves is seen as temporary. (Note that in including 'committees' in this heading we are thinking of committees that have a defined life as opposed to committees that are ongoing.)

Membership of these sorts of groups can be through volunteering oneself or through being drafted in. There may be many motivations for volunteering for such a group. Whether or not learning is the primary motivation it is learning that you will be engaged in, as it is the only route through which to realize whatever other aims you may have. And if, on the other hand, you were drafted into the group, it is through learning that you can gain from the experience and bring interest to it.

Examples

The existence of these sorts of groups will be familiar, and they may be formed for any number of purposes. Organizations may create task groups to handle specific events, such as a conference. The event may be a one-off that needs the co-operation of a number of departments so a temporary task group can seem the best option. One organization has created a steering group to manage the creation and launch of a major new leadership development programme. The learning and development function is leading this but has needed to bring in representation from various user departments in order to get buy-in and ensure a smooth launch.

The Health Trust and the Social Services department serving one locality have formed a working group. The membership is drawn from both organizations and the purpose is to bring together the separate criteria on which each assesses a patient. Each organization has historically, within their separate professional spheres, developed criteria having relevance to their particular requirements and responsibilities. As a result, they can each have different ideas about what should happen to the patient. This leads to problems for the patient and for both organizations. The aim of the working party is to merge their criteria in such a way that the resulting assessment, as conducted by either organization, will lead to the same recommendations.

Possible benefits

☑ An out-of-department perspective. Being part of such a group will involve you with people from other areas of the organization. This is an opportunity to enlarge your understanding of what goes on in those other areas and gain the perspectives they have on the organization as a whole. It gives you a better insight into what's going on. Whether or not those areas are your internal customers, it can be valuable to know how your department is viewed and the perceptions they have of what your department does.

☑ An out-of-organization perspective. As in the last example given above, some groups are formed with people from other organizations. This is also the case with professional bodies and associations of various kinds. Within such groups there is a wealth of insight available into how other organizations approach things. As in all such circumstances, awareness of what happens in other organizations can stimulate in you an external perspective on the all too familiar workings of your own organization.

☑ Increasing profile. Through membership of such groups, the profile of your department, and yourself, can be raised. People have volunteered for such positions precisely because they felt their department had insufficient profile in their organization. In being part of a group which goes on to accomplish a valued task there is the benefit of reflected glory. Additionally, those being considered for higher posts can be offered roles in such groups as a way of evaluating their likely contribution in a more senior role.

☑ Political influence. Because such groups are inter-departmental, or inter-organizational, they offer a field on which to wield political influence. Volunteering for, or finding oneself drafted into, such a group can be taken as an opportunity to develop your political savvy. As with **meetings** there is the same ability to observe how influence is gained and is used, and to practice your own arts of influence.

Possible limitations

☒ Takes up time. In some cases, the expenditure of time is minor, in others it is a major commitment. If such groups are not available to you within a work context they can be found outside work, but with the consequent claims upon your free time.

☒ Extra work. Often committees and working parties, in particular, generate tasks to be done outside of their meetings. Taking on such tasks, or being delegated them, may be burdensome, especially if the task has no learning benefit for you. Recognize, in this regard, that it is often the (understandable) tendency of such groups to allocate tasks to those who already know how to do them. This may be efficient for the group but does nothing for your learning.

☒ Groups may be run badly. This need not be a limitation if you are in a position, or can get yourself into a position, to influence how it is run. If that is not the case, you may find that what you can learn from an ineffective group is insufficient for the time expended.

Operating hints

⊃ Identify learning possibilities. If you are volunteering for such a group be clear what your learning goals are for that context. If you are drafted in, quickly seek out ways you can use the situation by listing the learning potential within it, and then decide on which of these potential learnings you will actualize. For instance, there are likely to be learning opportunities in relation to the content with which the group is dealing, its task, in relation to how the group operates, and how you might operate within it, in relation to networking with people in other areas and, often, at higher levels.

⊃ Learn how not to do it. If you find yourself stuck in a group which is ineffective there is a lot that can be learnt about what works by examining what doesn't work. This might not be your preferred approach to learning but it is a better use of your time than sitting around in seething frustration.

⊃ Have an exit. Endeavour to find a point of closure, a point at which you will be able to leave the group. The group may have a natural point of closure, with the completion of its allotted task, for instance. In other cases, committees rotate their membership and it is possible to step down. The thing to remember is that the group may not serve your learning goals forever, and it is better to give some thought to how you might depart from it before you begin to get involved in it. This can be especially important when you are drafted into a group. The point of accepting the assignment can be a good one at which to negotiate the terms of your membership. For many of the groups we have been speaking of it can be easier to elect to stay than to find a way to go. Therefore, having your exit prepared does not necessarily commit you to leaving while you are still learning from the experience.

4.31 *Travel*

Travel broadens the mind. The fact that it's a cliché doesn't mean it isn't true. More surprisingly, travel is almost always considered fruitful, even by those who had bad experiences at the time. No matter how stressful it might have been people usually feel they learnt something from it. Indeed, in our research on effective learning experiences, travel came out as almost universally positive, from a learning perspective. That is, even where people recalled bad experiences they reflected later that these produced positive and valuable learning.

Examples

- Attending an international conference in another country. Most conferences include an opportunity to get a flavour of the host country. In addition, in an international conference there is not only your own reaction to the host country but the reactions of those coming from other countries.
- Holidays are, for many today, synonymous with going abroad. It may be no more than the sun that is being sought, but if that sun is in another country there is always the opportunity to experience another culture.
- Visits to organizations in other countries.
- Working abroad means living in another country. It might even mean living there with your family, which can give a very different perspective.

Possible benefits

☑ Gives you another perspective. As Dr Johnson is reputed to have said, 'You learn about your own country by visiting other people's'. It makes you reflect on your own, familiar context.

☑ In another country we see things being done in another way. This stimulates a contrast and comparison between the two different ways of going about something.

☑ Our ideas about how to do things, and our ways of thinking, are built on the foundation of many unexamined cultural assumptions. The experience of another culture can challenge those assumptions, and prod us to question them. Through this process, we can arrive at different ways of thinking, different ways of approaching things. This is not necessarily a process of which we are conscious. But the result of having been in another country is that we return with new eyes.

☑ The tangible reality of the experience. On an informational level, we can learn about other countries through books and TV. While this can provide many benefits it is no substitute for actually being there. The texture of the real experience is so much richer.

Possible limitations

☒ We can take our own culture with us. Although it is something of a caricature, there are still people who go abroad expecting the people of the country they are visiting to respond in just the same way as at home. For some, the fact that they don't will only be interpreted to mean that these foreign nationals are being deliberately perverse. Those with so rigid a mind set are unlikely to learn much that is beneficial; they are only likely to reinforce their uninformed prejudice against foreigners.

☒ Many conference venues and sun sites for tourists aim to duplicate a Western context, with a hint of exoticism at the edges. Similarly, those working abroad can find themselves living in enclaves of people from Western cultures. All of this lessens the contact with the other culture, and thus lessens the learning benefits.

☒ Travelling can be stressful. Contact with another culture, precisely because it challenges our deeply-embedded cultural assumptions, can be stressful. We can feel at a loss, not knowing the customs of the country. Even finding our way around can be a mammoth undertaking in some places. As with any stress, when it reaches too high a level we go into defensive retreat. This can mean we bring down the shutters on the other culture. Often this is incomplete and, when we are out of the country and the stress is over, we may find we have learnt something of value from the experience.

Operating hints

⮑ Be open to experiencing the other culture. This may involve no more than preparing oneself with a receptive mind set. Alternatively, you might have read up on the other country, talked to those who have been there before, watched videos about it, and so on.

⮑ Recognizing that much of the value of travel is due to the contrast with what one is used to, you can purposefully look for differences and seek an understanding of what lies underneath them. Doing this will generate plenty of questions to fuel conversation with the local people.

⮑ The stress of culture contact can be lessened by recognizing that it is to be expected, simply because so many of the norms you rely on are absent. Knowing this, you can provide yourself with islands of familiarity via things that are part of your normal life, such as exercise regimes, reading novels, keeping your diary, telephoning home, visiting expatriate hang-outs, listening to the BBC's World Service or watching familiar TV programmes. Use such things simply to punctuate the experience when stress builds up. Otherwise enjoy the unfamiliar.

4.32 *Video Feedback*

Video equipment is ever more readily to hand, cheaper and increasingly easy for amateurs to operate. In consequence, the benefits that were only available from formal trainer-led workshops, where such equipment was provided, are now available to anyone who has or can borrow the kind of camcorder taken on holiday or to family events.

Seeing yourself on video, either in a role play or a rehearsal of, say, a presentation, instantly gives you the kind of feedback that cannot be gleaned from even the very best verbal description. You see yourself as others would see you.

Examples

It is now widely understood that many professional sports people use video in their training. That way they can sit down with their coach and see exactly what they were doing, regardless of what they thought they were doing, or what they intended to do. Frequently, they know what they need to be doing and seeing the video can be enough for them to be able to correct their movements; at other times it is helpful to have a coach on hand to explore what was going on 'behind the scenes', that is, in their mental and emotional psychology. Sports where it is particularly easy to gain from video feedback are golf, in terms of the swing; tennis, in being able to analyse the serve; and cricket, in terms of the stance before the wicket.

Another professional usage is in media training for executives. Those who may have to represent their organization on television can be trained in presenting themselves in that medium. This will involve many iterations of videoed interviews and then analysis of the recordings. In organizations, video feedback can be particularly useful for those who are preparing for a presentation. They can rehearse the presentation, revising both the content and how they present it in the light of their response to what they see.

Possible benefits

☑ In the training setting, video role plays are usually carried out with an audience, and this can be daunting for many people. If we separate the approach from the training room we can see how it can be used more fruitfully. For instance, you can just set up a camcorder on a tripod and practise your presentation in front of it and then replay the tape in order to assess how you did. You can repeat this process as many times as you like and no one needs to see it.

☑ A video of ourselves is as near as we can come to seeing ourselves as others see us. This has obvious relevance where other people's perceptions of us are important, whether that be in a presentation, an interview, an appraisal, or whatever.

☑ Seeing ourselves from the outside can allow us to make changes in our behaviour, that is, learn. Frequently, the very act of seeing something in ourselves we would like to change can be enough to bring about that change in our behaviour, and much more readily than if it were described to us by someone else.

☑ By stopping the video at a crucial moment of behaviour we are much more able to recall what we were thinking and feeling at the time than if someone merely asks what was going on with us when we did so-and-so. That facility in aiding recall is especially valuable when our behaviour does not simply change due to having seen ourselves. Then it can be helpful to explore what was happening in our internal world, as a means to change the outer behaviour through changing the inner movements of our psychology. As with seeing a behaviour, the precise recognition of what was going on internally is often enough for it to begin to change of its own accord.

☑ In a **coaching** situation, the use of video recording can be very helpful. The coach can set up and run the video recorder and assist in the processing of the material when it is played back. This is used for coaching on presentation skills, for example.

Possible limitations

☒ The requisite equipment needs to be available, and it may involve the presence of another person, either to work the camera (unless the activity is quite confined) or to act in a role play. Of course, the presence of another person can be of great value (especially in relation to the next point); the limitation is merely that the process would need more organizing.

☒ Those who are unfamiliar with seeing themselves on video may have responses to themselves which are quite at variance to those of other observers. When this is the case, and unless the views of others are obtained, the evaluation of their behaviour on the video may be decidedly skewed. This is especially so for those who have critical views of their own visual appearance or the sound of their own voice. Such reactions will get in the way of their being able to evaluate the video as anyone else might. It is often necessary to re-run the video a number of times until they are able to get beyond this reaction and attain a more dispassionate view of their image.

☒ The video medium carries with it the temptation to remain on the surface, fixed only on the visual appearance and the sound of the voice. As has been said, this can be sufficient. But to do so is unnecessarily to limit the value of the exercise. By stopping the tape and 'going backstage' to the thoughts and feelings that are motivating the behaviour a more rounded portrait can be obtained, giving greater value to the process.

Operating hints

⮑ Be clear about what you want to video and what you want to find out from the video.

⮑ It is often not appropriate to video people when they are engaged in the real life events on which they want to focus. This is the reason for using role plays. The nature of role plays, however, is that they are artificial situations and it is important for the parties involved to make them as realistic as possible. This is less a matter of props, and so on, than of mentally entering into the context and character of the activity. Often this is done by remembering, as vividly as possible, past similar incidents and, as it were, remembering them from the inside.

⮑ Do stop the video and question yourself as to what was happening to you on the inside, not only in areas where you would like to make changes but also at those times you think especially effective. What you can learn from when things are going well is every bit as valuable as what you can learn from the things you want to change.

⮑ Particularly when you are new to the process, obtain the views of others on how you come across. Ask them specific questions, not simply whether you come across okay. Ask about what you want to know about. If they are convinced that you are asking questions because you want to learn rather than because you want to hear something flattering, most people are willing to reveal much of their real response and some may be completely frank.

4.33 *Video Conference/ Webcam/ Teleconference*

These are all ways by which to banish distance, at least to some extent. Teleconferencing removed the need for a whole series of calls to people who needed to be party to a discussion or decision. All could be present at the same time and also hear the comments of each other, rather than their having to be funnelled through one co-ordinating caller. The video conference extended this, providing the visual input of expression and body language, plus allowing the use of visual material (for example, with a camera on the ceiling zooming into a paper on the desk).

Teleconferencing and video conferencing are also being used as a medium for seminars.

The webcam aims to bring the same facilities into wider usage, more economically. Increasing computer memory combined with video-editing facilities and inexpensive digital video-cameras opens up increasing scope for this mode of communication. The potential is developing for webcam discussions to be informed by video feeds from various locations, for example, showing how different production lines are operating or showing how various technical processes are to be carried out. The full flowering of this multi-input communication awaits further technological development.

Examples

- Discussion and decision-making meetings are obvious examples, and provide the primary uses for this technology.
- Teleconferencing seminars are taking place on all manner of topics. There are organizations set up solely to co-ordinate such seminar programmes.
- Many large international organizations have dedicated video conferencing suites in their main offices in different countries. These are booked by groups needing to bring together people from various sites.
- Online university programmes utilize webcam to ensure that the students who are sending in their papers for marking are, in fact, their authors. The tutor may be in London and the student in Hong Kong (to take a real example).
- Coaching via webcam or video conference link is a step up from the telephone in that it includes the visual element.

Possible benefits

☑ Video conferencing puts you in the same room (to an extent). It removes the need to travel. Much business travel is in order to get a number of people into the same room for discussion and decision making. While there is no substitute for face-to-face contact, much that is gained can be obtained more conveniently via video conferencing.

☑ Cheap in comparison. While there are expenses to all these modes, even the cost of video conferencing is insignificant compared to the time and expenses of flying half a dozen senior people halfway round the world. As the quality of webcam develops the costs will drop significantly.

☑ Increased creativity. All these modes can increase creativity in that a number of people are able to talk together. The way ideas can bounce around, and by so doing develop, is stifled by one-to-one telephone conversations. If everyone can talk and hear what others are saying, even when they are not in the same room, and even when there is only the audio, the ideas can still bounce.

☑ Similar to other **meetings**. When the technology works well and people are good at using it, such connections can bring the benefits of a normal **meeting.** You might, therefore, find it useful to refer to the section on meetings as the learning benefits identified there can apply here.

Possible limitations

☒ Teleconferencing with the unknown. Teleconferencing is less comfortable when there are a number of people present whom you do not know. If the group is small it is possible for them to say their names and for you subsequently to identify them by their voices. As it gets larger it can feel as if you are communicating with a horde of unknown people. This is an influence on the discussions that can follow teleconference seminars.

☒ Video conferencing is expensive. It is only large organizations, usually with offices in different countries, that can invest in a dedicated video conferencing facility.

☒ Video conferencing doesn't always work. The technology is sufficiently involved that it is not infrequent for groups to get together on two locations and be unable to get a video link. Apart from the frustration, there can be a considerable waste of time.

☒ Video conferencing is usually two-way. While a number of people might be present in each of the two locations, it is less common to have a number of video conferencing locations present at the same time. The quality of the visual input decreases drastically if the screen has to be divided to show different locations.

☒ Webcam is usually two-way. The point made about video conferencing is equally applicable to the use of webcam, the visual quality being even more of a problem.

☒ Webcam is low quality. At present, webcam is unable to provide the quality to show written materials adequately. These need to be transmitted by fax or email.

☒ Cameras make people uncomfortable. Currently, many people feel uncomfortable in front of the camera. Their continued awareness of it can be inhibiting. To a large extent, this will be an issue of familiarity. When webcams are in common use it is likely to diminish.

Operating hints

➲ Make sure you have use of good, and reliable, equipment. (This is less of a problem with teleconferencing.)

➲ Make sure you know how to use the equipment. This includes being able to make the connections between sites, manipulate the cameras, and so on.

➲ Consider how you will co-ordinate people's different contributions. This is somewhat like chairing a meeting but can be even more important in this context.

➲ Be clear about how the group will deal with any problems, that is, what are you going to do if the connections cannot be made. It is best to have thought out, and agreed, such things beforehand.

➲ For **mentoring** and **coaching** via a videoconference link it can be important to meet face-to-face first, if possible. However, we have seen examples where all mentoring and coaching sessions have been carried out over a video link and it has worked well.

➲ In a case where an interview was conducted over a webcam link, the audio dimension had to be handled by phone – and this can work fine.

4.34 *Visits*

Visiting another organization gives you an opportunity to see how other people do things, and there may be things you can learn from that. In addition, as with **travel**, experiencing another organization can give you a different perspective on your own organization. Visiting other organizations is relatively cost effective as there may only be travel expenses involved. If you are on a formal programme, it is easier to legitimate visits as it can be seen as something with proper approval.

Examples

On a consortium-based **Self Managed Learning** programme, the people in the learning groups came from different organizations. Each participant took it in turn to host the learning group meeting. This meant that each participant was exposed to five other organizations. Part of the learning group meeting would be given over to a guided tour of the organizational site, with the opportunity to meet some of the host participant's colleagues.

On in-house programmes, some learning groups have elected to visit other organizations. One example was a group from a city council which visited the offices of a building society. They had arranged to be given a room where they could have their learning group meeting and, in addition, were able to interview various people who worked in the organization. For instance, one of the group, who in the city council had responsibility for libraries, had arranged to see what those in the building society did about archiving.

Individuals have done the same. They have often used their presence on a learning programme as a justification for being able to make the visit. People seem able to understand that rationale far more than just announcing that you are interested in visiting. Of course, if you are engaged in work based learning you are, even if you have no learning colleagues, in effect on a learning programme for one.

Possible benefits

☑ Insight into another world. With all the similarities involved in making any organization work, it can be surprising how different organizations are from one another. Getting some kind of insight into how another organization works can challenge assumptions about 'the way things are' in your own organization. It is less easy to accept the way things are as an immutable 'given'.

☑ It can give new ideas. Sometimes there is something in the organization which can be taken on *in toto*. More often it is a matter of the differences in how things are done stimulating new ideas for your own organization.

☑ It gets below the level of tips and hints on what to do. You get the experience of how something is done.

☑ You get a sense of the organization's culture. It is very different reading about an organization, or even hearing a speech by its CEO, and having a first hand experience of it. Even though this first hand experience might not allow an understanding in depth, there may be something special that could be picked up by simply being there.

Possible limitations

☒ It takes time, both in making the visit and in arranging it. If you want to see a number of people or be shown around a number of areas you need to take into account that people will not always be ready for you just when you are for them.

☒ You will not get an in-depth understanding of the organization. Unless you have something very specific you want to find out about, you are only likely to get a overall impression of the organization.

☒ Your advanced preparation has to be good if you are to get what you want out of the visit. Additionally, when you are there you need to be good at questioning people if you want to get behind the generalities.

☒ Although it depends on the culture of the organization, people will tend to wear the public face of the organization. Because you will not be there long you often do not have the opportunity to develop the kind of relationship with people that is conducive to candour.

Operating hints

➲ Be clear on what you want to get out of the visit. Plan (and write down) the questions that you want to ask. Consider how the visit will meet your own learning needs.

➲ Consider how best to present your request to be allowed to visit. Obviously, it is best if you have a contact in the organization, or a contact who has a contact in the organization. If you have no contacts, it might be best to write a letter on your own organization's letterhead. Some organizations have a lot of people wanting to visit them, like the Body Shop, whereas it would be an unfamiliar request for others.

➲ After the visit, take stock of what you have gained from it. You may have follow-up queries, on reflection. At any rate, you may wish to write a note of thanks as a courtesy.

➲ It can be useful to go in a group, as each of you can pursue different issues and then you can compare notes afterwards.

4.35 *Volunteering*

According to the National Centre for Volunteering, volunteering is any activity which involves spending unpaid time doing something which aims to benefit individuals or groups (other than, or in addition to, close relatives) or to benefit the environment. Recent research shows that nearly 50 per cent of the adult population are involved in volunteering of some kind, men and women equally. These volunteers contribute, on average, four hours a week of their own time. They are involved in a range of activities of both a formal kind, through voluntary and other agencies, and informal volunteering carried out on a one-to-one basis. People's motives for volunteering vary and can include the desire to learn new skills and capabilities. This does not mean that they are only motivated by self-interest though. For most people there is a balance of motives in responding to a need in the community, both altruistic and self-interested, including the meeting of their own needs and those of family and friends.

Examples

The main areas of volunteering are sport, education, religion, health and social welfare. The main activities typically involve fundraising, organizing events, committee work and transportation. However, as expressed by the National Centre, you can do just about anything you want or can think of: you can volunteer to rescue people from mountains, to farm organically, build houses, write a magazine, judge criminals as a magistrate, or fix computers. There are organizations that cater for every interest and minority group imaginable. In some cases employers actively support their staff in volunteering, as a contribution to the local or wider community, and in the interests of meeting volunteers' career development needs. In practice this may mean that volunteers are provided with time off work or may volunteer as part of a group.

By way of a specific example, the largest 'formal' volunteer force in the UK is that of school governors. There are approximately 370 000 school governor posts at the maintained schools in England. At any one time, between 5 and 10 per cent of these posts are vacant, with some inner city areas having vacancy rates in excess of 20 per cent. Governors have a range of significant responsibilities, from promoting educational attainment, through managing the school's budget and participating in the appointment of the head teacher and other senior staff, to drawing up post-inspection action plans. Although the role is demanding, no special academic or professional qualifications are required.

As far as the uses of volunteering are concerned, potentially it's a case of 'spoilt for choice', given the enormous range of activities available. The role of school governor, for instance, offers 'work based' learning opportunities in the areas indicated in the outline of responsibilities above, together with the development of skills such as chairing meetings, speaking in groups, asking questions, making suggestions, clarifying decisions and so on. The important issue for the individual volunteer is being clear about why one particular area, organization, activity or role should be chosen rather than another. In the work based learning context the use, or usefulness, of volunteering depends on the contribution a particular form of it makes to the achievement of longer term personal, professional or career development goals. This, in turn, might be a comparative judgement in the light of current and anticipated learning opportunities in their normal place of (paid) work. Volunteering can complement existing work based learning opportunities or compensate for their inadequacy.

Possible benefits

☑ Greater freedom than in the normal workplace for people to make their own choices about roles and activities that will provide them with the learning they desire.

☑ Can provide learning that is enjoyable, has visible results and provides personal achievement.

☑ Can support or enhance the individual's position in the community.

Possible limitations

☒ Can present volunteers with either too little challenge or too much.

☒ Volunteers frequently cite poor organization on the part of the agencies or groups with which they are associated.

☒ Can take up too much time.

☒ Volunteers can experience lack of appreciation from the organization concerned.

☒ Volunteers might not be allowed to get involved with the more challenging and more interesting work. Some volunteers drop out because they feel that they are only allowed to do the menial work that employed staff don't want to do.

Operating hints

⮱ Diagnosis and planning. This covers you researching your own development needs and goals, and relevant groups or organizations, to achieve as close a match as possible between your interests and those of the voluntary body. However, it helps considerably if you find a group or organization associated with a cause or issue about which you feel passionately.

⊃ Drawing on and developing skills. This covers looking for volunteer work that achieves a balance between capitalizing on current skills and knowledge, and providing opportunities for development in new areas.

⊃ Pacing oneself. A problem commonly experienced by volunteers is over-commitment, so it's best for you to begin by committing less time than is available and then gradually increasing it to the appropriate level.

⊃ Prepare to be interviewed. Formal interviews are unlikely, unless the role concerned carries responsibilities for money or dangerous equipment, for example. However, an informal discussion is to be expected. The group or organization will want to know why you want to volunteer – the kind of information generated in 'Diagnosis and Planning' above. An informal meeting provides the prospective volunteer with opportunities to undertake the matching process indicated above, to meet other volunteers and staff and to check on issues such as payment of expenses, and the level of support/supervision to be expected from experienced volunteers or staff.

⊃ You may be able to get **coaching** or **mentoring** support through an organization where you do voluntary work. This can be especially important if such support is lacking in your own organization.

4.36 *Witnessing*

Work based learning groups have found that it can be valuable to ask people who are role models of effective performance how they do it. Individuals are brought into a learning context as witnesses before a group. In this role they are not required to lecture or teach; they come before the group to be questioned. We use the term 'witness' as it is the best metaphor for the role – the expert witness. The latter isn't on trial but is rather asked to come to court to be questioned with respect to an area of their expertise in order to get at the truth.

In a learning context a group will typically approach a person who is seen as particularly effective and quiz the person about how they do it. Ideally groups need to see a number of witnesses so that they can compare evidence from each of them.

Examples

In formally organized work based learning programmes the following might occur. Typically, there is more than one witness and they will be exemplars of the same role or ability. Each will say a little about themselves and their background. On that basis, sub-groups will form and identify the questions they would like to ask the witnesses. Each witness will then spend a little time with each sub-group, in rotation, answering their questions. The sub-groups draw general conclusions from what they have heard and feed these back to a plenary session, where the witnesses respond to those conclusions.

In one public sector leadership programme, the witnesses were three leaders drawn from, respectively, the commercial sector, another public sector and the voluntary sector. What they had in common was their role as leaders and it was about leadership that the programme participants were to form their conclusions. The participants were able to contrast and compare what they had heard and observed of the styles of leaders from other contexts with that of their own leaders, serving to enlarge their concept of leadership.

Possible benefits

☑ Rather than hearing prepared talks on leadership, the participants are given the opportunity to interact directly with the leaders and to ask about the things they considered relevant to them.

☑ Because the design is based on small participant groups, leaders tend to feel comfortable enough to be very open in their responses. Therefore, what they say is not pre-packaged, and is more valuable for that.

☑ Having a number of witnesses gives different perspectives on the area of which they are exemplars. Where possible, other differences, of background, ethnicity and gender, are also helpful in enlarging the scope of what is gained from them.

☑ Because of the interaction and intimacy of the process it can be very much more energizing than stand-up talks on the subject.

Possible limitations

☒ The process involves a good deal of organizing in advance, and managing at the time.

☒ It can be difficult to get the right kind of witnesses, with a sufficient mix of differences.

☒ Three witnesses to an area is still only three perspectives. Therefore, the witness session should be used alongside other learning modes to give a sufficient range of information and experiences in relation to the subject area.

Operating hints

➲ Groups need to prepare. This can begin in advance of the witness session, drawing on previous or vicarious experiences, reading, and so on, to provide an initial framework which can be filled in at the witness session.

➲ In the session, the group needs to think through how they will go about their interview with each of the witnesses. Sometimes agreed questions are allocated to each member of the sub-group; sometimes there is a spokesperson who asks the questions the group has generated. It is up to each sub-group to decide. They can do it how they like, but they need to recognize that they have the responsibility for how it goes. It can be useful for them to reflect on how it went afterwards, to see if there are any learning points for the future.

➲ If you are fortunate enough to be in a learning group, then it is worth considering this mode of working. You may need to persuade others of its efficacy as it can initially seem an unusual method, especially where people are more used to stand-up performances.

4.37 *Writing*

There are many times when we have to write, be it for a report or merely a memo. Here, though, we are looking at writing as a method of learning and development. All the same, this does not mean it can only apply to those cases where writing is a choice. One of the advantages of intentionally taking a 'learning orientation' is that we can bring it to bear on things which are not of our choosing and, thereby, gain benefits we would not otherwise gain.

Frequently, people are inhibited from writing by their idea of what might be expected of the results (by them or by some unspecified other, often the ghost of a school teacher past). Whilst there may be reasons for showing your writing to others, here the only purpose of writing is for learning. Accordingly, it matters not a jot whether others can read or understand what you have written; it is not written for them, it is written for you. When writing for learning, the only criterion your writing need satisfy is that it leads to learning.

Examples

- Writing up a **learning log**.
- Keeping notes on what we have read.
- Qualification programmes usually depend on writing to demonstrate what has been learnt.

Possible benefits

☑ Writing for learning can release us from the stranglehold of scholastic writing. What it needs is a change in the way we think about writing. A colleague of ours is fond of distinguishing between the processes of 'writing down' and 'writing up'. We write things *down* in rough notes, bits and pieces of thoughts, anything that strikes our fancy in relation to a given topic or situation. We write that *up* when we convert our rough material into a more readable form, when we impose shape upon it, and endeavour to make it fitting for a reader. All too often we eschew the first process, of writing things down, because we assume it must meet the criteria for something that is written up. If we do this we lose out on the benefits of writing. There are far more instances where we can use the process of *writing down* than where it is necessary to *write up*.

☑ Writing enables us to sort out our ideas. It is a way for us to find out what we think. Again, this is different from the school essay process of putting what we already know into words. This is using the process of writing as a way to explore a subject or experience. School taught us to get our thoughts clear *before* we wrote, but it is equally possible to fire our thoughts across the page and just get down everything a particular situation stimulates in us. After we have let rip with whatever came to mind, then there is time to make sense of it and to find where it takes us.

☑ Writing is one way to reflect on our experience. The very process of writing can slow down our racing thoughts, thereby allowing reflection. We can bring a new perspective or a new question to the thing we are thinking of, and our writing can unfurl new learning. There are always new perspectives and new questions.

☑ Much of our most important learning is about ourselves and our life circumstances. The process of 'freewriting' (explained more fully in Operating Hints) can be used in this exploration, and the research of James Pennebaker showed that it has significant benefits in terms of psychological and even physical health. Pennebaker got people to apply free writing to the vicissitudes of their lives. Consistently, the results showed that when people wrote quickly, paying no attention to the niceties of spelling or grammar, about what was troubling them in their lives or their situations, they benefited from this. The process of writing allowed them to get a distance from things and enabled them to make some sense out of what they were experiencing.

☑ Being able to make sense of our experience is a crucial human need. When things make sense then we feel more comfortable with them and much more able to cope, even if they are not to our liking. It is when we don't like our situation and are unable to make sense of what is going on or why it is going on that we get caught in a psychological spin which can affect our well being. Some advocates of freewriting suggest we write ten minutes per day on what is at the forefront of our minds, as a preventative medicine. Others suggest we take up the pen or pixels only when we feel the need. But by trying out the practice and being familiar with it, you can evaluate how you want to make use of it.

☑ Whether or not we have to write for others, whether or not our writing will be seen, it can still be useful to write, on occasion, 'as if' we are writing for others. This is especially the case when we are wanting to make sense of a particular subject area about which we are learning. By writing as if we are explaining the subject to a friend, or an audience of readers, we will force ourselves to organize our thinking, to marshal our argument and the facts that support it. The result is that it becomes very clear to us where our understanding falls short. When we find ourselves unable to write about a particular aspect, or our argument has gaps in it, this is a signal that our understanding is incomplete. Of course, understanding is usually incomplete; there are few subjects on which it is possible to know everything. The question is, rather, whether we know as much as we want to know. The point is that writing reveals this to us in a way that speaking may not. It is all too easy to gloss over gaps in our understanding with the verbal equivalent of 'arm-waving', and frequently listeners do not notice the gap, for they often know less about the subject than we do. In writing, when we are unable to 'join up' our thinking it shows.

☑ The same process can be applied to writing out the ideas we have read in a book. Do we understand what we have read; are we able to make it hang together? Write it out, and you will find out. In addition, there is another aspect that can usefully find a place in your writing, that is, your own ideas about the ideas you have been reading. Because the expectation of much of our schooling was that we be able to reproduce, parrot-fashion, what we have been taught, there is a tendency to carry this over into later life and assume this is the way to approach all non-fiction texts. Not at all. If you are reading something to learn from it, you are going to learn far more by bringing your own thoughts and experiences to bear on what the book is saying, even if they contradict one another.

☑ Writing can help us to integrate ideas. By engaging with them, as advocated, above, they cease to remain on the page as abstractions. We breathe some life into them, and make them more real, as we probe them with our questions and compare them with our own ideas. Then what we gain from them becomes ours. And we can put them into action and benefit from them.

Possible limitations

☒ The major limitation of writing is that it is something that needs to be done, that is, it takes time and it takes application. Often, when we come out of a situation that didn't go well or we have something we need to think through, we opt for short cuts (or so they seem at the time). We turn to distractions. We want out, and we want out now. They suspend what bothers us but they don't do anything to help us deal with it, other than giving us momentary respite. To do some writing may feel like the last thing we want to do, but usually that is because we are still thinking of it in a scholastic sense. Scholastic writing does take a good deal of concentration, freewriting requires much less; the process takes wing and our thoughts can sweep us along.

☒ Writing cannot be brought to bear when we are in the midst of a situation that is giving us trouble. In such cases, it is an after-the-fact method. It is something you use to ensure that you won't face the same kind of situation again without having more ideas and abilities with which to face it. However, the same restriction does not apply when it comes to dealing with our thoughts and feelings. Those we can tackle immediately. We can jump to the computer or grab a pen and notepad in the twinkling of an eye, and be working with what confuses or bothers us right at the moment we are being confused or bothered by it. It is unlikely for our state of mind to remain as it was for long; for it is in the nature of writing to generate ideas and to give form and shape to experience.

Operating hints

⮑ The method of freewriting can be useful in helping to release us from thinking of writing in terms of school essays. As developed by Peter Elbow, this is writing free of all constraints but one. In this writing no consideration is given to spelling, to grammar, to coherent argument, not even to sentences or paragraphs. The only constraint is that one must keep writing and writing fast.

⮑ You set yourself a time, say, fifteen minutes, and identify what you are going to write about. Then the only aim is to write continually, without stopping for thought, without correcting, and to continue writing even when you think there is nothing more you can say. The end result may have many repeated ideas, many times when all you have been able to write is that 'I don't know what to write' but, if you simply continue to write, new thoughts do seem to come to mind.

⮞ Sometimes those thoughts loop back to make connections with things you rushed down earlier and, without being able to think through the connections you write them in white-heat, off the top of your head. This process pushes your thinking, pushing out those only half-coherent or totally incoherent ideas, ideas you would never commit to writing were it not for the freewriting context.

⮞ The process can be used iteratively. Having written for 15 minutes on the subject, you can underline various observations and ideas that emerged. Then the clock can be set again to write for 15 minutes on those ideas. Again you will find ideas get pushed forward and developed, and new connections found. Sometimes the ideas become clearer; sometimes their import becomes wider or they take off in new directions.

⮞ The process can continue and, if you do need or want to bring it through to a finished piece of writing you can do so by letting a structure emerge as you go. That structure, written down and then written up at speed, often retains, even through the tidying-up process, a good deal of the spontaneity and liveliness of your freewriting – to produce an end result much more pleasing to the reader than one arrived at by a constraining struggle between yourself and the page.

⮞ Many people keep diaries and, in the last couple of decades or more, journal writing has had a vogue. Various purposes are proposed for these activities. Benefits to physical and psychological health can result, depending on the manner in which the writing is approached, and we will turn to this below.

⮞ One benefit that the daily activity of filling in a diary or journal can have is especially useful when working abroad. The unfamiliar environment, together with the fact that one's own familiar environment is missing, can be wearing. One of the greatest challenges of cross-cultural management is the need to develop 'emotional muscle'. While it might be expected that the biggest challenges have to do with dealing with the other culture, with its different social expectations and cultural norms, it is managing the effect this has on us that is a greater challenge. Thus the importance of emotional resilience should be acknowledged when most of the normal, and usually unnoticed, supports of our own life and our psychological equilibrium are absent, indeed may be even contradicted by the other culture.

⮞ In such cases, there is great value to having a regular practice, of which writing in a diary or journal is one example, which provides a thread of respite from the demands of another culture, a practice and period of the day when we can drop out of the unfamiliar context into a comfortable and familiar activity. The advantage when this activity is writing, is that the process of writing is one which assists us in making sense of our experience, thus of putting into perspective the emotional wear and tear and also the stimulation, freshness and excitement of dealing with another culture.

5 Conclusions and Directions

In this handbook we have made a case for the importance and centrality of work based learning in organizations. We have offered a wide range of approaches that can support and improve work based learning. We have not attempted to write an encyclopaedia on the subject but rather to provide ideas upon which others can build. We hope that what we have offered may spur the development of other approaches in addition to those that we describe.

In exploring a range of planned approaches we are not suggesting that work based learning can be totally planned and organized. On the contrary most learning at work is opportunistic and unplanned – things just happen that people learn from. This is how it has been for most of human history. Schools, colleges and universities are a relatively recent invention. The hunter-gatherer bands were the only form of human society for 90 per cent of our history on this planet. It was only with the coming of the agricultural revolution that such bands have been largely supplanted by today's more organized and controlled societies.

Prior to the industrial revolution there had been very little in the way of structured and controlled learning institutions and it was only late in the industrial era that mass schooling emerged. The problem we have is that all of us have been born in this era of mass schooling and have grown up in a world which assumes that this model is the most desirable. As we have stated earlier, this has led those in control of nation states to insist that the only legitimate learning is that which is controlled, directed and arranged through institutions, whether schools, colleges, universities or training organizations.

This approach not only demeans those who have had little involvement with institutional learning, it also undermines investment in the arenas where most learning takes place. Earlier we quoted from the UK's Chartered Institute of Personnel and Development, who have recognized that resources need to be switched from training courses to work based learning. Even with this support for our stance we know that getting such change will not be easy. The reasons for people clinging on to existing modes are explored further in Appendix III. However, we are aware that just showing something works better than current arrangements will not necessarily bring about change.

In this connection we can quote the example of the work of Reg Revans who showed the value of his action learning approach from the 1940s up to his death in 2003. Even though he was a university professor, and had substantial research to support his stance, he could not stop his own university from copying the worst of the US business school practices and ignoring the proven home grown alternative.

The picture is not, however, totally gloomy. Action learning has been developing and expanding along with variants of the approach. Even public sector bureaucracies are using such approaches more frequently. In the university world there are now formalized processes for gaining qualifications via work based learning (see, for example, Gallacher and Reeve, 2002, and the material in Appendix II). And such approaches are expanding and gaining greater recognition. It is also apparent that top managers can recognize that their key learning experiences have largely been through work based modes.

Note that in the previous sentence we said 'can' – often people do not recognize straightaway that they have learned mostly from work based experiences. One exercise that we use to tune managers into recognizing this is outlined here.

The process asks managers to go through a series of logical stages and we usually use a form for the purpose.

1 Everyone is asked to write a few notes on the purpose of their business. They may take this from a mission or vision statement. Wherever it comes from, what we want to get out of this exercise is: why does the organization exist? What is it here for?
2 We then ask people to make some notes on their own role in contributing to this purpose. What do they get paid for doing that relates to the organization's *raison d'être*?
3 Next we ask them to indicate the skills, knowledge, competences, qualities, and so on, that they bring to this role. We say that we assume that they must all be good at what they do, otherwise they wouldn't be in the roles that they are. Therefore they must bring to the role the ability to carry it out.
4 At this stage we ask for a few examples to put on a flip chart. We put these down on the left-hand side of a chart that we have divided by a vertical line. Examples might include business knowledge, strategic thinking, teamworking and so on.
5 We ask people to look back at what they have just written and to note down where these abilities (knowledge, skills, competences, and so on) have come from.
6 We then go back to the flip chart and ask for the answers of those who previously volunteered their abilities, and we put these alongside the previous answers.

What comes out is that pretty much everything they mention at the last stage is to do with learning. Even if they say 'experience' we can usually unpack that to show that they *learned* from their experience. And always the majority of the learning is work based, including such factors as learning from work colleagues, doing a challenging project, having a good manager who coached them, and so on.

The interesting issue here is the need to raise self awareness in people in order to make progress in developing work based learning. Goleman *et al.* (2002) suggest that self awareness is the cornerstone that supports the qualities needed in an effective leader. We can't, though, take it as a given that leaders will have this level of self awareness about their own learning. Exercises like the one above can assist the process and hence promote ideas about work based learning.

Trends

We'll mention a few trends here, some of which are helpful and some not. First, an unhelpful trend that we would like to see reversed. This is the trend to short-termism and quick fixes. Organizations used to send managers off on lengthy full-time residential programmes – in some cases up to ten weeks. This is now increasingly rare. Not that we want to defend such programmes – it's only that this change exemplifies a wider issue. People in organizations are not getting the time to learn in depth. Apprenticeships would last around five years and give a person the chance to absorb a field of activity in depth, including the values and ideals of a craft. When apprenticeship programmes were derided in the 1960s and 1970s for encouraging a 'sitting by Nellie' approach, what the critics didn't account for is that when the apprentice sat by 'Nellie' to learn what she did, they were not just learning the mechanics of the task; they were entering a 'community of practice' that needed this socialization process. They absorbed much of Nellie's work in a tacit and holistic way.

Task and job analysis and 'behavioural objectives' attempted to mechanize work practices in an atomized way. It was assumed that by learning the little bits, everything could be put together easily. Along with this, 'off-the-job learning' came to be more favoured; classroom learning was promoted by educational institutions as the main learning arena. Now none of this was, in itself, a bad thing. There were wasteful practices in apprenticeship schemes, and the classroom can supplement the work based learning. But it has to be *supplement* not *supplant*.

As this trend has gathered pace we now have training consultancies offering quick-fix lunch-time sessions that claim to create leaders through a series of one hour sessions. The UKHRD Digest is an emailed network where trainers and developers can log requests for assistance. One of the commonest requests goes along the lines of: 'Does anyone have a teambuilding/culture change/leadership exercise that is fun and can be run in half an hour?' There seems to be no end to the inventiveness of trainers to create useless fun exercises that demonstrate the blindingly obvious or trivialize important issues in organizations.

In Part 1 we pointed out the evidence quoted by Goleman *et al.* (2002) from neuroscience research that the neocortex is quick to learn facts but that ingrained habits and modes of working are learned in the limbic system. Limbic learning is slower and deeper than neocortical learning. And as they cite: 'When a limbic connection has established a neural pattern, it takes a limbic connection to revise it' (p. 104). They go on to assert that 'Because the limbic brain learns more slowly – and requires much more practice – than the neocortex, it takes more effort to strengthen an ability such as empathy than, say, to become adept at risk analysis' (pp. 104–5).

To complement the evidence from the neurosciences we can quote the work of Senge and his colleagues from the learning organization school (Senge *et al.*, 1994). They comment about the need for deep learning that happens over time and that cannot be rushed. They quote a Ford manager on one of their programmes as follows: 'If calculus were invented today, our organisation would not be able to learn it. We'd send everyone off to a three-day intensive programme. We'd then tell everyone to try to apply what they'd learned. After three to six months we'd assess whether it was working. We'd undoubtedly then conclude that this "calculus stuff" wasn't all it was made out to be and go off and look for something else to improve results' (p. 45).

What is interesting about the quote is that learning calculus is neocortical learning. So even in this domain there is need for time to learn and apply.

The mention of more intellectual (neocortical) learning leads us into the next problematic issue which is the overvaluing of such intellectual, detached learning. Many people would see work based learning as merely inefficient 'folk learning' that can be supplanted by classroom learning. A good example of this was the debacle of Long-Term Capital Management. This organization was led by detached analytical PhD holders, including university professors and two Nobel Prize winners, who thought that their models would prove unbeatable in the stock market against the old-fashioned traders. As Lowenstein (2001) commented, when the firm was at its peak 'Its intellectual supermen had apparently been able to reduce an uncertain world to rigorous cold-blooded odds – on form, they were the very best that modern finance had to offer' (p. xix).

The denouement, as described in Lowenstein's fascinating book, reveals what happened later, in one of the world's biggest financial disasters: 'Long-Term's final, cumulative loss was staggering...each invested dollar having grown to $2.85, shrank to a meagre 23 cents. In net terms, the greatest fund ever – surely the one with the highest IQs – had lost 77 per cent of its capital whilst the ordinary stock market investor had been more than doubling his money' (pp. 224–5).

Part of the problem with the over-valuing of detached analytical knowledge is a rejection of the idea of wisdom. The latter implies an experience that gives the wise person more than mere factual, analytical knowledge. That notion does not sit easily with many in educational establishments dedicated to the view that education is about detached unemotional knowledge transfer.

Here again Goleman *et al.* (2002) offer crucial evidence about one aspect of wisdom. They point out that leaders learn, from unconscious experience, what they call 'decision rules' that allow them to act almost automatically. They go on to say that:

> Whenever we face a moment in which these decision rules pertain, the brain applies them silently, coming to its wisest conclusion. Accordingly, the brain won't inform us of these judgements with words; instead, the emotional brain activates circuitry that runs from the limbic centres into the gut, giving us the compelling sense that *this feels right*. The amygdala, then, lets us know its conclusions primarily through circuitry extending into the gastrointestinal tract that, literally, creates a gut feeling. Gut feelings offer a guide when facing a complex decision that goes beyond the data at hand (p. 44).

It's clear that this gut feeling is part of what is called wisdom and is a learned attribute that comes from live experience. As the kind of research that Goleman *et al.* draw on becomes better known we ought to find that work based learning methods that encourage the growth of wisdom are more accepted. But it isn't guaranteed. (Appendix III has more on why it may be a problem.)

One author who has commented on the difficulties of getting new learning accepted is Schein (1995). He has suggested that there are two important 'anxieties' in organizations. First, there is 'Survival Anxiety'. 'It is the anxiety that unless we change, we will not meet our goals, achieve our ideals, or, at the extreme, survive at all' (p. 3). He balances this with 'Learning Anxiety' – the anxiety 'that if I let myself become a learner I will become incompetent and, at worst, lose my identity' (p. 3). He suggests that it is too crude and simplistic to imagine that, if Survival Anxiety is greater than Learning Anxiety, learning will take place. This is because high Survival Anxiety can induce defensiveness and denial. He suggests that we need to reduce Learning Anxiety instead. In this he offers one solution, namely, the creation of a parallel system within the organization that can foster new learning. Such a system might be a group of people such as a task force that has a remit to, amongst other things, create psychological safety so that people are able to lower their defences and be prepared to learn new ways of working.

Our espousal of learning groups (in the section on **Self Managed Learning**) fits the need for a structure that helps people lower their defences and open themselves to change. Effective mentoring and coaching that goes beyond the superficial 'quick fix' can also assist this process. And there are many other examples that we have explored in other parts of this handbook. The methodology is there but maybe Schein is right that new structures inside organizations would assist the use of such methodology. Boards are often enmeshed in fire fighting (despite the notion that they should be strategic) and cannot give sufficient attention to learning and development. Hence they are more likely to retreat into the tried and trusted (but inefficient) training course solutions simply because they are the most familiar.

The parallel system would ideally need to have representatives from different levels in the organization as well as different departments. It needs also to be a volunteer group of people that act as 'learning champions'. This approach was used in a financial services organization. The HRD Director sent round a note to ask who wanted to promote work based learning and she then invited them to a meeting. She was pleasantly surprised at how many people turned up and how much energy they were prepared to put into developing more of a live learning culture in the organization. We should add that when she joined the organization she had stopped all training and then waited for managers to ask for what they needed. She found that, without the crutch of a training catalogue for managers to put people onto courses, people started to look more carefully at what they actually needed. This and other actions that she initiated significantly shifted the organization towards a more balanced and cost-effective approach to learning and development.

For the future

It is dangerous to predict the future and that is certainly so in relation to work based learning. However, we can use the views of others to offer some pointers to possibilities. For instance, Susan Greenfield, the noted neuroscientist, suggested at a conference in 2002 that all the standard (explicit) knowledge we need can be captured by the new technology and all we will have to do is to wear a watch into which we can ask our questions. The watch will be connected to this knowledge source so that we can get instant access to standardized and codified information.

The implication of this notion along with other ideas about the development of technology, implies that information-giving courses could become redundant. Of course this does not mean that all courses would disappear, as the argument would be that the interaction of participants on the more attitude changing courses would still be necessary. But Greenfield's quite sober suggestion of major change in the future due to new technology is important. Already the Internet has revolutionized learning for many people.

Technological changes link to potentially immense changes in working practices. For instance, email has radically changed business communication in a relatively short space of time. What these other changes might be is hard to predict. However, we can safely predict continuing change, and therefore the need for continuing and continuous learning. Hence the notion commonly labelled 'learning how to learn' becomes more and more important. The approaches to learning that we have indicated in this handbook are part and parcel of such a 'learning to learn' framework and orientation. It also takes us back to our espousal of a more strategic approach to learning. We would re-iterate our view that just randomly using the methods that we have outlined is not being strategic. It requires all of us to look at the big picture and utilize methods that are fit for purpose.

A Declaration on Learning – A Call to Action

This appendix reproduces the 'Declaration on Learning' that was created by leading figures in the field of organizational learning. It provides a valuable backdrop to ideas and approaches covered in this handbook.

CONTENTS
- Origins of the Declaration
- The challenge
- Our assertions about the nature of learning
- The benefits of effective learning
- What certain key terms should – and should not – mean
- The signatories

Origins of the Declaration

As people who have researched and written extensively about effective learning, we came together in an experiment to see how far we could agree on statements about learning that would be of benefit to others and, in particular, help policy makers and those in leadership roles. We were excited by the common ground we discovered. We are united in the belief that learning is the core process for the positive development of individuals, organizations and society as we enter the twenty-first century.

Learning can be the most vital, engaging and enjoyable aspect of our personal and collective experience. Equally, learning can be difficult and the source of much of our pain and failure. The ability to learn about learning and to harness the learning process is the key to our ability to survive in a complex and unpredictable world.

The challenge

Learning reinforces the informed, conscious and discriminating choices that underpin democracy.

National policy makers must:

1   Make learning to learn one of the fundamental goals of education and training and reduce the excessive focus on knowledge and skills that can quickly become obsolete.

2   Support and invest in uncertificated learning as much as in certificated learning. Abandon the preoccupation with controls that inhibit learning (for example, accreditation, inspection, audit and pre-defined standards).

3   Recognize there is no such thing as a non-learner; all people are learners. The challenge is to secure the kinds, amount and pace of learning that benefits individuals, organizations and society as a whole.

4   Encourage and support the self-management of learning (for example, allowing learners to set their own goals and to choose how and when to learn to meet needs identified by themselves rather than by others).

5   Create schemes that remove financial obstacles to learning for individuals and socially disadvantaged groups.

6   Use participative democratic processes to promote inclusion and co-operation as a basis for learning.

Learning is the only source of sustainable development.

Leaders in organizations should:

1   Commit to, proclaim and celebrate continual learning as one of the organization's most valuable capabilities.

2   Include the right to learn and develop continually in all contracts of employment.

3   Build into the agreed roles of all managers the primary need to focus on encouraging others to learn and reinforce this through personal support and coaching.

4   Be a role model for learning, by doing such things as asking questions you do not know the answers to, demonstrating how you have learned from your mistakes, articulating and sharing your own learning.

5   Have effective strategies to link individual and collective learning, both within and between groups and organizations.

6   Routinely encourage curiosity, inquiry and diversity of thought as the norm to ensure dialogue about strategy and decision making at all levels.

7   Encourage people to challenge, innovate and experiment.

Learning to learn is the most fundamental learning of all.

Teachers, trainers and developers must:

1   Be role models for effective learning.

2   Support learning from live problems and experience, as a central activity of work.

3   Encourage and support reflection.

4   Encourage *everyone* to have learning goals and development plans.

5   Respond to both the complexity of situations and the diversity of learners and avoid simplistic solutions that fail to create worthwhile learning.

6   Ensure everyone has the opportunity to learn how to learn effectively and to exploit the full range of opportunities available to them every day.

7   Support people through the discomfort and uncertainty sometimes associated with learning (for example, through mentoring, support groups and networks).

8   Invest time and effort in bringing people together to learn from each other.

9   Empower others to take responsibility for, and to manage, their own learning. Stop defining for others what they need and how those needs should be met.

Learning is the key to developing your identity and your potential.

As an individual learner you should:

1   Take responsibility for yourself as a learner – both in terms of what you seek to learn, and how – by setting your own learning goals, actively seeking the conditions or experiences that will help to achieve the goals, making demands on the system, refusing to tolerate obstacles to effective learning.
2   Make your learning (both in terms of goals and the means to achieve the goals) as conscious, self-disciplined and explicit as possible. Routinely review whether you are making progress towards your learning goals.
3   Share your learning with others as an investment with a high return in terms of personal learning.
4   Learn to exploit everyday experiences as learning opportunities – experiment, try out alternatives, ask others, invite challenge.
5   Learn with and through others as a prime vehicle for learning.
6   Explore and consciously exploit the wide range of resources for learning (for example, the Internet, coaches, mentors and colleagues).
7   Always seek and learn from feedback as well as inquiry.

Our assertions about the nature of learning

Learning is frequently associated with formal teaching and training which, too often, comes to be seen as irrelevant to daily life and work. Most learning takes place outside controlled classroom environments and this needs to be recognized – especially by educators and governments. It is unhelpful to link learning solely to the achievement of qualifications where systems of accreditation are often assumed to represent the totality of a person's learning and can result in unfair discriminatory practices and mere tests of short-term memory.

The critical task for government policy makers and leaders in organizations is to maximize the learning ability of people by encouraging and supporting individual and collective learning. In this way organizations, communities and societies can change and adapt more effectively.

Learning can be looked upon as a *process*, for example reflecting and questioning (which can be made more effective through consciously learning to learn), or an *outcome* (which may or may not be planned).

1   Learning is not just about knowledge. It is also about skills, insights, beliefs, values, attitudes, habits, feelings, wisdom, shared understandings and self-awareness.
2   Learning outcomes can be incremental (building gradually on what has already been learned) or transformational (changing ways of being, thinking, feeling and acting).

3 Transformational learning may be a struggle, take time and involve conflict over aims and outcomes.
4 By its very nature, learning is essentially individual but can also be collectively generated in groups and organizations.
5 There is no one right way to learn for everybody and for every situation.
6 We can learn from any experience – failure, success, having our expectations confirmed or having them confounded.
7 Learning processes can be conscious (which helps us exercise our control over the process) or unconscious and serendipitous.
8 Learning processes can be both planned and opportunistic. Combining the strengths of both can enhance learning effectiveness.
9 Learning outcomes can be desirable or undesirable for the learner and for others – therefore, learning always has a moral dimension.
10 Learning (both as a process and an outcome) can be both a cause of change and a consequence of change. There is no learning without change, though there can be change with insufficient learning.
11 Questioning, listening, challenging, enquiring and taking action are crucial to effective learning.
12 The learning process occurs inside the person, but making the outcomes explicit, and sharing them with others, adds value to the learning.
13 When self-managed, learning becomes more effective.
14 Learning as a process can be subject to obstacles (for example, social exclusion, lack of resources or confidence) but the desire and ability to learn is hard to suppress.
15 Wanting to learn, and seeing the point of learning, is often crucial and makes it more likely that unexpected opportunities to learn will be exploited.
16 Mood influences the quality of learning. While not a prerequisite, enjoyment of the learning process is a significant enabler.

The benefits of effective learning

The following benefits assume that the learning in question is morally acceptable in intent, process and outcome. (This of course leaves open the question of whose morality.)

For society:

1 Society, and the communities of which it is comprised, survives, adapts and thrives through developing and sharing learning.
2 A focus on articulating, valuing and sharing learning contributes to a more cohesive society where everyone's contribution is valued.
3 Individual and collective learning reinforces the informed, conscious and discriminating choices that underpin democracy.
4 Learning has the potential to create a society where diversity is valued and everyone can lead more fulfilled lives.
5 Learning (as distinct from education) helps people become active citizens in a constantly changing world.

For organizations:

1   Regular and rigorous use of learning processes increases everyone's capacity to contribute to the success of an organization by challenging, reshaping and meeting its goals.
2   Learning from and with all stakeholders enhances and helps clarify purpose, vision, values and behaviour.
3   A focus on learning, planned and unplanned, produces a wide range of solutions to organizational issues.
4   Learning helps achieve a balance between the pressures of long-term effectiveness and short-term efficiency.
5   Learning enables an organization to balance the demands of its stakeholders and its environment.
6   Learning, when shared, reduces the likelihood of repeated mistakes.

For individuals:

1   Learning is the key to developing our identity and our potential.
2   Learning to learn is the key to effective learning.
3   Learning enables us to meet the demands of change.
4   The capacity to learn is an asset which never becomes obsolete.
5   Embracing learning helps us to understand that learning is a great deal more than just formal education and training.
6   Learning increases the range of our options. Learning about our past can help us understand the present and prepare for the future.
7   Learning expands the horizons of who we are and what we can become.
8   The continuing desire to learn fuels curiosity and progress, and restrains prejudice and parochialism.

What certain key terms should – and should not – mean

Term	Should be	Should not be
Lifelong learning	A learning approach to all life and work experience, using formal education and training as a last resort.	Ongoing compulsory formal learning events and monitoring against competency requirements.
Open learning	User-friendly learning opportunities minimizing constraints of time, place, cost, access, content and process.	Repackaged and recycled correspondence and distance learning packages.
Learning society	A society in which individual and collective natural learning is a way of life and a major dynamic	A monopolistic take-over by the institutionalized education and training industry.

	in social processes, encouraged and supported by formal education and training provision.	
Learning organization	An organization which promotes learning and sharing, supported by values, processes and investment, to enhance its capacity to create its own future.	An organization that regards training as the only legitimate mode of learning.
Self and personal development	A liberating and emancipating process for individuals as employees and citizens.	Self-subjugation, discipline and enforcement of conformity to corporate and state norms.

The signatories

We never set out to say all there is to say on the subject of learning, or to impose our views on others. Rather, we point to the richness and diversity of approaches to learning as an indication of its potential to achieve desirable transformations. Our goals are to stimulate discussion about the importance of learning and to resist the encroachment of narrow, dogmatic approaches that limit learning, in whatever context they occur.

This declaration reflects the thinking of us all and our passion about the importance of learning. We offer it as a basis for dialogue and action.

Margaret Attwood
Tom Boydell
John Burgoyne
David Clutterbuck
Ian Cunningham
Bob Garratt
Peter Honey

Andrew Mayo
David Megginson
Alan Mumford
Michael Pearn
Mike Pedler
Robin Wood

A Work Based Model for Gaining Qualifications

This appendix outlines the approach adopted by one university to provide work based learning qualifications. It is not reproduced here as an ideal model – it is just the largest scheme in operation in the UK. The description below has been provided for us by the university concerned.

The National Centre for Work Based Learning Partnerships at Middlesex University

PARTNERSHIP

Partnerships with a range of organizations make use of the university's well-established facility for the accreditation of in-house courses, and recognition of professional qualifications. This facility enables employees' existing training and professional experience to be converted into academic credit, and can be topped up to Bachelors degree, postgraduate diploma or Masters degree level through the development and conduct of work based project activities. These activities are agreed between the organization, employee and university and are a means to develop:

- individual employees – by making them more effective work based learners and providing them with the opportunity to gain academic qualifications;
- the organization – through the creation of new knowledge and the application of learning to achieve corporate objectives.

Examples of partnerships

Since 1993, the National Centre for Work Based Learning Partnerships has developed partnerships with organizations in both the private and public sector. For example, the in-house management development programmes of Bovis and Marks & Spencer have been accredited at postgraduate level by Middlesex University and as a route to Masters degree. As a result of the partnership with the Corporation of London, work required of employees in the achievement of 'Best Value' can be used as the focal point of individually negotiated work based learning programmes. The project-based focus of the work based learning programmes makes the approach particularly attractive to the self-employed and to small enterprises.

ACCREDITATION

Accreditation is the process of assigning value to learning in terms of a number of academic credit points (a measure of quantity of learning achievement) and Higher Education level (a measure of complexity of learning achievement). The use of academic credit points and levels facilitates the recognition of learning from other sources (for example, from training courses and experience) as it can be evaluated and the result expressed in the common currency of academic credit. It also facilitates recognition and transfer of qualifications or parts of qualifications not only between UK universities, but also increasingly within the European Union and the USA.

The main forms accreditation takes are as follows:

- In-house company programmes – a member of the university staff works with the organization to map the learning outcomes of company courses onto the requirements for academic achievement at undergraduate or postgraduate level. A credit rating for the company programme may thus be achieved.
- Professional qualifications which do not already have a nationally recognized academic credit rating can be considered for accreditation by Middlesex University.
- Academic qualifications, such as DMS or postgraduate diploma, carry nationally recognized academic credit ratings.
- The learning achieved on-the-job by experienced practitioners can be accredited by Middlesex University.

It is possible to import credit from each of these sources into a work based learning programme leading to an undergraduate or postgraduate qualification.

Work based learning routes to higher education qualifications

QUALIFICATIONS AT DIFFERENT LEVELS

The full range of university undergraduate and postgraduate qualifications are available via Middlesex University's work based programme, all of which can incorporate accredited learning from the other sources described above. Qualifications require academic credit at one or more levels:

- Level 1: characterized by knowledge and straightforward comprehension.
- Level 2: characterized by application of knowledge and comprehension.
- Level 3: characterized by high level analysis and synthesis.
- Level 4: characterized by self-directed research and development, depth of understanding and the creation and articulation of knowledge of significance to others.

Examples of qualifications incorporating these levels are:

- Certificate of Higher Education – a 120 credit point qualification at Level 1.
- Diploma of Higher Education – a 240 point qualification, including at least 100 points at Level 2.

- Honours Degree (BA Hons or BSc Hons) – a 360 credit point qualification including at least 120 points at Level 3 and a further 100 at Level 2.
- Postgraduate Diploma – a 120 point qualification including at least 80 points at Level 4.
- Masters Degree (MA or MSc) – a 180 point qualification including at least 120 points at Level 4.

Work based learning and NVQs

The work based learning approach also relates well to National Vocational Qualifications (NVQs) by:

- Increasing awareness and ability to assemble portfolios of learning achievement (good basis for all levels of NVQ);
- Producing project evidence which can be collected within an NVQ portfolio (particularly relevant for NVQ at NVQ Levels 4 and 5);
- Providing progression from NVQs into the university qualification framework (particularly relevant for NVQ Level 3 [progression to Higher Education Level 1], NVQ Level 4 [progression to Higher Education Level 2/3] and NVQ Level 5 [progression to Higher Education Level 3/4]).

Progression through a work based learning programme

The flow chart shown in Figure A.1 shows how individuals in a range of contexts might gain a work based academic qualification. Time scales are indicative only (for part-time students) and may be negotiated:

Stage 1:

- Where a large organization has gained accreditation of an in-house graduate development programme, a new graduate can import credit from this into a work based learning programme leading to a postgraduate qualification.
- Other employees in either large or smaller organizations may already have professional qualifications. Depending on the academic level of these, they may use credit from them towards an under or postgraduate qualification.
- Experienced practitioners may well have achieved considerable on-the-job learning. They have the opportunity to claim academic credit for this and put credit gained towards an undergraduate or postgraduate qualification.
- Many individuals may also be in a position to identify particular projects on which they must work, for example, to meet departmental objectives or to forward a particular aspect of a small business. These too may form the basis of an accreditation claim.
- The development of a comprehensive accreditation claim, including learning from experience, typically takes three months.

Stage 2:

- At the programme planning stage, the individual creates a learning agreement in negotiation with his/her employer and the university. A case for the coherence of the programme as a whole (including any accredited learning) must be made and a

Stage 1

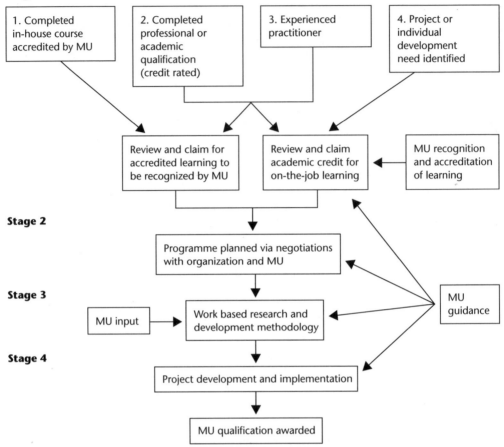

Figure A.1   Flow chart showing a sample of four work based learning routes to academic qualifications

proposal drawn up for the work based project activity with which the programme will conclude. Employer involvement is critical in order to inform and confirm the work based relevance of the proposed project(s).

Stage 3:

• University support and guidance is offered at each stage of the programme, but there is particular input on work based research and development methods to provide structure and strategy to underpin project activity. This stage focuses on enhancing project design, implementation, evaluation and dissemination.
• Stages 2 and 3 are typically done in the same three month period.

Stage 4:

- The work based project(s) may differ widely in content (depending on organizational and personal need), but they always have the same general outcomes. They use, develop and demonstrate the skills and knowledge of those who undertake them and they enhance the systems, product and performance of the organization in which they take place.
- Projects typically take 3–6 months.

Examples

Below are some examples of work based programmes and projects undertaken by real students (anonymized).

AN EXAMPLE OF A MASTERS PROGRAMME INCLUDING ACCREDITED LEARNING

The table below shows how the 180 credits needed for a Masters degree qualification were achieved in a programme which incorporates accredited learning from in-company courses and experiential learning.

Title: MA Work Based Learning Studies (Project management)

	Module	Level 4 credit
Stage 1: Claim for academic credit from existing learning	Accredited learning from in-house management development programme:	
	• Presentation skills	5
	• Customer focus	15
	• Commercial awareness	10
	• Health, safety and environment	10
	Claim for academic credit from on-the-job learning:	
	• Project management	20
	• Team leadership	10
	• Business development	10
	• Budget management	10
Stage 2: Programme planning	Programme planning	10
Stage 3: Work based research and development methodology	Work based research methods	20
Stage 4: Project development and implementation	Work based project	60
Total credit		180

AN EXAMPLE OF A MASTERS LEVEL WORK BASED PROJECT

Title: 'Delivering community development and training in a borough council – a framework for the millennium'.

Summary: The project reviews existing community training and development provision within a borough council and explores options for alternative models. It is based on the premise that current operation is not compatible with the future strategic needs of the organization, especially in the light of recent political directives (Best Value in particular). The project recommends preferred options for future provision as well as strategies for continual review of this service. These comprise implications for council-wide practice as well as arrangements adopted for partnerships with other client bodies. The project required full collaboration with key stakeholders in the organization and the primary research methodology was participative Action Research, yielding a combination of qualitative and quantitative data.

EXAMPLES OF TITLES OF WORK BASED PROJECTS FROM A RANGE OF FIELDS

Field–Vehicle Entrapment Training:
A combination of survey and action research approaches to identify a 'standard entrapment' scenario and thus improve rescue training.

Field–Curriculum Development:
A combination of action research and documentary analysis to produce a work based model for curriculum innovation.

Field–Engineering Management:
An action research approach to produce a research-based proposal for the regeneration of an engineering plant.

Field–Small Business Survival:
A combination of case study and literature survey to identify factors relating to small business survival.

Field–Medical Centre Management:
A group project drawing upon individual experience, expertise and literature search to produce a training package for medical centre managers.

Field–Design and Build:
A combination of case study and literature search to identify the potential advantages for a major construction company of design and build projects.

Why Isn't Work Based Learning More Supported?

Colin Coulson-Thomas conducted a significant two-year research project on training and development in organizations. In a perceptive article he summarized some of his findings as follows:

> Many trainers appear to 'follow fads'. They buy 'off the shelf' learning resource packs, rather than assemble or create bespoke responses to specific situations and circumstances. They persuade senior management that all members of staff should receive some standard programme, regardless of individual interests and needs. Enormous sums of money are therefore spent exposing diverse people, working on very different activities, to common experiences that may have little relevance to their particular requirements and priorities (Coulson-Thomas, 2001, p. 28).

In addition to this evidence, the Confederation of British Industry has suggested that over £2 billion of the UK's annual spend on training is wasted. Others have suggested higher figures than this. And the Detterman and Sternberg (1993) research suggests that perhaps only about 10 per cent of training actually transfers to the workplace.

Some facts to add

1   The National Health Service (NHS) in the UK invests over £2.5 billion per annum on education and training (Department of Health, 2001).
2   The research conducted by ourselves, along with that from the universities of Hull, Lancaster and Sussex, confirms that most learning related to organizational performance occurs outside education and training activity (Cunningham, 1999; Cunningham, Bennett and Dawes, 2000). Indeed it seems that there is an 80:20 rule operating here, that is, at most 20 per cent of effective, useful learning occurs in formal (education/training) settings and at least 80 per cent in so-called 'informal' settings. (We are using here the UK government's language as evidenced in reports such as the Department of Health [2001] and the Cabinet Office Performance and Innovation Unit 2001.)

A question. If these facts are correct (and indeed there is no evidence that we know of that would challenge them), then is the ratio of spending in the NHS reflecting the importance of informal (work based) learning? That is, is the investment by the NHS in work based learning in excess of £12 billion per annum? It is difficult to calculate the investment in informal (work based) learning, but we'd be very surprised if it came anywhere near this. And we still have to address the evidence analysed by Coulson-Thomas (2001) and others about the wasted investment in formal training.

So we may need to consider if investment in learning, not just in the NHS but also in most other organizations, is allocated wisely. And if not, why not. In order to do this we need to step back a bit and consider why formal education and training has such a hold and why work based methods are relatively neglected. These other methods would include those recognized in the Department of Health report (2002) mentioned earlier, namely 'coaching on the job, mentorship, learning sets, job rotation, secondments, project work, sabbaticals' (p. 14). If we take a more strategic view of development approaches we could include Action Learning, Self Managed Learning and Learning Organization strategies in this category.

Action learning as a case

The approach we will use as a case is action learning. This approach has a long pedigree, dating back over more than half a century. Reg Revans has been able to show considerable pay-off for organizations from action learning.[1] Let us take a highly rated action learning programme, namely, the GEC 'Developing Senior Managers Programme', which ran in the early 1970s. Some facts about this programme include:

1   It was personally backed by the MD, Arnold Weinstock, who at that time was winning polls as the UK's number one business leader.
2   GEC itself was a large, highly profitable company with an excellent reputation.
3   The programme successfully developed future managing directors for GEC companies.
4   The programme was carefully evaluated and shown to be cost effective.
5   The book about the programme (Casey and Pearce, 1977) sold well and was highly praised in book reviews and so on.

Yet, the long-term impact of all this on other organizations has been small compared with the investment in standard management training courses. There are successful action learning programmes but they are only a tiny part of the UK investment in management development.

The case of action learning can be replicated with other development approaches that do not fit the bog-standard training model. And we should emphasize here that this is not an anti-training diatribe. Training activity that is part of an overall organizational strategy has its place. But the Declaration on Learning (see Appendix I) does say that, for instance, lifelong learning should be seen as 'a learning approach to all life and work experience, using formal education and training as a last resort'. It also says that lifelong learning should not mean 'ongoing compulsory formal learning events and monitoring against competency requirements'.

Why is there a problem?

Cialdini (2001) offers a range of reasons why people are influenced to behave in the ways that they do. We believe that his research throws some light on why some of the most effective learning approaches are the least used. We will quote a few of his examples that seem to fit the situation we face here.

CONSISTENCY

Most people like to feel that they are consistent in their behaviour. There is a tendency for many people to want to fit what they do into a pattern, even if it may not seem rational. Cialdini quotes many research studies to demonstrate this. For instance, people betting on a horse are more likely to feel confident that the horse will win after they have placed their bet than before. Now the chances of the horse winning have not changed, so this change of attitude does not appear to be rational. However, as Cialdini points out: 'Once we make a choice or take a stand, we will encounter personal and interpersonal pressures to behave consistently with that commitment' (p. 53).

Another piece of research he quotes is where people in a smart residential neighbourhood were asked, by a supposed volunteer worker (actually a researcher), if they would allow the installation of a huge billboard saying 'DRIVE CAREFULLY' in their front gardens. Only 17 per cent of people agreed.

The researchers used a different tactic in another neighbourhood. A supposed volunteer worker went round and asked people if they would display a three-inch square sign 'BE A SAFE DRIVER' in their windows. Nearly everyone agreed. Then two weeks later a different volunteer worker went round and made the same request about the huge billboard saying 'DRIVE CAREFULLY'. This time 76 per cent of people agreed. Cialdini's interpretation is that people wished to be consistent in their views and therefore felt obligated to act on them. People had identified themselves as in favour of safe driving and therefore acted on the basis of their self concept.

What's the relevance in our field? We'd suggest that many trainers' self concept is of being a classroom-based operator, someone who knows more than the learners, who has a right and a duty to tell them what they should learn, and who would feel inconsistent in deviating from that. Similarly for managers, when they have been on training courses themselves (even if they have found them of limited use) they can feel obliged to maintain a consistent stance and so to support the use of courses that are of limited value.

SOCIAL PROOF

Cialdini quotes a sales and motivation consultant who suggests that 'Since 95% of people are imitators and only 5% are initiators, people are persuaded more by the actions of others than by any proof we can offer' (p. 101). Hence the action learning case (and the case that can be made against other approaches that seem different from a standard training course) – 'if most people are investing most of their development spend on training, that's what must be done – irrespective of any evidence that other approaches are more cost effective.'

Cialdini's principle of social proof states that: 'The greater the number of people who find any idea correct, the more a given individual will perceive the idea to be correct' (pp. 110–11). He cites many examples from advertising which rely on this principle, for example, 'best selling brand', 'fastest growing'. He suggests that the influence process is more marked where people perceive that others similar to themselves behave in particular ways. He analyses, for instance, cults such as Jonestown where hundreds of seemingly intelligent people committed suicide. This he puts down to copycat behaviour – 'if others who believe as I do are doing this then this must be the right thing to do.'

He also has startling statistics showing that after a well-publicized suicide there follows a significant rise in suicides, in that geographical area, from people who feel themselves to be in the same circumstances as the person who has died.

In our field, if a person identifies with colleagues who are working in a particular way, they are more likely to copy that behaviour, even if there is evidence that there are better ways of doing things. (Note that we are here only talking in generalities. It is evident that some people will not be influenced by the approaches that we have discussed and the ones that follow.)

POSITIVE ASSOCIATION

A positive association with a product helps to sell it. Hence the use by advertisers of endorsements by famous people such as sports stars. More interesting is the evidence of associations that are less obvious. One piece of research (Cialdini, 2001) compared male responses to advertisements for a car. One advertisement showed the car with a seductive female model in front of it and the other showed just the car. Male respondents shown the advertisement with the model rated the car more highly than the second group (shown the same car but without the model), yet denied that the model had had any influence on their views.

In our field the same technique is used to sell MBAs by mentioning important managers who have taken an MBA. The fact that there are many successful managers without MBAs is ignored. Also there are many MBA holders who have proved unsuccessful. Research carried out at INSEAD showed that, while many of their MBA holders ended up in top jobs, this was more to do with family connections than the possession of an MBA. This research is, of course, ignored by business schools.

AUTHORITY

Most people are heavily influenced by authority figures: the famous Milgram (1974) experiment is one exemplar of this phenomenon.[2]

In another research study in a hospital setting, Cialdini (2001) shows how just the assertion of a position of authority can influence behaviour in quite startling ways. A researcher pretended to be a physician and phoned twenty-two separate nurse stations in a US hospital. He identified himself as a consultant and directed the answering nurse to give a potentially dangerous dose of a drug to a specific patient. In 95 per cent of cases the nurse went straight to the medicine cabinet and was prepared to administer the drug even though a) it was against hospital policy for prescriptions to be transmitted by phone; b) this particular medication was unauthorized; c) the dosage suggested was obviously dangerous; and d) the instruction was given by a man she had never met or even talked to on the phone before. The interpretation is that just the assertion of a position of authority is enough to make many seemingly intelligent people act in ways that they would not normally.

In another piece of research, Peters and Ceci (1982) took twelve articles that had been published 18 to 32 months earlier by authors from prestigious universities. They re-submitted the same articles to the same journals, only this time they put on them invented names of authors from the unknown 'Tri-Valley Centre for Human Potential'. Nine of the articles went through the review process undetected and eight were rejected, even though the very same journal had previously published the article (but with the names of prestigious authors from prestigious universities).

In the development field there are many assertions of authority used. One comes from government sources. For instance, as we have mentioned, the UK government asserts that a person not using formal education or training is a non-learner. This assertion is clearly wrong, since in the same document the place of 'informal (work based) learning' is accepted. If informal learning exists then the assertion that anyone not on a formal course is not learning is clearly nonsensical. However, it suits the UK government and the education and training establishment to mislead the public.

In organizations the assertion of authority (for example, by senior managers) can be used to compel people to go on courses even if they don't see the value of them. In some cases managers use the instruction to go on a course as a let out to avoid them having to take responsibility for assisting their staff to develop. It is just a whole lot harder for the manager to provide work based learning (such as coaching) than to send someone off on a course.

Trainers can also use their authority, especially with junior staff, in order to bolster their own position. Part of the hidden curriculum of the course environment is to engender in people the notion that this setting is the prime place for important learning. As Vail (1996) comments, on what he calls 'the institutional learning model':

> The institutional learning model, to retain its power, needs to remain tacit in the learner's mind. It makes a lot of assumptions about what is good for the learner that a learner might well object to or want to renegotiate if given the opportunity. The institutional learning model is built in part on an implicit belief that learners should not bother with philosophical considerations about that model (p. 84).

Other evidence

In addition to the issues that Cialdini analyses, we can offer a few more examples of likely problems.

1   Is it possible that some of those who hold positions of power do not actually want people to learn in significant ways? Learning is a process that produces change. For some senior managers, the idea that 'their people' might change can be quite threatening. Hence they have a personal investment in sending people on ritualistic courses that people can enjoy but that will not produce major change. In the process they can be seen as 'good guys' as they appear to 'invest in people'.

2   Is the impact of branding too great? Just as there was the famous mantra that 'no one ever got fired through buying IBM' it seems that, for trainers and HR people the equivalent syndrome is 'no one ever got fired for sending managers to Harvard Business School (or any other prestigious business school)'. People and organizations promoting approaches that do not fit the standard model don't have the same brand cachet. And to suggest learning through work or other 'informal approaches' can seem pretty sloppy in comparison.

3   Are people too concerned to massage their CVs? The problem is linked to the one above. A person may choose to go on a course in order to add it to their CV and not because they have a serious desire to learn. Unfortunately there are still many recruiters who are fooled by this ploy. They take at face value a proffered CV when, for all they know, the person may have slept through all the impressive courses that they have attended. The difficulty for those who don't play this game is that their work based learning may not be recognized by inept recruiters so there is continued pressure to play the inflationary CV massaging game.

4   Do trainers and academics lack the confidence to learn new ways of working? Are they too wedded to the kinds of 'command and control' methods that they criticize? The classroom environment can seem very safe compared with taking on, say, mentoring or coaching responsibilities. The latter roles have to be responsive to what the learner raises and hence are less under the control of the 'trainer'. Is there an important fear factor at work here? Collins (1999) certainly suggests that desire for control by academics gets in the way of learning innovations in business schools. He commented on a small innovation to give students more say in class and reported a fellow professor as saying: 'I can't imagine doing that. I mean, you never know what might happen. I could never give up that much control in my classroom' (p. 74).

5   Is just plain and simple ignorance a major factor? Are people in positions of power just ignorant of how learning happens and of the research evidence? We suspect that this is true for a very large number of managers. And, given that their HR and training people don't help them to understand the issues, it might be a forgivable error on the part of managers. But the fact that HR and training people are ignorant of these issues cannot be forgivable – it's just plain professional incompetence. But perhaps professional competence is not high in this area. An article in the *Sunday Times* (Eglin, 27 January 2002) quoted research conducted by Adrian Furnham and Strategic Dimensions where they claim that many HR professionals are poorly equipped to do their jobs.

6   Is some supposed training just rest and recreation ('R and R'), as the Americans call it? Is it perhaps reasonable to give people a break from work in pleasant surroundings and not actually care about whether they learn anything useful? Maybe. But it's frustrating if you aren't alerted to this when you are presenting to such groups. One of us recently addressed a conference held at a hotel adjacent to a famous golf course. It was clear that people were there mainly to play golf and the conference was organized as an excuse for people to be there. We just wish the organizers had told us this instead of pretending that it was a serious learning event.

7   Do organizations feel that they have to put everyone through particular courses in order to cover their backs? It seems that many public sector bodies compel people to attend courses in areas such as sexual harassment, racism and bullying in order to defend themselves against any potential legal or other action. The downside of this is that the course can have the opposite effect to what is intended. Much of the anti-racism training of the 1980s gained a poor reputation and induced cynicism in many people, rather than producing active efforts to combat racism. Lee Jasper, the Race Adviser to the Mayor of London, commented: 'For the last 20 years the government has spent millions of pounds on race-awareness training, anti-racism training and anti-discriminatory training... Massive effort and expenditure and ranks of consultants and expert race trainers have failed to change the organisation culture of the police' (2002, p. 31). Indeed it's clear that work based approaches such as coaching and learning

groups are much more effective in getting people to address these serious issues. However, such methods are more difficult to implement than putting on standardized mechanistic courses.

8   Do trainers sometimes get too much of an ego boost from conducting or organizing entertaining training sessions such that they lose sight of the need to assist people to learn? Happiness sheets have a lot to answer for. There is little evidence that such supposed evaluations have much actual value. We remember interviewing senior managers who had attended an extremely prestigious course, which included lectures from well-known people, a visit to Brussels to meet senior EU officials, grand dinners with CEOs of major companies, and so on. When we asked them what they had liked and disliked about the course, they all said that the aspects mentioned above were the ones that they liked best at the time. The session they had most disliked was a one-day workshop on coaching. When we quizzed them about what they had applied back at work, implementing what they learned on the coaching workshop was the most mentioned item.

Conclusion

Education and training have a role in helping people to learn. People do go off on courses and learn things of use to them and their organizations. We have no desire to dismiss what the UK government and others label as 'formal learning'. However, we do object to this language, as the implication is that so-called informal or work based learning is of a lower status (remember the idea of non-learners). What would be useful is if there was recognition that education and training have a minor (but important) role to play – and that if they are to play that role effectively we need an over-arching strategy for learning which encompasses approaches with a proven track record.

One way of reading our analysis is to take a pessimistic view of the likelihood of changing the situation. If Cialdini is right that only 5 per cent of people are initiators then maybe it's only these that will recognize the need to take a more rational, evidence-based approach. One piece of evidence that supports Cialdini is from Warren Buffett. Here is one of the world's richest men (and the most successful investor in history) saying that he makes his money by not following the crowd. The dot.com mess is a good example. As Buffett says, why buy shares when they are overpriced and shun them when they are under priced. The answer for the majority of less successful investors is in the herd instinct that Cialdini says is linked to some of the factors above.

One hopeful sign that Cialdini underestimates is that there are people who aren't influenced by the techniques that he exposes. For instance Hampden-Turner (1971) re-examined Milgram's (1974) research and found that the people most susceptible to influence were the traditional authoritarian personalities (both on the political right and left). There was a significant minority who refused to obey and they were people of a more libertarian stance – the kind of people in organizations who are genuine supporters of empowerment policies and practices.

So all is not lost. This could be especially relevant if we take the example of Warren Buffett. Poor (follow-the-herd) investors may go bust or lose their jobs, so there may be a possible Darwinian effect here – survival of the fittest. Applied to the organizational world we have the example of companies like Semco in Brazil that buck the trend and become successful. To revert to the GEC example, it prospered under the leadership of Arnold Weinstock when other companies didn't. We are not suggesting that, on its own, action learning was responsible for that. Our contention would be that the same attitude in Weinstock not to follow the herd (and not to be swayed by ill-informed journalists) was involved in other business decisions and that collectively these decisions encouraged GEC's financial success.

The positive possibility, then, is that if companies take more rational business decisions about development, they may succeed in the long run and hence we may find a swing towards a more balanced approach. (But then look at what happened when Weinstock left GEC and his successors did follow the crowd!) Also we are reminded of Keynes' remark that in the long run we are all dead. Markets don't operate efficiently. Poor performers in the City can survive because of the herd. We may not have so much of the old school tie syndrome today, but it's apparent that people at the top of organizations support each other. The cross-membership on board remuneration committees ensures that directors' rewards are more often than not disconnected from performance.

Furthermore, the difficulty is that a Darwinian model does not apply to the public sector. The government can continue to use its muscle to fund approaches that fit its own agenda and undermine investment in cost-effective development approaches. This has been happening in the education sector and it's difficult to see how the rigidities of the National Curriculum, school league tables and excessive testing can be counteracted.

Notes

1. The International Foundation for Action Learning has a large library of materials (over 1000 articles and books) that amply justify Revans' assertions about the value of action learning. (Contact t.e.webber@btn.ac.uk or p.wright@lancaster.ac.uk)
2. The following is a rather simplified version of the research on obedience to authority, conducted by Stanley Milgram: Milgram (1974) wanted to see how obedient people would be to authority figures. He asked for volunteers for an experiment which was ostensibly about learning and memory. Those who came forward were told that there would be a person in the next room who was being tested on their learning and memory. If the person (learner) made a mistake, the volunteer was to press a switch to deliver an electric shock to the learner. The learner was given tasks to do during which he did actually make mistakes. As the learner progressively made mistakes, the volunteer was instructed to increase the intensity of the electric shocks until they were apparently in the dangerous area.

    The 'learner' was actually part of the research team and no real electric shocks were delivered. However, the volunteers did not know this. They were instructed by a researcher (in a white lab coat) to keep on increasing the level of 'pain' until the learner was shouting out, apparently in severe distress. Most volunteers were prepared to administer what they thought were dangerous levels of electric shocks, just because the researcher told them to do it.

Bibliography

Adult Learning Inspectorate – Annual Reports – published at ww.ali.gov.uk. The 2002 report contains criticisms of work based training.

Aley, J. (2002), 'Software doesn't work. Customers are in revolt. Here's the plan', *Fortune*, 25 November, pp. 63–9. A penetrating article on the follies of simplistic IT decisions.

Area Protection Committees (June 2002), 'Learning from past experience – a review of Serious Case Reviews', Department of Health (www.doh.gov.uk/acpc/learning.htm). An example of learning at the organizational level.

Argyris, C. (1980), 'Double Loop Learning in Organisations' reprinted in Kolb, D.A., Rubin, I.M. and McIntyre, J.M. (eds) *Organizational Psychology: Readings on Human Behaviour in Organizations*, London: Prentice Hall. This paper is also reprinted in other collections.

Argyris, C. (1990), *Overcoming Organisational Defences: Facilitating Organisational Learning*, Boston: Allyn & Bacon. One of his best books – since he has tended to write about the same issues in a number of books, others of his works are likely to cover similar ground.

Argyris, C. and Schön, D. (1974), *Theory in Practice*, San Francisco: Jossey-Bass. A classic text on learning – not easy going.

Baker, W. (2000), *Achieving Success Through Social Capital*, San Francisco: Jossey-Bass. Baker has produced a 'pop' text on the subject, but he does have some interesting practical exercises on subjects such as networking.

Bateson, G. (1973), *Steps to an Ecology of Mind*, London: Paladin. Brilliant on learning and performance but very hard going if you are not used to his abstract style.

Beard, P.R.J. (1992), *The Reality Behind the Myth: The MBA Experience*, London: The Association of MBAs. Interesting research on MBA holders and their views about learning.

Belbin, R.M. (2001), *Managing Without Power*. Oxford: Butterworth Heinemann. Belbin raises some interesting, and controversial, ideas in this text. He also updates his well-known team roles – and some may find that helpful in thinking about team performance.

Bell, E., Taylor, S. and Thorpe, R. (2002), 'A step in the right direction? Investors in People and the Learning Organisation', *British Journal of Management*, vol. 13, pp. 161–71. This is a useful research paper which provides real evidence of the problems of IiP.

Brown, J.S. and Duguid, P. (1991), 'Organizational learning and communities-of-practice', *Organization Science*, vol. 2, no. 1, pp. 40–57, February. These are two of the important writers on communities of practice.

Burgoyne, J. and Reynolds, M. (eds) (1997), *Management Learning*, London: Sage. This is a relatively academic collection, but there is useful material on managerial learning related to performance.

Campaign for Learning (2002), *An Introduction to Our Work, The Learner* (The Annual Report of the Campaign) p. 2. This page has a definition of learning.

Casey, D. and Pearce, D. (1977), *More than Management Development: Action Learning at GEC*, Aldershot, Hants: Gower. Still a useful text on a case of the use of action learning.

Chambers, E.G., Foulon, M., Handfield-Jones, H., Hankin, S.M. and Michaels, E.G. (1998), 'The war for talent', *The McKinsey Quarterly*, no. 3, pp. 44–57. This is the classic article. Since then there have been other McKinsey pieces on this topic but the original gives you the flavour of the argument.

Chartered Institute of Personnel and Development (2002), *Who Learns at Work?* London: CIPD, February. A very useful survey of the attitudes of learners.

Chartered Institute of Personnel and Development (2002), Training and Development Report, London: CIPD. Useful material on costing.

Chief Medical Officer (2000), *An Organisation with a Memory*, London: Department of Health. An excellent report on the systemic issues of learning in modern organizations. Not just relevant to the health service.

Cialdini, R. (2001), *Influence: Science and Practice*, Boston: Allyn and Bacon. This is a general text on why people are influenced to do what they do. It has relevance in explaining some of the social factors that inhibit the transfer of learning.

Cohen, D. and Prusak, L. (2001), *In Good Company*, Cambridge, Mass.: Harvard Business School Press. A 'pop' text on social capital. Worth looking at the introduction, for definitions, and so on. The rest of the book may be of lesser interest.

Coleman, J. (1988), 'Social capital in the creation of human capital', *American Journal of Sociology*, vol. 94, pp. 95–120. A classic text on social capital – but his work is summarized in books referenced here.

Collins, J. (1999), 'Turning goals into results', *Harvard Business Review*, July–August, pp. 71–82. A good article on a range of issues that has some good comments about real empowerment.

Coulson-Thomas, C. (2001), 'Entrepreneurship for organisational success', *Journal of Professional HRM*, 22 January, pp. 25–31. Contains a useful summary of a large research project on training and development.

Cox, G. (2002), 'Directors too must reach for the sky', *Institute of Directors News*, November. A short piece on After Action Reviews.

Cummings, T.G. and Worley, C.G. (1993), *Organisation Development and Change*, 5th edn. St Paul, MN: West. This gives material on the organizational level of performance. There are various editions of this book, but don't worry if you look at a newer or earlier edition – they are not markedly different.

Cunningham, I. (1999), *The Wisdom of Strategic Learning*, 2nd edn., Aldershot, Hants: Gower. The book contains an argument for a strategic approach to learning, including ideas on a 'learning business'. Links individual and organizational level issues.

Cunningham, I., Bennett, B. and Dawes, G. (eds) (2000), *Self Managed Learning in Action*, Aldershot, Hants: Gower. The research on learning in organizations is summarized here. As it's an edited collection it's easy to dip in and out.

Cunningham, I., Dawes, G. and Bennett, B. (1998), *Exercises for Developing Coaching Capability*, London: CIPD (also published in the USA by AMACOM as The Coaching Skill-Builder Activity Pack). A pack of materials designed for developing coaching capability in all managers in organizations.

Dasgupta, P. and Serageldin, I. (2002), *Social Capital: A multi-faceted perspective*, The World Bank.

De Geus, A. (1997), *The Living Company*, Cambridge, Mass.: Harvard Business School Press. A popular text emanating out of the author's experiences in Shell.

Department for Education and Skills (2002), First Release Statistics 'Government supported work-based learning for young people in England 2001–02: volumes and outcomes' (Ref SFR 14/2002). English statistics on areas such as Modern Apprenticeships.

Department of Health (1999), 'Continuing professional development quality in the new NHS', p. 11, London: Department of Health.

Department of Health (2000), 'An organization with a memory', London: Department of Health.

Department of Health (2002), 'Working Together – Learning Together', London: Department of Health (available at www.doh.gov.uk).

Detterman, D.K. and Sternberg, R.J. (eds) (1993), *Transfer on Trial: Intelligence, Cognition and Instruction*, Norwood, NJ: Ablex. This is a classic academic text. Some of it is heavy going, but it's a very stimulating collection that allows you to get different perspectives on the issue.

Dixon, N. (1976), *On the Psychology of Military Incompetence*, London: Jonathan Cape. This is not as irrelevant as it sounds. Dixon shows how poor performance impacts on people and why people often perform badly.

Eglin, R. (2002), 'Personnel experts' myth exploded', in *Sunday Times*, 27 January, p. 7 ('Appointments' section). Trenchant comments about the state of HR/personnel.

Elbow, P. (1973), *Writing Without Teachers*, New York: Oxford University Press.

Elbow, P. (1981), *Writing With Power: Techniques for Mastering the Writing Process*, New York: Oxford University Press. Both Elbow texts relate to the section on 'Writing' in Part 4 of this handbook.

Eraut, M. (1998), 'Learning in the workplace', *Training Officer*, vol. 34, no. 6, July/August, pp. 172–4. Michael Eraut has done much valuable research on work based learning.

Eraut, M., Alderton, J., Cole, G. and Senker, P. (1998), 'Development of knowledge and skills in employment', Research Report No. 5, University of Sussex Institute of Education.

Evans, P. and Bartolomé, F. (1980), *Must Success Cost So Much?*, London: Grant McIntyre. An early study on managerial lifestyles, stress and so on.

Fleishman, E.A. (1953), 'Leadership climate and human relations training', *Personnel Psychology*, vol. 6, pp. 205–22. Early research on the problems of transfer of learning.

Frankola, K. (2001), 'Why Online Learners Drop Out' at www.workforce.com/ feature/00/07/29/. Short article on e-learning.

Fukuyama, F. (1999), *The Great Disruption*, London: Profile. A wider discussion of social capital for those who want to consider the societal issues around this notion.

Gallacher, J. and Reeve, F. (2002), 'Work-based Learning: the implications for Higher Education and for supporting informal learning in the workplace' at www.open.ac.uk/lifelong-learning. Short article available on the Open University website, along with other articles that might be of interest.

Gallwey, W.T. (2000), *The Inner Game of Work*, London: Orion. This is based on Gallwey's original ideas on sports coaching. He shows how his ideas have relevance in organizations. A highly recommended text for coaches.

Gary, L. (2002), 'Becoming a resonant leader', *Harvard Business Review* 'Burning Questions', July, pp. 4–5. Gary does a neat summary of the Goleman *et al.* 2002 book (see below).

Goleman, D. (1995), *Emotional Intelligence*, London: Bantam. The original text that popularized the idea of EI.

Goleman, D., Boyatzis, R. and McKee, A. (2002), *Primal Leadership: Realizing the Power of Emotional Intelligence*. Cambridge, Mass.: Harvard Business School Press. A useful development from Goleman's earlier work.

Guide to Work Based Learning Terms (1989), Work Based Learning Project, Blaydon, Bristol, Further Education Staff College. It does what it says in the title.

Hampden-Turner, C. (1971), *Radical Man*, London: Duckworth. An old but valuable text based on Hampden-Turner's Harvard PhD.

Handy, C. (2000), *21 Ideas for Managers*, San Francisco, CA: Jossey-Bass. As usual, an easy read from Charles Handy.

Hofstede, G. (1980), *Cultures Consequences*, London: Sage. The classic text on cultural differences.

Hofstede, G. (1985), 'Cultural differences in teaching and learning', Paper to Colloquium on Selected Issues in International Business, Honolulu, Hawaii, 10–11 August. This reference is placed here only to show that there is a paper on the subject of cross-cultural learning. Hofstede (1980) is his standard work – and is more appropriate reading.

Honey, P. (1997), *The Best of Peter Honey*, Maidenhead, Berks: Peter Honey Publications. A very practical collection of previously published articles, including the classic Honey and Mumford material on learning styles.

Honey, P. (2002), 'Learning and the bottom line', *Training Journal*, August, p. 7. Trenchant comments about the value of learning in organizations.

Honold, L. (2000), *Developing Employees Who Love to Learn*, Palo Alto, CA: Davies-Black. A useful practical collection of material from a practitioner who knows her stuff.

Huczynski, A. (2001), *Encyclopedia of Development Methods*, Aldershot, Hants: Gower. A useful encyclopedia that covers more than learning issues.

Hüppi, R. and Seemann, P. (2001), *Social Capital: Securing Competitive Advantage in the New Economy*, London: Financial Times Prentice Hall. A company-based report on the idea of mobilizing social capital.

Jasper, L. (2002), 'Macpherson: was it all a waste of time?', *RSA Journal*, vol. 2, no. 6, pp. 30–32. Some stinging comments about the wasted effort in training.

Kegan, R. (1994), *In Over Our Heads: The Mental Demands of Modern Life*, Cambridge, Mass.: Harvard Business School Press. This is quite a heavy going text but it contains useful insights.

Levy, M. (1987), 'The core skills project and work based learning'. Sheffield, MSC/FESC. The reference here is just in case anyone wants to look at other definitions.

Levy, M. (2000), *Accidental Genius: Revolutionize Your Thinking Through Private Writing*, San Francisco, CA: Berrett-Koehler. Does what it says in the title.

Liedholm, C. and Brown, B. (2002), quoted in 'A Poor Grade for E-Learning', at www.workforce.com/section/11/article/23/26/48.html. A short piece on problems with e-learning.

Lowenstein, R. (2001), *When Genius Failed*, London: Fourth Estate. A fascinating description of the failure of supposed rational analysis and, by implication, its educational roots.

Mabey, C. and Iles, P. (eds) (1994), *Managing Learning*, London: Routledge. Another collection of papers – more academic than some others.

Mabey, C., Salaman, G. and Storey, J. (1998), *Human Resource Management: A Strategic Introduction*, Oxford: Blackwell, 2nd edn. Again a more academic approach to the issues.

Malone, S.A. (2003), *Learning About Learning*, London: Chartered Insurance Institute. This book is a kind of encyclopaedia of aspects of learning though some of the advice offered is rather odd, as is the choice of topics covered.

Matthews, P. (1999), 'Workplace learning: developing an holistic model', *The Learning Organisation*, vol. 6, no. 1, pp. 18–29. Reviews some interesting ideas – but in a rather confused way.

McCall, M.W., Lombardo, M.M. and Morrison, A.M. (1988), *The Lessons of Experience*. Lexington: Lexington Books. Classic US study on work based learning.

McConnell, D. (2000), *Implementing Computer Supported Cooperative Learning*, London: Kogan Page, 2nd edn. Thorough text that starts from first principles about co-operative approaches to learning and shows how the technology can be used for a genuinely interactive approach.

Milgram, S. (1974), *Obedience to Authority*, New York: Harper and Row. The classic text on its subject.

Mumford, A. (ed.) (1994), *Handbook of Management Development*, Aldershot, Hants: Gower, 4th edn. Useful collection of papers on aspects of management development.

Naylor, M. (1997), 'Work-Based Learning', *ERIC Digest*, no. 187. This paper focuses on school-based learning for children.

Nicholson, N. (2000), *Managing the Human Animal*, London: Texere. A controversial text on applying evolutionary psychology to organizational performance. Quite anti-learning (and very misguided in lots of ways – but it should stimulate debate).

O'Reilly, D., Cunningham, L. and Lester, S. (eds) (1999), *Developing the Capable Practitioner*, London: Kogan Page. Useful collection of papers, some more oriented to the educational world.

Pearn, M. (ed.) (2002), *Individual Differences and Development in Organizations*, Chichester: John Wiley. An academically-oriented collection, though with some very useful chapters. Part IV of the book is probably the most useful as it focuses more on methods.

Pearn, M., Mulrooney, C. and Payne, T. (1998), *Ending the Blame Culture*, Aldershot, Hants: Gower. The best text on learning from mistakes.

Pedler, M., Burgoyne, J. and Boydell, T. (1991), *The Learning Company*, London: McGraw-Hill. This provides a focus at the organizational level of learning.

Pennebaker, J. (1997), *Opening Up: The Healing Power of Expressing Emotions*, New York: Guilford Press, revised edn. A text on using writing for learning about yourself, and for emotional discharge.

Performance and Innovation Unit, Cabinet Office (2001), Report on Workforce Development (available at www.cabinet-office.gov.uk/innovation/2001/workforce/report/).

Peters, D.P. and Ceci, S.J. (1982), 'Peer review practices of the psychological journals: the fate of published articles submitted again', *Journal of Personality and Social Psychology*, 41, pp. 847–55. Article on the influence process in academic circles.

Putnam, R. (1995), 'Bowling alone: America's declining social capital', *Journal of Democracy*, vol. 6, no. 1, pp. 65–78. A classic text, which is summarized in books, so only to look at if really interested in some historical roots of the issue.

Raelin, J.A. (1998), 'Work-based learning in practice', *Journal of Workplace Learning*, vol. 10, no. 6/7, pp. 280–83. Raelin has published a number of useful texts and this paper is an easy way into his work.

Rajani, R. and Rosenberg, D. (1999), 'Usable?...Or Not?...Factors Affecting the Usability of Web Sites', at www.december.com/cmc/mag/1999/jan/rakros.html. Article on e-learning and so on.

Ratiu, I. (ed.) (1987), Multicultural management development – Special issue of the *Journal of Management Development*, vol. 6, no. 3. Ratiu has done significant work in this field but has been under-rated.

Revans, R.W. (1980), *Action Learning: New Techniques for Management*, London: Blond and Briggs. Reg Revans is excellent on the linkage of learning to action. There are a number of books by him – this just happens to be our favourite. He is not always easy to follow, but if you persevere you'll find his material more rewarding than pale imitators.

Reynolds, L. (2002), 'Keeping it business focused', *Training Journal*, June, pp. 8–11. A 'pop' piece that makes a case for 'business focused' training. Has practical advice for trainers.

Roberts, Z. (2003), 'Fast-track learning', *People Management*, 10 July, pp. 14–15. A review of bite-size learning by a journalist.

Schein, E.H. (1995), 'Building the Learning Consortium', at www.sol-ne.org/res/wp/10005.html. A useful paper on a range of learning issues.

Senge, P.M. (1990), *The Fifth Discipline*, London: Random House. The classic US text on learning organizations. It is an over-rated book – and quite limited – despite its length.

Senge, P.M., Roberts, C., Ross, R.B., Smith, B.J. and Kleiner, A. (1994), *The Fifth Discipline Fieldbook*, London: Nicholas Brealey. This is a collection with a wide range of material – some new, some old.

Simon, H.A. (1991), *Models of My Life*, New York: Basic Books. This is an excellent autobiography of someone who was a brilliant learner.

Smith, W. (2003), 'Bite-sized learning gains strength', *Director*, March, p. 36. A short article that promotes bite-sized learning.

Staley, A. and MacKenzie, N. (2000), 'Enabling curriculum re-design through asynchronous learning networks', *Journal of Asynchronous Learning Networks*, vol. 4, no. 1, June, pp. 1–14. For practitioners only.

Stewart, V., Stewart, A. and Fonda, N. (1981), *Business Applications of Repertory Grid*, Maidenhead: McGraw Hill. This text can help you to understand further the repertory grid technique.

Storey, J., Edwards, P.K., and Sissons, K. (1997), *Managers in the Making: Careers, Development and Control in Corporate Britain and Japan*, London: Sage. Valuable research studies comparing the UK with Japan.

Throp, N. (2000), 'Superhighway 61 revisited', *People Management*, 20 July, p. 49. Short article on aspects of e-learning.

Trompenaars, F. (1993), *Riding the Waves of Culture*, London: Economist Book. The big rival to Hofstede in the culture market.

Vail, P. (1996), *Learning As a Way of Being*, San Francisco: Jossey-Bass. Vail is a clear writer who makes a strong case for the negative influence of institutional educational processes – and hence about what does transfer into the workplace.

Wenger, E. (1998), *Communities of Practice*, Cambridge: Cambridge University Press. Heavy going in places, not for the faint hearted.

Wenger, E., McDermott, R. and Snyder, W.M. (2002), *Cultivating Communities of Practice*, Cambridge, Mass.: Harvard University Press. An organizationally oriented text – goes the other way from Wenger in being too shallow. Read the opening two chapters and skim the rest.

Westerbeck, T. (2000), Interview with Bill Wiggenhorn, Motorola, at www.academyonline.com/corp_ed/index.htm.

Woodall, J. (1999), 'Corporate support for work-based management development', *Human Resource Management Journal*, vol. 10, no. 1, pp. 18–32. A very useful research study that can be recommended for management development practitioners.

Yamnill, S. and McLean, G.N. (2001), 'Theories supporting transfer of training', *Human Resource Development Quarterly*, vol. 12, no. 2, pp. 195–208. An academic article which covers what it says in the title.

Index

How to Plan and Manage an e-Learning Programme
Roger Lewis and Quentin Whitlock
0 566 08424 4

Assessing the Value of Your Training
The Evaluation Process from Training Needs to the Report
to the Board
Leslie Rae
0 566 08535 6

The Situational Mentor
An International Review of Competencies and Capabilities
in Mentoring
Edited by David Clutterbuck and Gill Lane
0 566 08543 7

How to Get Best Value From HR
The Shared Services Option
Peter Reilly and Tony Williams
0 566 08495 3

Implementing Virtual Teams
A Guide to Organizational and Human Factors
Abigail A.V. Edwards and John R. Wilson
0 566 08468 6

Trainer Assessment
A Guide to Measuring the Performance of Trainers and
Facilitators
Leslie Rae
0 566 08457 0

Outdoor and Experiential Education
A Holistic Approach to Programme Design
Andy Martin, Dan Franc and Daniela Zounkova
0 566 08628 X

GOWER

John Clare's Guide to Media Handling
John Clare
0 566 08298 5

Making the Connections
Using Internal Communication to Turn Strategy into
Action
Bill Quirke
0 566 08175 X

How to Measure Customer Satisfaction 2ed
Nigel Hill, John Brierley and Rob MacDougall
0 566 08595 X

The Goal
A Process of Ongoing Improvement 2ed
Eliyahu M. Goldratt and Jeff Cox
0 566 07418 4

Benchmarking
Sylvia Codling
0 566 07926 7

The New Guide to Identity
How to Create and Sustain Change Through Managing
Identity
Wolff Olins
0 566 07737 X

It's Not Luck
Eliyahu M. Goldratt
0 566 07627 6

GOWER

Join our email newsletter

Gower is widely recognized as one of the world's leading publishers on management and business practice. Its programmes range from 1000-page handbooks through practical manuals to popular paperbacks. These cover all the main functions of management: human resource development, sales and marketing, project management, finance, etc. Gower also produces training videos and activities manuals on a wide range of management skills.

As our list is constantly developing you may find it difficult to keep abreast of new titles. With this in mind we offer a free email news service, approximately once every two months, which provides a brief overview of the most recent titles and links into our catalogue, should you wish to read more or see sample pages.

To sign up to this service, send your request via email to **info@gowerpub.com**. Please put your email address in the body of the email as confirmation of your agreement to receive information in this way.

GOWER